D1359526

Successful Strategies for Teaching Undergraduate Research

Edited by Marta Deyrup and Beth Bloom

THE SCARECROW PRESS, INC.
Lanham • Toronto • Plymouth, UK
2013

Clinton College Library

Published by Scarecrow Press, Inc.
A wholly owned subsidiary of The Rowman & Littlefield Publishing Group, Inc.
4501 Forbes Boulevard, Suite 200, Lanham, Maryland 20706
http://www.scarecrowpress.com

Estover Road, Plymouth PL6 7PY, United Kingdom

Copyright © 2013 by Marta Mestrovic Deyrup and Beth Bloom

Individual chapters copyright © 2013 by their authors.

All rights reserved. No part of this book may be reproduced in any form or by any electronic or mechanical means, including information storage and retrieval systems, without written permission from the publisher, except by a reviewer who may quote passages in a review.

British Library Cataloguing in Publication Information Available

Library of Congress Cataloging-in-Publication Data

Successful strategies for teaching undergraduate research / edited by Marta Deyrup and Beth Bloom.
pages cm
Includes bibliographical references and index.
ISBN 978-0-8108-8716-9 (pbk. : alk. paper) -- ISBN 978-0-8108-8717-6 (ebook)
1. Research--Methodology--Study and teaching (Higher) 2. Information literacy--Study and teaching (Higher) 3. Library orientation for college students. I. Deyrup, Marta Mestrovic.
LB2369.S827 2013
808.06'6378--dc23
2013011864

♾™ The paper used in this publication meets the minimum requirements of American National Standard for Information Sciences Permanence of Paper for Printed Library Materials, ANSI/NISO Z39.48-1992.

Printed in the United States of America

Contents

Preface

Marta Mestrovic Deyrup and Beth Bloom

For years, Beth and I have been interested in how undergraduate students do research and the influence (or lack of influence) that teachers, professors, and librarians have on these students. It was only after receiving a 2010 Google Research Grant that we seriously began to examine the *how* rather than the *why* of student behavior. As part of a larger study on information-seeking behavior, we asked three undergraduate cohorts at our institution to use a browser-based tracking tool called Open Hallway and record out loud their methodology as they prepared their research assignments. What we found was that students essentially fell into three categories: those who already had a predetermined conclusion and were looking for information that would support their thesis, those who were browsing through information in hopes of finding a thesis, and those who believed that if searched correctly, the Internet would produce information that was an exact match to their topic.

This book is about the *why*. We were both students of Carol Kuhlthau at the Rutgers University School of Communication and Information. Carol is a well-known educator and author of *Seeking Meaning: A Process Approach to Library and Information Services* (1993), *Guided Inquiry: Learning in the 21st Century* (2007), and *Guided Inquiry Design: A Framework for Inquiry in Your School* (2012). Our research and teaching have been influenced by her theories, as is the case with many of the authors in this book. Beth and I both believe research skills can be taught, provided that this teaching is based upon collaboration among all those involved, librarians, professors, writing instructors, and, most importantly, the students themselves. We believe that learning to do research, as Carol has demonstrated, is a process that does not come all at once. The student must persist through false starts, trial and error, and patient digging for information until he or she comes to the realization that yes, indeed, he or she has done enough and, in the process, has come to truly understand the topic he or she has chosen to investigate. This journey also requires that students go through a period of self-doubt and confusion, followed by the growing realization that he or she has done it right. It is this self-confidence in their own abilities that we hope will stay with them their entire lives.

Marta Mestrovic Deyrup

This book is a product of a lengthy information literacy-focused partnership between Marta and myself. Together we have produced tutorials, written courses, and brought about the acceptance of information literacy as a fundamental competency in the new Core Curriculum at our university. This alliance also resulted in a successful bid for funding from Google to study the online research behaviors of undergraduate students. Our study revealed much about student research behaviors, much of which is supported in the literature on this topic, but our findings also raised some questions. What happens in students' minds as they approach their research? Do they prepare themselves to think critically about the goals of their research? Do they read the assignment and then just start typing—dive in, so to speak? Where were the studies on this aspect of information-seeking behavior?

Librarians have written on myriad aspects of information literacy: the student centered classroom, research behaviors, the effectiveness of various instruction models and theoretical constructs, learning theory, and so forth. However, absent from this conversation has been the focus on the research question, how researchers approach inquiry given a writing assignment. Seeing this gap in literature, we approached colleagues who are actively involved with what Maria T. Accardi calls the "research question and the research questions" to ask them their thoughts. What evolved from this discussion was the conviction that there was a need to produce a work that address the entire process of information literacy instruction, from the research assignment to the research question, and including partnerships with teaching colleagues, in addition to pedagogies. With the research question as a central theme, we sought out experts on various aspects of the library instruction process. Their contributions have helped create this work—and answer our own questions. With this book, we hope to contribute to the ongoing discussion about new pedagogies and enhanced relationships with faculty colleagues—and present a more comprehensive means to address the research process.

Beth Bloom

Introduction

Undergraduates and Library Research: What's Changed, What Hasn't, What Now?

Mary W. George

There are four elements that, combined together, shape the library research lives of undergraduates: the students themselves, as individuals and as members of social groups; faculty; librarians; and information resources. But that list omits three complicating factors: technology, methodology, and incentive. I hold that the four basic elements never change their essential natures. Twenty-first-century students, whether they are in the traditional young adult cohort or are nontraditional in some way, are still bundles of enthusiasm, uncertainty, and distractions. Faculty continue to believe that their role is to convey great ideas and spark complex understandings in their students. Librarians remain passionate about connecting researchers at all levels with tools and sources, in their own collections or anywhere from earth to ether. And most information resources are stable in both type and content: A biographical essay is still a biographical essay whether it exists in print in a multivolume reference set, on a microfilm reel, in a proprietary electronic database, or on the Web.

Enter today's information technology, however, and all the dynamics shift. Now, students, faculty, and librarians alike expect research miracles from mouse clicks or screen taps and are annoyed when the "link doesn't work," which is how they describe any setback, without reflecting that it might be their expectations or tactics that don't work. Petabytes have been written on how and why people's research expectations, search behavior, and critical evaluation of sources have been skewed by the Internet, so I will not reprise them, but I would like to comment on the other two complicating factors: library research methodology (what I sometimes call planned processhood) and incentive. My belief is that if, and only if, faculty and librarians conspire to impress the idea of research *process* on undergraduates, will our collections, both physical and virtual, be well-exploited. Cooperation to this end will also reduce students' misunderstandings and neuroses about library research and help them become astute information seekers after college.

Let's consider the views and roles of the collaborators. When college faculty and academic librarians agonize over the research skills of undergraduates, they rarely speak to one another, and, if they do, the conversation needs an interpreter. Faculty are most likely to commiserate among themselves about students' superficial choice and use of sources. Even when a professor concludes that a student's work is original—i.e., that there is no whiff of plagiarism and sources are adequately cited—and even when that work displays a cogent argument, he or she will often bemoan the lack of historical context or a theoretical approach that "any serious student" should acknowledge. The trouble is that although faculty grumble amongst themselves about this problem—and have done so for decades—they do not recognize that they are a large part of the solution.

So are college librarians, who likewise encounter undergraduates at all levels who are, anxiously or blissfully, ignorant regarding valid methods of information seeking. Generalist reference librarians and their subject specialist colleagues share amazing stories about students who announce a vast topic but have no background knowledge about it and assume that all necessary sources are so-labeled, online, short, and in English. Worse yet are the students who treat library research as a nuisance, an unnecessary diversion as they state the conclusion they have already reached.

For the past half-century, academic librarians have tried every trick they can think of to inform and excite undergraduates about the research resources available to them. Librarians have created workbooks, class- and topic-specific research guides, online tutorials, games, and countless instruction sessions employing every pedagogical approach known to academe. They have stepped outside the traditional reference zone to connect with students via social media or mingle with students in learning communities, commons areas, dormitory spaces, academic departments, or cozy cafés. Occasionally they have assisted faculty with the design of research assignments, although usually without having a role in evaluation; however, too often there is little communication between faculty and librarians, or it is phrased something like, "I want them [my students] to use *Psych Abstracts* and *Mental Measurements Yearbook*." But this does not specify what evidence the teacher will actually be looking for in the completed assignment. Once librarians understand what a professor regards as a successful research project, they can introduce students to the best tools at the best time and provide opportunities for individual consultation, in person or online, as students progress through the term.

So what has been the effect of these efforts at collaboration to date? The result has been positive public relations in many cases, but little retention by students of concepts or strategies, and little glimmer of the confidence that shines from someone who has mastered a complex activity. There is precious little long-term proof that students can transfer research reasoning from one project to another even within the same discipline—let alone across fields or to their off-campus lives.

When it comes to library research instruction in whatever guise, faculty provide both the carrot and the stick by how they craft their assignments and weight their grades. If they have been disappointed with student research in the past, then I would argue that they should require students to document and comment on their thought process, tools, search methods, and judgment criteria *throughout all stages of their work,* submitting a chronological research log (written "raw," not reconstructed) with their term paper or other project. Why? Because none of these matters is self-evident from the student's finished product. This exercise in reflection is as important a learning moment as an outline or annotated bibliography, and, as such, it deserves serious assessment and some degree of feedback.

But who should assess students' research logs, and how? That can be a sensitive question requiring negotiation between faculty and librarians. I would advocate that the logs be submitted in searchable form and that students be asked to place in boldface type what they consider to be the major steps they took and tools they used, so that whoever reviews their process can quickly scan each log for significant points, or lack thereof, using a grading rubric students know in advance. The key here is to relate the student's research process to the research question they chose to explore. Students are already used to the directive "show your calculations" in their math and science courses, so it should be no surprise when they are asked to detail their reasoning in other fields. Furthermore, when students know that their project must in some way connect to their research activity, the temptation to plagiarize magically disappears.

Faculty are, in fact, double role models—as researchers themselves and evaluators of the research done by others, whether as peer reviewers or critics once a work is out. Professors and other experts, for example, guest speakers on campus, should make a practice of explaining to students how complex research projects unfold from the flash of an idea to the final publication, with particular attention to the literature review, methodology applied (and why), research design, information sources used, both false and productive leads, and major decisions made along the way. When students realize that although there is a standard approach to the study of X, rough spots are inevitable and must be dealt with, often by the researcher assuming a different point of view. Then they will be less unnerved by the bumps they encounter as novices. The retrospective and introspective candor of scholars is priceless.

Faculty members and librarians must face these changes and challenges together and devise flexible, measurable ways to ensure that undergraduates understand, demonstrate, retain, and can transfer the basic tenets of library research, going beyond passive Google searching to active knowledge searching. The contributions in this volume suggest means to that end.

I

The State of Teaching Today

ONE

Research Questions and the Research Question: What Are We Teaching When We Teach Research?

Heidi L. M. Jacobs

> Information literacy lies at the core of lifelong learning. It empowers people in all walks of life to seek, evaluate, use, and create information effectively to achieve their personal, social, occupational, and educational goals. It is a basic human right in a digital world and promotes social inclusion of all nations.—"Alexandria Proclamation on Information Literacy and Lifelong Learning" (2008)

> I had to work all weekend. I can't find anything for my assignment. I just need to get it done. Do you have time to help me tomorrow?"—Sunday night email from an undergraduate history student (Fall 2011)

There are times when I, an information literacy librarian, feel my job is to teach research in ways that will help guide our campus's students and society at large toward the temptingly admirable and admittedly lofty goals of information literacy, as described in the "Alexandria Proclamation on Information Literacy and Lifelong Learning": "to empower people in all walks of life to use, create, and evaluate information in ways that will help them achieve their goals and in ways that will promote social inclusion of all nations.[1] There are also times, while I work with my campus's students in class, at the reference desk, in my office, or via email, when research seems like something I just have to help them get through. I will admit I often feel torn between the ideals of information literacy that I aspire to work toward and the day-to-day realities of student life. There are also the ideals and realities of the professor teaching the course: They expect librarians to introduce students to the processes and challenges of scholarly research and the critical thinking skills required for effective research, while also helping students find appropriate resources in a timely manner so they can write strong, well-researched papers.

I know I am not alone in feeling conflicted between the ideals of information literacy and daily realities. This chapter does not offer any quick-fix solutions to the conflicts that most—if not all— information literacy librarians encounter. Instead, I posit that one of the ways we can negotiate this seemingly unbridgeable rift between the ideals and realities of teaching research is to think reflectively about the research question, which is central to so much of what we talk about when we discuss information literacy, writing, and research. By research question, I mean both the Research Question (the broad, probing questions about what research means in today's society, our profession, our current curricula, and our students' lives) and the research question that students are assigned for research assignments.[2] Instead of focusing on "how to" questions, I want to focus on "how might we" questions. How, for example, might we use the Research Question and the research question as sites of inquiry to work toward some of the ideals embodied in the "Alexandria Proclamation" *and* help the students who "just need to get it done"? How might we bring students' lives, skills, interests, passions, and commitments into the research process and the Research Question? How might we get students, librarians, and faculty to engage with the Research Question so that research questions become true engagements with the world rather than exercises in information retrieval?

Before I discuss the role of these two kinds of questions, I want to say a few words about the late-night emails I often get, asking for help a few days or hours before a deadline. While there are always exceptions, the students on my campus work hard in their school lives, family and personal lives, part-time jobs, and other commitments. It is imperative that we read their asking for help to "just get it done" within this context and understand the complexity of their lives. It is easy to fall into the trap of assuming our students don't take their education seriously or value the intellectual work required to complete assignments carefully and critically. We too often forget that a surprisingly high number of students balance full courseloads with part-time jobs. On my campus, some students work nearly full-time hours; some work midnight shifts in auto plants and come to morning classes after work; some have children or other family responsibilities. When I get requests for help from students working against deadlines, more often than not, it is their nonscholarly commitments, not laziness or time mismanagement, that push them up against deadlines. Ideally, many students would love to be full-time students focused only on their studies. The economic realities, however, are such that progressively fewer students have the luxury of having this kind of focus. I raise these issues not as a lament or an excuse; I raise them because when we talk about student research processes, ideals, and realities, we need to be aware that few students have the ideal amount of time needed for conducting research. I also raise these issues because my discussion of students' research shortcuts must be contextualized within the various factors with which our students contend. Furthermore, I want to underscore the complexity of our students' lives, because it is a reminder that our students have many experiences and skills to draw on and are not blank slates.

As a way of discussing the broad Research Question and the research questions with which our students grapple, I offer two examples of the kinds of questions I see at the reference desk or when working one-on-one with students. Both questions are versions of research questions I've seen, but the specifics have been modified: "gun control: yes or no" and "select two short stories by Hemingway and discuss his depiction of women within the discourse of misogyny." In the case of the question about gun control, students would, in an ideal situation, examine each side of the issue objectively, consult balanced and nuanced arguments, and, then, based on what they read, present a case for or against in their essays. What we often see at the reference desk or when we help students with these for-or-against type questions is something quite different. Confronted with limited time, many students forego inquiry into and exploration of the issue, select either for or against, and then find research to support the answer they've selected based on what they already know or believe. I have also seen, on more than one occasion, students who will select a position based on which side of the argument has the most articles available in downloadable formats. In either case, the act of research is not one of inquiry, exploration, and critical thinking, but one of expedient information retrieval.

In the case of the Hemingway example, research becomes a way to fill in the blanks left open by the assigned question: "Find two short stories with depictions of women and explain why they are misogynistic." I have sat with many a student, both of us searching for articles that fit the assigned question, while more interesting topics of the student's own devising wither under the confines of the assignment. Here, too, research has been reduced to finding existing literary criticism on the topic, assembling it with some new critical analysis of the student's own and writing a paper where the major research question seems to be how does one find what the professor has already found.

These experiences are disheartening for a librarian who would like to believe that we can do what the "Alexandria Proclamation" describes. Indeed, one could take the opportunity to suggest—as we are taught in library school—that when the student with the gun-control topic comes to the desk, our reference interview should guide him or her to five solid and reputable sources from each position, encourage her or him to read and consider each side carefully, and then, based on their reading, develop an argument for or against gun control. Or, we might want to suggest that the student with the Hemingway topic rewrite the question into something he or she is more interested in or that asks more challenging and interesting questions about Hemingway and gender; however, when a student with a Monday afternoon deadline comes for help during a late Sunday afternoon reference shift, even the most ardent supporters of the "Alexandria Proclamation" would be hard pressed to focus on the larger, loftier information literacy goals and ignore the reality of the student's looming deadline or the possibility of a failing grade for an off-topic paper.

To be fair, both assigned questions have, at their core, a generous impulse: provide a question that guides students toward a focused topic. Indeed, having an open topic can be a daunting experience for students, especially those new to academic writing and research; however, both the gun control and Hemingway questions run the risk of taking the inquiry out of the research process and making research simply a matter of database searching and retrieval. In both cases, it is easy to blame the student for taking shortcuts within their research and bypassing what librarians and professors see as the most important parts of the research: inquiry. When we examine the questions from a pedagogical perspective, we can see that the questions themselves are, inadvertently it would appear, set up in ways that funnel students away from the act of asking new and innovative questions of texts and subject matter and toward the act of supplying an answer to the question without fully engaging in inquiry.

Although both questions have the potential to engage students with inquiry and problem posing, in reality, they tend to emulate what Paulo Freire calls the "banking" concept of education. Freire argues that in this kind of education, students are turned into "'containers,' into 'receptacles' to be 'filled' by the teacher."[3] "Education," Freire argues, "thus becomes an act of depositing, in which the students are the depositories and the teacher is the depositor. Instead of communicating, the teacher issues communiqués and makes deposits that the students patiently receive, memorize, and repeat."[4] In this context, the major problem with the Hemingway research question is the assumption that students are incapable of coming up with a question about or an interpretation of Hemingway's stories on their own; questions like this one function as an empty vessel into which students pour a predetermined answer. Although the gun-control question has the potential to be a problem-posing venture, more often than not, these kinds of questions have the potential of becoming empty-vessel queries because of the way that the research process has been approached by teacher, librarian, and student: Students are given a question and are expected to fill that question with an answer.

The questions I am getting at here are not about whether librarians should abandon all hopes of achieving the larger information literacy goals, or what role pragmatism should play in the work with our students. The questions I'm raising are ones about the Research Question and the research question: How do we address research in our curriculum? How do we ask research questions? What are we considering when we construct research questions? And what do students, librarians, and teaching faculty bring to the table as we pose problems about research and information literacy?

In theory, the research assignment carries with it tremendous possibilities for student engagement. In its ideal form, it builds on natural curiosity, encourages exploration, and positions students as critical thinkers and active creators of knowledge. In practice, more often than not, research assignments with library components fail to live up to their potential. As Virginia A. Chappell, Randall Hensley, and Elizabeth Simmons-O'Neill describe, research assignments and library instruction

> have long been shaped by a paradigm in which faculty produce the questions by giving an assignment, librarians tell students where to find the answers, and the resulting term papers demonstrate the writers' retrieval and summary skills. Unfortunately, the student's role in all this as thinker and writer is minimal. The term papers function primarily as information conduits.[5]

Within the fields of composition and information literacy, the research paper is referred to in ways that suggest it is a necessary evil within academia. Composition and rhetoric scholars Robert Davis and Mark Shadle relate the following:

> Research writing was conceived in the modern era as a way of writing the making of knowledge, and this writing was, at least in theory, open to all. Anyone, according to this modern mythology, was capable of making a breakthrough, given the right disposition, intelligence, and training. The research paper as we now teach it, like many things modern, scarcely lives up to this promise. It is, typically, an apprentice work, not making knowledge as much as reporting the known.[6]

"Research writing," they further contend, "is disrespected and omnipresent, trite and vital, central to modern academic discourse, yet a part of our own duties as teachers of writing that we seldom discuss."[7] Likewise, within information literacy scholarship, the teaching of research is a central concern, but we've yet to fully engage with what it means to teach research: Our scholarly journals are replete with articles about best practices and how to teach research, but few take on the questions of *why* we teach research. As with many scholars in composition, information literacy librarians would like to believe, as Davis and Shadle describe, that

> research writing teaches valuable skills and encourages students to commit to the academic ideals of inquiry and evidentiary reasoning. However, it may be as often the case that the research paper assignment teaches students little more than the act of producing, as effort-

lessly as possible, a drab discourse, vacant of originality or commitment.[8]

A number of scholars in both composition and information literacy have
suggested alternatives to the standard research assignment, and, indeed,
changing the central assignment is important.[9] However, I believe it is
crucial that we consider the Research Question alongside the research
questions that we assign, and that we involve students, faculty, and librarians in these discussions.

Although Russel K. Durst's book *Collision Course: Conflict, Negotiation,
and Learning in College Composition* does not draw explicit connections to
information literacy or the teaching of research or librarianship, his ideas
about the "collision course" between composition students and teaching
faculty are deeply relevant to what we do as information literacy librarians when we navigate the expectations and hopes of teaching faculty,
students, and ourselves.[10] Durst's book is based on the "overarching
view that students and teacher often have very different—and in many
ways opposing—agendas in the composition class, that these differing
agendas lead to significant conflict and negotiation throughout the
course."[11] Most first-year students, Durst argues, come to composition
classes as

> career-oriented pragmatists who view writing as a difficult but poten-
> tially useful technology. These students would generally prefer to learn
> a way of writing that is simple, quick, and efficient, applicable in all or
> most situations, and either reducible to a formula or straightforward
> set of rules, or free from rules, prescriptions, and restrictions.[12]

Teachers of composition, however, "typically stress much more complex
and demanding notions of critical literacy."[13] Influenced by the work of
Freire and critical literacy theories, many composition teachers "emphasize self-reflection, multiperspective thinking, explicit consideration of
ideological issues, rigorous development of ideas, and questioning of
established ways of thinking."[14] Librarians teaching information literacy
are often caught in a confluence of conflicting hopes and expectations:
Some professors want more critical information literacy elements, while
others want none; some librarians want to explore the more political and
theoretical aspects of critical information literacy, yet feel compelled to
help students with a more pragmatic approach to research assignments;
some students are taken with the ideas of critical information literacy, but
many just want to get the assignment done.

For librarians, Durst's examination of the "collision course" between
students and teachers is useful for two reasons. The first is how he navi-
gates the student/teacher, pragmatism/critical literacy "collision course."
He advocates an approach to composition that fosters what he calls "reflective instrumentalism."

> This approach preserves the intellectual rigor and social analysis of current pedagogies without rejecting the pragmatism of most first-year college students. Instead, the approach accepts students' pragmatic goals, offers to help achieve their goals, but adds a reflective dimension that, while itself is useful in the work world, also helps students place their individual aspirations in the larger context necessary for critical analysis. [15]

In his reflective instrumentalism, Durst balances critical inquiry with pragmatism; such an approach is worth considering in information literacy work. How, for example, might we acknowledge students' pragmatic goals related to library research while incorporating reflection on their larger contexts and individual aspirations?

The second reason Durst's work is important to librarians' information literacy work is his insistence that we think reflectively about our teaching practices. One of the key purposes of *Collision Course*, he writes, is to "place the teaching of composition—as in consideration of such issues as 'What do we mean by good writing, given the many different contexts in which writing takes place, and how do we help students become good writers'—back into the professional conversation." [16] Similarly, information literacy work would be well served by bringing questions of this nature into our professional conversations. Elsewhere, I argue for the need for reflective pedagogical praxis with information literacy work. [17] Here, however, I want to focus upon the need to apply that kind of reflective thinking to the pedagogy of research. What is good research? What are good research habits of mind? Why do we have students conduct research? What are our goals in having students do research? What are the pedagogical goals behind specific kinds of research activities? What engages students about research? How might we locate research where students are? What are the pedagogical realities behind the research questions we ask? What are we inadvertently teaching when we teach research in particular ways?

The raising of questions is nothing new to discussions of the teaching of research writing. In the seminal *The Craft of Research*, for example, Wayne C. Booth, Gregory G. Colomb, and Joseph M. Williams describe the importance of questions within the research process. They write, "To engage your best critical thinking, systematically ask questions about your topic's history, composition, and categories." [18] They also note the importance of framing the significance of their research questions into problems, saying the following:

> [Y]ou join a community of researchers when you can state that significance *from your readers' point of view*. In so doing, you create a stronger relationship with readers because you promise something in return for their interest in your report—a deeper understanding of something that matters to *them*. At that point you have posed a *problem* that they recognize needs a solution. [19]

Although Booth, Colomb, and Williams's discussions of questions and problem posing are useful strategies to help students complete their research, these questions and problem posing do not extend much beyond the topic itself or the mentioned reader (who, we might safely assume, is the teacher who will assign a grade). We need to find ways to inspire students to engage with research questions and the Research Question in ways that are wider-ranging than engaging one's reader in this artificial context (the reward for engaging this particular reader is, presumably, a higher grade). We need to find ways to engage students with the meta-level of inquiry: What are the questions of research questions? What are the problems of research problems? We need to find ways, in the words of Gerald Graff, to teach the conflicts and engage our students in those questions. "Good education," he writes, "is about helping students enter the culture of ideas and arguments . . . teaching students to engage in intellectual debate at a high level is the most important thing we can do."[20] How might we help students enter the culture of ideas and arguments about research? How might we—as librarians, teachers, and students—use this "culture of ideas and arguments" to find better ways to explore research questions? How might we engage in the world of knowledge creation? In short, how might we transform the research assignment to embody the ideals and potentials it possesses?

One of the things we need to keep ever present in our minds as we teach research is this: What, precisely, is the problem we are posing when we give research assignments to students? Is the problem how to find resources? Is it how to navigate an information-rich world? Is it how to think critically about the information world and, as Maura Seale describes, the "politics and processes of knowledge production"?[21] Is it how to think creatively and critically about the world? Or, are the problems we inadvertently pose only how to complete a research assignment? As Freire argues,[22] the "educational goal of deposit-making" must be replaced with the "posing of the problems of human beings in their relations with the world."[23] While many educators might think of their research questions as ventures in problem posing, it is important to remember that Freire emphatically states that problem-posing education is related to "posing of the problems of human beings in their relations with the world" not the problems related to filling a vessel with knowledge.[24]

At this point, we need to consider the difference between problem solving and problem posing. Problem solving assumes that there is an answer to be found and a replicable process to finding that answer. Problem posing, on the other hand, is a more reflective, iterative, recursive process where questions beget additional questions. Of course, students do need to learn how to solve problems, but we can find ways to challenge them with problem posing as well. As Freire writes, "In problem-posing education, people develop their power to perceive critically *the way they exist* in the world *with which* and *in which* they find themselves;

they come to see the world not as a static reality, but as a reality in process, in transformation."[25] To engage students fully with problem-posing education, we need to make sure we are not only presenting them with problem-solving endeavors.

This point can be well-illustrated with an example from Durst's description of two students in a composition class: "Larry and Chuck, for example, knew they were not going to solve the problems of guns in schools and toxic waste at Fernald [a local site], respectively. The problem they actually attempted to solve was that of writing a paper for their English class."[26] Like the students who select a perspective on gun control based on the availability of material or the students who search for articles they know their professors have in mind for the Hemingway topic, Larry and Chuck were not engaged in the act of problem posing. Instead, they were engaged in a very specific and limited kind of problem solving: How do we complete this assignment?

Larry and Chuck were navigating what Henry Giroux calls the "hidden curriculum"[27] or what James Elmborg has more recently referred to as "playing the game of school": "learning abstract and sometimes useless-seeming information, and learning to put that information into a framework with other information."[28] The point of this game, writes Elmborg, "is not to make sense of the world, but rather to prove to teachers and future teachers and future employers that one can play this game."[29] If we are committed to engaging students with problem-posing education, we need to consider critically what we are asking when we ask research questions. What are students taking away from their research questions? Are students posed problems relating to themselves in the world and in the world where they will feel increasingly challenged and obliged to respond to that challenge? Or are they playing the game of school? If our research questions consist only of teaching students how to solve the problems in the game of school, we need to seriously reconsider the kinds of questions we ask.

I am not suggesting that the Research Question can be solved by simply providing students with a particular kind of research question or by teaching research in specific ways. Rather, I am suggesting that the Research Question needs to become a site of collective inquiry for students, faculty, and librarians and a site of problem-posing for all three groups. As Jonathan Cope writes, "There are occasions when critical [information literacy] calls more for the asking of new questions than it does for the provision of clear, instrumental answers."[30] Indeed, I believe it is time to ask new questions of research and what it means to teach it, learn it, and engage with it. This chapter is, emphatically, not a how-to chapter or an examination of best practices. Instead, it poses the problem of how we might approach the problem of the Research Question and research questions. In considering how we might go about thinking through a problem-posing approach to research, as well as navigating the collision course of librarians, students, and teaching faculty, I return to Freire, who argues that problem-posing education must "break with the vertical patterns characteristic of banking education."[31] If we can work to create an environment where teaching faculty, librarians and students can engage with the Research Question and research questions as, in Freire's words, "critical co-investigators," we can begin to work toward an educational experience about research where students are "increasingly posed with problems relating to themselves in the world and with the world" and where they "will feel increasingly challenged and obliged to respond to that challenge."[32] At present, faculty, librarians, and students are not critically co-investigating the Research Question, but they are instead independently navigating their own collision courses.

Although research questions are recurrent topics within discussions of research and writing, we often talk around the Research Question or address it obliquely. It is a commonly held belief that research skills are important for students, yet we never talk about precisely why we believe this to be true. It is simply taken as a given that research is an important thing to learn. As we consider the research question and the Research Question, it is assumptions such as these that need unpacking. We need to be more explicit about posing the problem of the Research Question with our students, our colleagues, and ourselves. Why do we teach research? Why is it part of the curriculum? What do we hope to achieve by having our students do research assignments?

Having dialogues with ourselves, our librarian colleagues, our teaching colleagues, and our students about the Research Question can turn research from something that is a ubiquitous and rarely questioned requirement into something that is vital, evolving, and up for critical questioning by all parties. Engaging students in the Research Question better positions them to become active agents and critical coinvestigators in their research questions. Working to position students as active agents within the broader Research Question helps us work toward developing true research questions within the Freirean problem-posing context. In so doing, we also create room for students, faculty, and librarians to begin to have conversations about how research and, correspondingly, information literacy can "empower people in all walks of life to seek, evaluate, use, and create information effectively to achieve their personal, social, occupational, and educational goals" and how it is a "basic human right in a digital world [that] promotes social inclusion of all nations."[33] Accordingly, we can help ourselves, our colleagues, and our students to see the Research Question and their research questions as something larger than an assignment, where the problem to be solved is less about how to write an English paper and more about the world and how we exist within it.

NOTES

1. "Alexandria Proclamation on Information Literacy and Lifelong Learning," International Federation of Library Associations and Institutions, *IFLANET*, November 9, 2005. Available online at www.ifla.org/III/wsis/BeaconInfSoc.html (accessed August 29, 2012).

2. There is a tendency to use the term *information literacy* as an umbrella term for any kind of library instruction. In practice, the term *bibliographic instruction* is often swapped out for *information literacy* when, in fact, they are two different ventures. In this chapter, I distinguish bibliographic instruction (the teaching of tools-based skills) from information literacy, which has a much broader focus.

3. Paulo Freire, *Pedagogy of the Oppressed*, trans. Donald Macedo (New York: Continuum, 2002), 72.

4. Freire, *Pedagogy of the Oppressed*, 72.

5. Virginia A. Chappell, Randall Hensley, and Elizabeth Simmons-O'Neill, "Beyond Information Retrieval: Transforming Research Assignments into Genuine Inquiry," *Journal of Teaching Writing* 13, nos. 1/2 (1994): 211–12.

6. Robert Davis and Mark Shadle, "'Building a Mystery': Alternative Research Writing and the Academic Art of Seeking," *College Composition and Communication* 51, no. 3 (February 2000): 423.

7. Davis and Shadle, "'Building a Mystery,'" 417.

8. Davis and Shadle, "'Building a Mystery,'" 419.

9. See, for example, Davis and Shadle, "'Building a Mystery'"; Tom Romano, Blending Genre, Altering Style: Writing Multigenre Papers (Portsmouth, NH: Heinemann, 2000); and Laura Brady, Nathalie Singh-Corcoran, Jo Ann Dadisman, and Kelly Diamond, "A Collaborative Approach to Information Literacy: First-Year Composition, Writing Center, and Library Partnerships at West Virginia University," *Composition Forum* 19 (Spring 2009): 1.

10. Russel K. Durst, *Collision Course: Conflict, Negotiation, and Learning in College Composition* (Urbana, IL: National Council of Teachers of English, 1999).

11. Durst, *Collision Course*, 2.

12. Durst, *Collision Course*, 2.

13. Durst, *Collision Course*, 3.

14. Durst, *Collision Course*, 3.

15. Durst, *Collision Course*, 117.

16. Durst, *Collision Course*, 6.

17. Heidi L. M. Jacobs, "Information Literacy and Reflective Pedagogical Praxis," *Journal of Academic Librarianship* 34, no. 3 (May 2008): 256–62.

18. Wayne C. Booth, Gregory G. Colomb, and Joseph M. Williams, *The Craft of Research*, (Chicago: University of Chicago Press, 2008), 41.

19. Booth, Colomb, and Williams, *The Craft of Research*, 51–52.

20. Gerald Graff, *Professing Literature: An Institutional History, Twentieth Anniversary Edition* (Chicago: University of Chicago Press, 2007), xvii.

21. Maura Seale, "Information Literacy Standards and the Politics of Knowledge Production: Using User-Generated Content to Incorporate Critical Pedagogy," in *Critical Library Instruction: Theories and Methods*, edited by Maria T. Accardi, Emily Drabinski, and Alana Kumbier (Duluth, MN: Library Juice Press, 2010), 229.

22. In "Untested Feasibility: Imagining the Pragmatic Possibility of Paulo Freire," *College English* 63, no. 5 (May 2011), Kate Ronald and Hephzibah Roskelly write that, "we need to remember and take heart from Freire's warning: 'To read is to rewrite, not memorize the content of what is being read' (*Critical Consciousness*, 100). Recognizing his popularity among educators in the United States, Freire cautions, 'It is impossible to export pedagogical practices without reinventing them. Please, tell your fellow Americans not to import me. Ask them to recreate and rewrite my ideas' (*Politics of Education*, xii–xix)" (612). We need to be cognizant of the impulse to import his ideas

and work toward rewriting and recreating them in our particular contexts. Freire, *Pedagogy of the Oppressed*, 79.

23. Freire, *Pedagogy of the Oppressed*, 79.

24. Freire, *Pedagogy of the Oppressed*, 83.

25. Freire, *Pedagogy of the Oppressed*.

26. Durst, Collision Course, 114.

27. Henry Giroux and David Purpel, *The Hidden Curriculum and Moral Education: Deception or Discovery ?* (Berkeley, CA: McCutchan, 1983).

28. James Elmborg, "Critical Information Literacy: Definitions and Challenges," in *Transforming Information Literacy Programs: Intersecting Frontiers of Self, Library Culture, and Campus Community*, edited by Carroll Wetzel Wilkinson and Courtney Bruch (Chicago: Association of College and Research Libraries, 2012), 92.

29. Elmborg, "Critical Information Literacy," 92.

30. Jonathan Cope, "Information Literacy and Social Power," in *Critical Library Instruction: Theories and Methods*, edited by Maria T. Accardi, Emily Drabinski, and Alana Kumbier (Duluth, MN: Library Juice Press, 2010), 21.

31. Freire, *Pedagogy of the Oppressed*, 80.

32. Freire, *Pedagogy of the Oppressed*, 81.

33. "Alexandria Proclamation on Information Literacy and Lifelong Learning," www.ifla.org/III/wsis/BeaconInfSoc.html.

TWO

Understanding the Relationship between Good Research and Good Writing

Barbara J. D'Angelo

Much has been written about the relationship between research and writing in the literature of the library and information science and rhetoric and writing disciplines, both theoretically and pedagogically. This is not surprising given the prominence of the research paper assignment and the emphasis on critical thinking in higher education writing courses. Librarians and writing faculty have formed natural partnerships in creating effective pedagogies to help students learn good research practices in the context of their writing assignments.

To understand what we mean by "good research" and "good writing," however, we must first understand what is meant by these terms. *Writing* is often used as a generic term to refer to the genre or product produced; however, all writing is contextual. A poem, for example, has different characteristics from an essay, just as an essay has different characteristics than a technical report. Similarly, research is often taught as a skill set in which an individual is expected to master the techniques of using databases (or search engines) to effectively find information. Yet, research—the collection, analysis, and use of information—is also contextual. The conflation of these terms often leads to misconceptions and confusion about what they are, how they relate to one another, and, therefore, how to teach them. Indeed, students often wonder why they need to learn to do "academic" research, how to use a library, and why they must write academic-style essays and papers when their jobs or careers may involve a very different set of research and writing practices.

Is there, then, a definable relationship between "good research" and "good writing?"

The relationship between information and writing is symbiotic; one cannot exist without the other. One cannot write without information, whether that information comes from the writer's memory bank or experiences or, more likely, from collecting information through the process of research. On the other hand, research is meaningless if it is not presented in some way. And, while information can be presented orally or visually, it can be argued that the majority of information is still presented textually, whether in a traditional print genre or digitally.

As a result, the relationship between research and writing may seem simplistic: Writing needs research to find information or content; research needs writing to communicate the information found. However, the relationship between these two constructs is much more complicated. Both research and writing are contextual processes grounded in rhetorical theory. By extension, the pedagogical approaches that are built upon understanding research and writing as rhetorically situated processes are the basis of the relationship between "good research" and "good writing."

Rhetorically situated processes are grounded in an understanding that the presentation of information is based on an awareness of an audience, that is, an understanding of whom the communication is directed toward, as well as its purpose—the reason for writing. As rhetorically situated processes, research and writing are connected to constructivist learning theory in which information is sought and used to create knowledge. In college courses, this is reflected in two ways. First, the learner uses research and writing to learn disciplinary content (and demonstrate the learning of it). Second, the learner seeks information and writes to demonstrate understanding of the conventions of the discipline, including genre conventions. In the field of history, for example, research may incorporate literature searches and/or analysis of primary documents, with the results reported in research papers, articles, books, or such digital formats as blogs. In the field of engineering, research may include literature searches and usability studies, with the results reported in storyboards, white papers, or recommendation reports.

This chapter explores the relationship between research and writing through a review of current theoretical and pedagogical perspectives and expands upon those perspectives by exploring the relationship between research and writing processes as described in Carol Kuhlthau's studies on the information search process and Linda Flower and John Hayes's studies on the writing process. For the purposes of this chapter, the terms *research* and *information literacy* (IL) will be used interchangeably. While IL may be seen as a broader term than research, it encompasses research practices and is the commonly acceptable phrase for information- and research-based instruction in U.S. colleges. In addition, rhetoric and writing is the phrase commonly used to describe the discipline of writing studies and, therefore, will be used throughout the chapter.

BACKGROUND

The relationship between research and writing has been explored extensively in the information science and rhetoric and writing disciplinary literatures. Jean Sheridan, for example, describes how librarians and writing faculty can learn from each other by focusing on writing and research as processes.[1] James Elmborg calls upon librarians to understand the history of the Writing across the Curriculum (WAC) movement to begin to define a theoretical basis for IL.[2] He expands upon the connections between IL and writing in his call for more collaboration between writing centers and libraries, focusing on process-oriented approaches and advocating for the alignment of writing and research as one holistic process.[3] Many describe partnerships with first-year-composition courses and programs for the teaching and assessment of research and writing. For example, Jennifer Nutefall and Phyllis Mentzell Ryder detail a partnership between librarians and faculty to develop a new first-year writing course for freshmen at George Washington University.[4]

INFORMATION LITERACY AND WRITING: WHAT'S RHETORIC GOT TO DO WITH IT?

Rolf Norgaard's influential articles on the ties between IL and writing provide a basis for understanding the rhetorical foundation for both.[5] Norgaard encourages an intellectual engagement between the fields of library and information science and rhetoric and writing to engender a broader conversation to link the two disciplines theoretically. He points out similar misconceptions both fields have to battle. Often, inside and outside the academy, both writing and research are viewed as neutral and context-free mechanical skills. Seen in this way, the teaching of writing is focused on the mechanics of grammar, structure, and style. Similarly, IL is focused on the mechanics of searching for information and citation practices. Little to no attention is paid to context for the research or writing so that content is deemphasized. The traditional research paper or five-paragraph essay often assigned in courses is typical of such an approach—an approach that encourages students to find information to "data dump" into an end product, with information used simply to fill up space. Indeed, recent results from the Citation Project seem to support this contention. Researchers concluded that the students they studied in first-year writing courses "sentence-mine" from sources rather than fully read, understand, and use them.[6]

To avoid a reductionist view and misconception of IL as a mechanical skill, Norgaard argues that IL should be "rhetoricized." Rhetorical theory allows both IL and writing to be viewed as situated within a specific context and influenced by cultural, historical, social, and political systems. Norgaard also points to the rhetorical canons as a way to rhetoricize IL. In particular, the rhetorical canon of invention provides a link between IL and writing.

The five canons (or parts) of rhetoric are invention (making persuasive arguments), arrangement (organization of discourse), style (use of language), memory (memorization of information), and delivery (presentation of information). While the canons originated in classical rhetoric and oral speech, they also serve as the basis for writing theory and pedagogy. Ideally, the canons are considered holistically to prepare and present discourse. Historically, however, one or more of the canons have predominated in teaching and the act of composing. In current-traditional forms of writing pedagogy, for example, the canons of arrangement and style predominate so that the teaching of writing becomes focused on mechanics and style. As a result, the canon of invention is subordinated and content deemphasized. However, the canon of invention experienced a resurgence of interest during the latter part of the twentieth century in both theory and practice in the field of rhetoric and writing. Scholars note the connection between discourse and its relationship to the content it communicates.[7] Through invention, a writer finds and discovers information to communicate and with which to make a persuasive argument. As such, the canon of invention ties research to the process of composing through a common interest in inquiry to make and mediate meaning. In pedagogical terms, invention is associated with active learning strategies that emphasize discovery (e.g., problem-based learning), finding information for a purpose, and the presentation of that information. Hook, for example, describes the use of invention and reinvention strategies in research and writing processes.[8]

Thus, rhetorical invention, known more commonly in pedagogy as inquiry, is a key link establishing the theoretical connection between research and writing. Research, then, can be seen as a contextual and process-oriented literacy that fosters an intellectual process that makes and negotiates meaning driven by inquiry. As a result, Norgaard proposes that we "write information literacy" to place it within rhetoric and writing theory to facilitate a shift in conception about what it is.[9] Furthermore, as rhetorically theorized constructs, writing and IL are intrinsically connected to constructivist theories of learning in which the learner actively engages in inquiry and reflective practices to assimilate and construct meaning or knowledge from information.

Researchers advocate that IL be seen as a context-based construct tied to liberal education, lifelong learning, and to learning as a social good.[10] Christine Bruce, for example, delineates seven different conceptions of IL based on user experience.[11] Her research shifts the definition of IL away from being based on skills or attributes toward an understanding of IL based on the individual's relationship with her or his information environment—that is, within the context of the task. Mandy Lupton studied conceptions of IL by analyzing the research students did to write a course essay. She concluded that students' approaches to research fell into three categories: fact finding, balancing information, and scrutinizing and analyzing.[12] Fact finding illustrates the conception of IL associated with current traditional teaching that results in the search for information to meet course requirements. Thus, writing is a product with little concern for context. In comparison, the third category, scrutinizing and analyzing, reflects a deeper learning experience in which students seek and use information to create meaning, build their knowledge base, and communicate for a purpose and to an audience—that is, within a rhetorical context. Louise Limberg also shows a more rhetorical approach to research, in which the context and purpose of information seeking more fully develops the students' ability to construct knowledge from different perspectives rather than seek the right answer.[13] Furthermore, studies have shown that instructors view research and information seeking in the context of making meaning, in opposition to traditional models emphasizing learning discrete skills.[14]

Rhetorical theory serves as the theoretical basis for a connection between research and writing, as well as a foundation for pedagogical practices as manifested in standards and outcomes created by the professional bodies of both disciplines. "Information Competency Standards for Higher Education," hereafter referred to as IL Standards, details five standards and accompanying performance measures and objectives as a framework to define and assess IL in higher education.[15] Almost simultaneously, the Council of Writing Program Administrators (WPA) developed the *WPA Outcomes Statement for First-Year Composition* (*WPA OS*). Emerging from different disciplines, the *WPA OS* and IL Standards are remarkably similar in intent.[16] Rhetorical context can be clearly seen in the IL Standards in the articulation of finding, using, and presenting information within a purpose. In addition, the IL Standards articulate the reevaluation and revision of search strategies as new information is found and integrated with the old so that research is defined as a recursive process. Similarly, the *WPA OS* articulates revision and reevaluation so that writing is also conceptualized as a recursive process. Given disciplinary roots, the *WPA OS* focuses on writing, and the IL Standards center on information seeking (or research); however, both emphasize rhetorical constructs and the importance of audience and purpose. The IL Standards and *WPA OS* have guided curriculum design and pedagogical practices for IL instruction and writing and have been integrated for course design.[17] They have also been integrated to develop program-level outcomes for IL and writing for undergraduate majors.[18]

PROCESSES

The concept of research as a process emerged at approximately the same time as the writing process movement in the late twentieth century, and it built upon rhetorical theory and constructivist theories of learning. Carol Kuhlthau delineates research as a process, from topic selection to search closure to the communication of information. During nearly the same time period, Linda Flower and John Hayes reported on their research to outline a model for the writing process. While conducted in separate disciplines and on seemingly distinct topics, the models consist of similarities that highlight and emphasize constructivist learning and the connection between good research and good writing and the pedagogical path to achieve both.

Information Search Process

In her book *Seeking Meaning: A Process Approach to Library and Information Services*, based on research into the information search process (ISP), Kuhlthau proposes a process approach for library services.[19] Kuhlthau conducted longitudinal research through a series of studies with students and a variety of information-intensive professionals. Her findings resulted in the construction of the ISP as a six-stage model. Kuhlthau's holistic ISP model articulates six stages reflecting the cognitive, affective, and physical aspects individuals experience while conducting research to complete a task. They are as follows:

1. Initiation: Identification of an information need during which the individual contemplates the task, engages in brainstorming, and discusses the topic and other strategies that are typically associated with prewriting. This stage is dominated by confusion and uncertainty as the individual struggles to define the task.
2. Selection: Identification of a general topic or problem area during which the individual conducts background research and analyzes a particular topic's fit within the task or assignment criteria. This stage may also be associated with confusion and anxiety as the individual attempts to match potential topics with requirements.
3. Exploration: Initial searching and seeking of information in which the individual searches for and reads information to become more informed about the general topic, with the goal of narrowing and refining. This stage is associated with doubt and confusion as the individual analyzes and sorts through differing, and perhaps competing, perspectives to formalize a topic.
4. Formulation: Identification of a focused topic area in which the individual uses the information found and analyzed during the exploration stage to focus on a specific topic area (creating a thesis

statement, for example). This stage is associated with confidence and optimism and, at times, increased motivation and engagement.

5. Collection: Searching and collecting information relevant to the focused topic area in which the individual collects information specific to the focused topic to expand and support it. The individual conducts more focused searches and organizes information. This stage is associated with confidence as the individual works toward completion of the task.

6. Presentation: The individual ends the search process as a result of finding redundant or irrelevant information or because of impending deadlines; presentation of information to others. Feelings associated with this stage may be satisfaction, relief at completing the project, or disappointment.[20]

Although presented in stages, the ISP model is sequential but not necessarily linear; reflection guides the process as the user moves from identifying an information need to search closure; however, this sequence does not preclude recursiveness as information is found and the topic is developed and refined.[21] In addition to the aforementioned six stages, Kuhlthau describes the concept of "information impact" (the purpose of the information needed and how will it be used) and its importance as a motivational factor in the ISP. Individuals enter into a search for information to accomplish a task; therefore, goals related to that task influence their motivation for seeking information. As a result, the ISP is highly rhetorical in that it is based on the context within which the individual seeks information. These same conceptions of process articulated in the ISP can be seen in Flower and Hayes's writing process model.

The Writing Process

In their landmark 1981 article in *College Composition and Communication*, Linda Flower and John Hayes describe a cognitive process theory of writing.[22] The writing process, as presented by Flower and Hayes and successive researchers, is now a standard pedagogical foundation for writing courses and college writing textbooks. Hayes and others have continued research on the writing process since Flower and Hayes's original publication of the model. The stages of the process are often delineated in more detail and articulated using different language from that first used by Flower and Hayes; however, for the purposes of this chapter and comparison with the ISP, the focus will be on Flower and Hayes's original work, as it still serves as a foundation for understanding and conceiving the writing process.

Flower and Hayes's cognitive theory of writing describes writing as a goal-directed process in which writers move through hierarchical thinking processes as they compose. The model incorporates three interacting units: the task environment; the writer's long-term memory; and the writing processes of planning, translating, and revising. They described these writing processes as tool kits that writers call upon when needed as they compose within a process model that is dynamic and fluid. As a tool kit, processes incorporate techniques or strategies for the writer to use to accomplish a task.

Planning, for example, incorporates the generation of ideas, goal setting, and organizing. Writers establish two types of goals during the planning stage. Process goals are the procedures or strategies writers use and continually refine as they move through completion of the task. Content goals are related to the information to be presented to the audience, and they are continually revised into a more complex network of goals and subgoals as the writer reviews and evaluates a composition and integrates information and learns to revise. This process of reviewing and evaluating to refine goals can clearly be seen in the Kuhlthau's ISP model as the individual moves through selection, exploration, formulation, and collection of information to establish a thesis or research question, and then to search for and use information to support (and revise) that thesis. In other words, both the ISP and the writing process are recursive in nature, as writers use reflection continually to revise their information needs and writing as they proceed through a task.

The translating stage of the writing process model reflects the writer's attempt to take ideas and put them into writing so that he or she makes meaning from information based on goals set during the planning stage. Composing during this stage incorporates the writer's analysis and integration of collected information with his or her own experience and the rhetorical situation represented in the task environment. The reviewing stage, then, involves two subprocesses: evaluating and revising the text as the writer reviews and revises what he or she has written.

Reflective of the recursive nature of the ISP and the writing process, writers move back and forth between stages and call upon specific techniques and strategies when needed. While reviewing, for example, a writer may return to the planning stage as he or she evaluates his or her written draft to develop additional goals to fill in informational gaps. Alternatively, he or she may return to the translating stage to construct or reconstruct meaning as he or she analyzes and integrates information.

In placing Kuhlthau's ISP model beside Flower and Hayes's model of the writing process, the tie between research and writing becomes obvious. Flower and Hayes's model focuses more explicitly on composing, while Kuhlthau's model of the ISP concentrates more heavily on collection of information; however, these differences can be accounted for by disciplinary emphases in which library and information science focuses on the seeking of information, while rhetoric and writing focuses on making meaning and its communication.

Despite disciplinary differences, Kuhlthau's and Flower and Hayes's process models clearly identify both research and writing as contextual rhetorical processes. Kuhlthau's description of the ISP is similar to the planning phase of the writing process. An information need (or broad topic) is identified, requiring the individual to generate ideas and set goals. Flower and Hayes's model describes organization as a writing process strategy, similar to strategies used in the initiation and exploration stages of the ISP, in which researchers and writers discover structure by categorizing information to make decisions related to audience and other goals. In rhetoric and writing, these strategies are often referred to pedagogically as prewriting techniques in which the individual engages in brainstorming activities, discussions, and initial reading or evaluation of the task criteria. Likewise, strategies Kuhlthau uses in the focus formulation and collection stages are similar to those described in Flower and Hayes's model (note taking, outlining, and other techniques) to organize and categorize information collected to first formulate a refined thesis and then organize collected information to support that thesis.

GOALS AND MOTIVATION

Beyond techniques and strategies, both Kuhlthau and Flower and Hayes discuss the importance of goals and motivation to the processes of research and writing. According to Flower and Hayes, the writer's ability to develop and refine goals is influential in how well they write. Kuhlthau describes this same concept as "information impact."[23] In both researchers' studies, goal setting (or information impact) influenced the search for information and writing. Kuhlthau notes that experienced researchers seek information to create value and add to meaning. Flower and Hayes contend that experienced writers continually modify goals as they learn when gathering and analyzing information. These descriptions are consistent with constructivist learning theory's description of deep learning versus surface learning.

Surface learning is characterized by the use of information and writing that results from current traditional forms of teaching and learning in which mechanics and style are emphasized and content is deemphasized. Deep learning, on the other hand, is characterized by the search for information based on goals related to context (the task, the audience, the purpose) and by writing that integrates information found to synthesize and create meaning. Deep learning is the goal of constructivist pedagogy by placing students in such active learning paradigms as problem-based learning, role-playing and scenarios, experiments, or other techniques that guide students through discovery. For librarians and instructors, then, the key is to find ways to facilitate students' engagement with a topic so that they are motivated to search for and use information in a deep way.

FROM THEORY TO PROCESS TO PEDAGOGY: INQUIRY

Strategies that engage and motivate students in the inquiry process lead to deep learning. The ISP and writing process models illuminate these strategies and guide instructors to develop methods to facilitate inquiry and writing by understanding the cognitive and affective modes as part of learning. For example, Limberg reports on study results in which attention to early stages of the research and writing processes when students explore the topic and develop research questions are more effective than traditional instructional approaches in which students are taught to search specific databases or formulate search terms.[24] Limberg calls this an emphasis on information *use* rather than information *seeking*. This approach is consistent with rhetorical strategies that emphasize invention and making meaning from information as a deeper approach to learning sought by constructivist paradigms. It is also an approach that shifts teaching away from practices associated with the traditional research paper to more meaningful research/writing processes.

Sandra Jamieson and Rebecca Moore Howard hypothesize that students in first-year courses may not have an understanding of what writing a college research paper means and suggest that pedagogy must adjust to overhaul how research writing is taught.[25] Perhaps one way to do this is to focus on students' lack of understanding of the research writing task by creating activities that facilitate their analysis of the task environment: the assignment itself, the audience they are addressing, and the purpose for which they are conducting research and writing. This calls for more attention to students' work during early phases of the ISP (initiation, selection, exploration) and writing processes (planning). Doing so facilitates an approach that coaches students and facilitates their ability to understand how to use information, as well as seek it.

Lupton's research shows that the task environment (topic and discipline) impacted students' experiences (or motivation) related to IL; she concludes that it is important to design assignments and learning activities in a way that facilitates students' use of information as evidence and argument creation.[26] Learning strategies like problem-based learning lend themselves to this process so that students are immersed in the task environment and must use their research and writing to find information, set goals, and work toward a solution. In such learning strategies, the instructor and librarian become facilitators to help students brainstorm, find, and sift through various perspectives; organize information; and integrate information so that they create meaning. Problem-based learning strategies are recursive in nature, as students must weigh different approaches to a solution and may find themselves continually returning to the problem (or exploration) stages to reset goals and develop new information collection strategies before finally settling on a solution.

CONCLUSION

In higher education, disciplinary differences often result in silos that isolate individuals. Partnerships among disciplines, for instance, rhetoric and writing and library and information science, often help break down those silos. The spirit of Rolf Norgaard's call for librarians and writing instructors to hold deeper conversations and "write information literacy" is a call to tear down those disciplinary silos so that we work together and bring together our disciplinary expertise in seeking and making meaning effectively to develop pedagogies that engage and motivate students.

Norgaard claims that IL should be viewed as a process-oriented literacy in which inquiry is part of a process for making and mediating meaning. As such, it is linked to pedagogies familiar to writing instruction in which research and writing are goal-oriented and recursive. The relationship between good research and good writing is grounded in the nature of assignments that encourage students to use inquiry to guide exploration of a problem or task and establish goals within a rhetorical context. Doing so encourages recursive strategies in a process-oriented approach, which uses information to gain knowledge and seek meaning in a sophisticated way. Pedagogical strategies that engage students lead to self-motivation to encourage information use and stronger writing. As a result, it is clear that viewing both research and writing as context-oriented rhetorical processes that share theoretical roots and process-oriented pedagogical connections is the key to understanding the relationship between good research and good writing.

NOTES

1. Jean Sheridan, ed., *Writing-across-the-Curriculum and the Academic Library: A Guide for Librarians, Instructors, and Writing Program Directors* (Westport, CT: Greenwood Press, 1995).

2. James Elmborg, "Information Literacy and Writing across the Curriculum: Sharing the Vision," *Reference Services Review* 31, no. 1 (2003): 68–80.

3. James Elmborg, "Libraries and Writing Centers in Collaboration: A Basis in Theory," in *Centers for Learning: Writing Centers and Libraries in Collaboration*, edited by James Elmborg and Sheila Hook, 1–20 (Chicago: Association of College and Research Libraries, 2005).

4. Jennifer Nutefall and Phyllis Mentzell Ryder, "Teaching Research Rhetorically," *Academic Exchange Quarterly* 9, no. 3 (2005): 307–11. Available online at http://rapidintellect.com/AEQweb/6mar3163z5.htm (accessed August 29, 2012).

5. Rolf Norgaard, "Writing Information Literacy in the Classroom: Contributions to a Concept," *Reference and User Services Quarterly* 43, no. 2 (2003): 124–30; Rolf Norgaard, "Writing Information Literacy in the Classroom: Pedagogical Enactments and Implications," *Reference and User Services Quarterly* 43, no. 3 (2004): 220–26.

6. Sandra Jamieson and Rebecca Moore Howard, "Sentence-Mining: Uncovering the Amount of Reading and Comprehension in College Writers' Researched Writing," in *The New Digital Scholar*, edited by Randall McClure and James P. Purdy, 111–33 (Medford, NJ: Information Today, 2013).

7. Janice M. Lauer, *Invention in Rhetoric and Composition* (West Lafayette, IN: Parlor Press, 2004).

8. Shelia Hook, "Teaching Librarians and Writing Center Professionals in Collaboration: Comprehensive Practices," in *Centers for Learning: Writing Centers and Librarians in Collaboration*, edited by James Elmborg and Sheila Hook, 21–41 (Chicago: Association of College and Research Libraries, 2005).

9. Norgaard, "Writing Information Literacy in the Classroom."

10. Christine Bruce, *The Seven Faces of Information Literacy* (Adelaide, Australia: Auslib Press, 1997); Bruce Johnston and Sheila Webber, "Information Literacy in Higher Education: A Review and Case Study," *Studies in Higher Education* 28, no. 3 (2003): 335–52; Christine E. DeMars, Lynn Cameron, and T. Dary Erwin, "Information Literacy as Foundational: Determining Competence," *Journal of General Education* 52, no. 4 (2003): 253–65; Duane Ward, "Revisioning Information Literacy for Lifelong Meaning," *Journal of Academic Librarianship* 32, no. 4 (2006): 396–402.

11. Bruce, *The Seven Faces of Information Literacy*, 1997.

12. Mandy Lupton, *The Learning Connection: Information Literacy and the Student Experience* (Adelaide, Australia: Auslib Press, 2004).

13. Louise Limberg, Mikael Alexandersson, and Annika Lantz-Andersson, "What Matters? Shaping Meaningful Learning through Teaching Information Literacy," *Libri* 58, no. 2 (2008): 82–91.

14. Stuart Boon, Bruce Johnston, and Sheila Webber, "A Phenomenographic Study of English Faculty's Conception of Information Literacy," *Journal of Documentation* 63, no. 2 (2007): 204–8.

15. Association of College and Research Libraries, "Information Competency Standards for Higher Education" (Chicago: Association of College and Research Libraries, 2000). Available online at www.ala.org/ala/acrl/acrlstandards/informationliteracy-competency.htm (accessed August 29, 2012).

16. Barbara J. D'Angelo, "Information Literacy and Writing: A Rhetorical Analysis of Standards and Outcomes." Paper presented at the Annual Conference of the Council of Writing Program Administrators, Tempe, AZ, July 2007; Norgaard, "Writing Information Literacy in the Classroom."

17. Nutefall and Mentzell Ryder, "Teaching Research Rhetorically."

18. Barry M. Maid and Barbara J. D'Angelo, "The WPA Outcomes, Information Literacy, and Challenges of Outcomes-Based Curricular Design," in *Teaching and Assessing Writing: A Twenty-Fifth Anniversary Celebration*, edited by Norbert Elliot and Les Perelman, 99–112 (New York: Hampton Press, 2012).

19. Carol Kuhlthau, *Seeking Meaning: A Process Approach to Library and Information Services*, 2nd ed. (Westport, CT: Libraries Unlimited, 2004).

20. Kuhlthau, *Seeking Meaning*.

21. Carol Kuhlthau, "From Information to Meaning: Confronting Challenges of the Twenty-First Century," *Libri* 58, no. 2 (2008): 66–73.

22. Linda Flower and John Hayes, "A Cognitive Process Theory of Writing," *College Composition and Communication* 32, no. 4 (1981): 365–87.

23. Kuhlthau.

24. Limberg, Alexandersson, and Lantz-Andersson, "What Matters?"

25. Jamieson and Howard, "Sentence-Mining."

26. Lupton, *The Learning Connection*.

THREE

Toward the "Good" Research Assignment: A Librarian Speaks

Roberta Tipton

The John Cotton Dana Library is the third-largest of a 26-unit research library system. Dana is the main campus library at Rutgers-Newark, a highly diverse, urban, doctoral-granting academic institution, with just fewer than 12,000 students. About 7,500 of these students are undergraduates.[1] Our reference and instruction activities serve both well-prepared and underprepared undergraduate students in a variety of subject areas, including biology, business, psychology, nursing, social work, history, philosophy, public administration, geology, chemistry, and urban education.

Most research assignments we see are doable and lead (some might say force) a student to reach beyond received wisdom to construct new knowledge of his or her own. As Carol Kuhlthau has articulated so well in her information search process (ISP) model, authentic research is at best a process fraught with doubt and confusion for the researcher.[2] Under favorable circumstances, however, student research leads to the kind of informational self-reliance ("lifelong learning") held out as the ultimate goal of information literacy.[3] Unfortunately, poor research assignments have an impact larger than their numbers would indicate, frustrating the student learning process while wasting the time of everyone concerned. Academic librarians are in an ideal position to take positive steps to prevent and ameliorate the negative effects of poor assignments and encourage the writing of better ones, either by collaborating with teaching faculty or by writing them ourselves. As our head of reference at Dana, Natalie Borisovets, says about helping students, "We can't save the whole world, but we can save some of it."[4]

HOW DO ASSIGNMENTS GO WRONG?

What we've got here is a failure to communicate. — *Cool Hand Luke*

Conflicts and misunderstandings over assignments are all too common. See if you recognize any of the following scenarios:

1. The students do not understand the expectations of the assignment and are too inexperienced or intimidated to ask their professor. (This can actually be a librarian opportunity. As nongrading authorities in this context, librarians can be asked things that students would never dare ask the professor. This gives us a chance to help set the students on the right track.)
2. The professor has not yet explained the assignment or has just passed it out at the beginning of a library class, so the students have no concept of what they are supposed to be doing/feeling/ thinking at this time.
3. The professor has given a perfectly good assignment, but the students have not read the material they are to analyze even once (certainly not twice) and have no idea why you are focusing upon certain themes at the reference desk or in the library instruction class.
4. The professor has a conference and has just remembered that a library session will keep the class going for another week. There is often no library assignment at all. (This is worse than substitute teaching; this is babysitting. We try to avoid doing it if we can.) Mary Mancuso Biggs and Mark Weber wrote about this situation in 1979, and nothing much has changed since then.[5]
5. The professor tells the students on the assignment sheet to consult the reference librarians if they need help but does not inform the librarians. Unfortunately, there are 120 students in the class, and all of them converge on the reference desk with the same question within a short period of time. (A brief librarian visit to the class would have prevented this mob scene.)
6. The instructor is currently a Ph.D. student and has temporarily forgotten what an undergraduate assignment should look like. As a result, the assignment requires a level of scholarly interpretation and analysis that is beyond most of us on the planet, let alone an undergraduate.
7. The professor has given what Nina McHale calls a "rogue assignment": ill-conceived scavenger hunt, wrong information, missing resources, and the like.[6] Perhaps the professor just arrived from

another university (or industry or a different environment) and never bothered to check whether your library has the resources he or she assumes his or her students can use. Perhaps a combination of budget cuts and the constant changes in library holdings have sabotaged a previously useful assignment by altering the titles of sources. Now the librarian must take the initiative to solve the problem.

Surely someone has solutions for these too-familiar assignment issues. Surely the library literature has some answers.

CHARACTERISTICS OF EFFECTIVE AND INEFFECTIVE ASSIGNMENTS

To see the many ways in which librarians and teaching faculty have thought about and worked successfully with research assignments is encouraging.[7] To find that we keep returning to this issue every few years with a new solution to problematic assignments is discouraging in the extreme. This constant reinvention indicates that no one solution can be completely effective in every context. It falls upon librarians, and teaching faculty to adopt the approaches that work in their campus environments.

A. Ehrhardt, J. D. Gerletti, and C. C. Crawford, who were teaching faculty in three different subject areas (English, public administration, and education), wrote an article on college library assignments published in 1954 and republished in 1958.[8] Their article suggests a number of actions leading to useful college library assignments. These include 1) directing students to desirable references by choosing useful resources, providing a bibliography with location information, and making arrangements with the library in advance; 2) relieving congestion at the library by suggesting items to buy, giving both students and librarians sufficient advance notice, and placing scarce items on reserve; and 3) checking library assignments through the measurement of student performance.[9] Ehrhardt and colleagues advocate short-circuiting plagiarism, conducting direct assessment of student learning, and consulting with librarians—all very modern ideas consistent with current information literacy and assessment practices.

Librarians have written extensively on the subject, attempting to codify what makes good and poor assignments. Mara L. Houdyshell presents a table of characteristics of effective assignments and pitfalls to avoid.[10] Pixey Anne Mosley offers an "assignment checklist" for "good" assignments and a section on "phrasing of assignments" that presents explanatory material about poorly phrased assignments.[11] Like Mosley, Patricia Morris Donegan prepared and delivered faculty workshops. She presents a table of "dos and don'ts" for effective library assignments.[12]

Necia Parker-Gibson emphasizes a respect for variations in student learning styles and a realistic evaluation of the effort/reward relationship from the student's point of view.[13] Donna Miller draws from available resources, including the published literature and online pages by other librarians, adds her own ideas, and synthesizes a strong list of descriptions and characteristics of effective assignments, along with an "avoid" list.[14]

Monty L. McAdoo offers a list of "common reasons assignments fail." They are as follows: 1) students are ill–prepared, 2) assignment contains flaws, 3) flawed assignment is repeated, and 4) librarian lacks rapport with faculty member.[15] McAdoo's work also includes a detailed analysis of different kinds of assignments and what librarians can do to help them succeed.[16]

If we were to summarize all of these thoughtful recommendations for creating good assignments, the list might look something like this:

1. Know your audience. Understand what students know and do not know when you begin.
2. Have precise learning objectives for the assignment. (Information literacy standards and Bloom's taxonomy can be helpful here.[17]) Find meaningful methods of determining if your objectives have been reached.
3. Be clear about what is required and where to find necessary research materials. Encourage feedback so that ambiguous elements can be made plain for this round and the next time you give the assignment.
4. Assign only resources actually available to the students.
5. Give an assignment with enough flexibility so that every student is not looking for exactly the same source. Where possible, offer individual choices to increase student interest and cut down on plagiarism.
6. Break complex assignments down into understandable pieces.
7. Teaching faculty: Talk with the librarians. Invite them to help you design library assignments or visit your classroom to explain research tools and approaches to your students.
8. Librarians: Talk with the teaching faculty. Get to know them and their concerns. Course and curriculum objectives are key to meaningful assignments.
9. Teaching faculty and librarians: Talk with the students in an understandable way. Clue them in to the scholarly conversation.

So, if there is so much agreement about what should be done, why don't we always do it the right way? The answers might lie in the situations of the players (students, teaching faculty, librarians) and how they interact with one another.

LIBRARY ASSIGNMENTS AND LIBRARIAN–TEACHING FACULTY COOPERATION AND COLLABORATION

Evan Ira Farber reviews the history of thought about librarian–teaching faculty cooperation since the 1930s and the effects of cooperation on library assignments. He outlines two extreme views: 1) librarian as faculty "handmaiden" and 2) librarian as completely independent actor. He then argues for cooperation as a middle ground.[18] Biggs and Weber, writing back in 1979, frame and articulate many persistent issues involved with classroom instruction, with faculty cooperation, and with teaching one-on-one at the reference desk while working with students and library assignments.[19] Michael Mounce, Rubina Bhatti, William B. Badke, and Monty L. McAdoo place library assignments firmly in the dual contexts of information literacy and collaboration with teaching faculty.[20]

Badke cites Harry L. Hardesty and R. K. Baker's work on faculty cultures and faculty perceptions. He contrasts the teaching faculty emphasis on content and relatively narrow questions with the library faculty/information literacy emphasis on process and broader organizational concerns.[21] Ultimately, Badke suggests demonstrating value and reaching information literacy objectives through a separate information literacy course in each discipline.[22]

Bhatti mentions the difference in focus between short-term and long-term goals for research instruction.[23] Alicia B. Ellison reminds us that librarians and teaching faculty can work collaboratively to achieve both course content and information literacy goals.[24] It is significant that the earlier literature uses the word *cooperation*, while later sources tend to use *collaboration*, implying a closer, more egalitarian, more active relationship between library faculty and teaching faculty.[25] Badke asserts that "effective collaboration is not the norm. . . . But we keep trying."[26] I would add that we keep trying because the benefits of effective collaboration are many and sometimes far-reaching.

Ways to cooperate or collaborate with teaching faculty in achieving effective assignments include librarian-led workshops, participation in faculty development activities, and proactive contacts with faculty and their departments.[27] Mosley and Donegan, in particular, offer thorough and carefully outlined descriptions of the rationales and objectives of librarian-led assignment workshops for teaching faculty.[28] Daniel Brendle-Moczuk and Nicole J. Auer and Ellen M. Krupar write of the desirability of librarian-graded assignments.[29]

McAdoo suggests a transactional model involving the student, the librarian, and the faculty member in an "assignment life cycle" of development, distribution, completion, and evaluation.[30] By looking at the stages of the assignment life cycle and the transactions between the participants in the various stages, McAdoo uncovers many of the thorny issues related to research assignments. The teaching faculty member usually develops and evaluates the assignment, but the student and the librarian are often only involved in receiving and completing the assignment. McAdoo suggests that librarians get involved with teaching faculty and curriculum on the departmental and institutional levels, as well as one-on-one, to develop a better understanding of assignments and encourage better assignment outcomes.[31]

WHY GIVE A LIBRARY ASSIGNMENT AT ALL? THE SITUATION OF THE TEACHING FACULTY

"When I first started teaching, I gave a traditional term paper. I soon learned not to do that."—An academic administrator and former professor

Teaching faculty would have an easier time if they never gave any research assignments at all. There would be no incoherent or trite papers to grade. No one would have to deal with plagiarism, which is too easy in our copy-and-paste technological universe. A disheartening phenomenon we see is the professor who, fed up with the whole library assignment/plagiarism problem, has students work on analytical papers only from a carefully chosen set of provided materials. The problem with this scenario is that it subverts some of the purposes of a college education. Looking at Bloom's taxonomy, no college student would have to practice any higher-level evaluation or synthesis based on anything except provided materials.[32] In terms of information literacy or research competency, few students would be motivated to go beyond received wisdom or Internet freebies to find out anything for themselves.[33]

A good research assignment requires time, effort, and attention. Teaching faculty, like academic librarians, are already overbooked. They have to contend with research, publication, committee meetings, student gripes and appointments, test preparation, administration, grading papers, reporting grades, and basic course preparation. In addition, library assignments, and teaching in general, are not necessarily the activities that will enhance one's academic career.[34]

Even under the best circumstances, college teaching is sometimes a difficult business. Consider the following scenarios:

1. A professor probably has a wide variety of students in the class, some of whom are underprepared for the work at hand.
2. An instructor might have little control over the curriculum that he or she is teaching.
3. Many professors have little or no formal preparation in teaching, although that does not prevent from learning to be good teachers.[35] (Many academic librarians have little formal preparation in

teaching, for that matter, but teaching is discussed and encouraged by colleagues and is often rewarding for librarian careers.)

4. The instructor might be a graduate student or an inexperienced college teacher. In that case, he or she will not discover *how* prepared or underprepared the students are until he or she sees the results of the first research assignment. (Experienced instructors learn to give a diagnostic assignment early in the course.)

5. He or she might be an adjunct, short of time and spending hours each week driving from job to job just to make ends meet. When will he or she become familiar with *your* library? Will the department tell you he or she exists so that you can reach out? Obtaining even a phone number or an e-mail address for an adjunct is often a challenge.

Mosley discusses misconceptions about libraries and student preparedness sometimes held by faculty. These include the following: 1) libraries are all alike and available worldwide; 2) all students know about the library from their freshman English class; 3) students say that they took the library tour, therefore they know all about the library; 4) libraries never change; and 5) anyone with a college degree knows how to use an academic library.[36] In addition, we find that many teaching faculty have never encountered librarians in the classroom, and they are surprised that librarians can and do teach.

THEY'RE JUST NOT THAT INTO YOU: RESEARCH ASSIGNMENTS AND THE UNDERGRADUATE STUDENT

> The librarian suggested a book that solved my problem. I mean, a book! I never thought of that. Books are so—medieval.—Overheard statement made by an undergraduate student

> We have very good students on this campus, but they can be very naïve.—Director of a writing center

> They don't know what they don't know.—A librarian colleague

A new academic librarian was disappointed to discover that many undergraduate students did not like libraries or research.[37] For those of us who have been teaching and doing reference for a few years, this is unfortunately old news. Constance A. Mellon identified and named library anxiety in 1986, and the years and technological changes since then appear to have done little or nothing to eliminate it.[38] In fact, to "library anxiety" one could now add the condition of "library indifference."

An elementary school librarian once bragged to me at a conference that her students started using library databases in the second grade, and some undergraduate students do come to college with good research skills. Even so, I encounter college students every day who have never used any search engine except Google, nor ever thought it necessary to darken the doors of any physical library before now. We are often dealing with college students whose library anxieties and library indifference are deepened by their lack of previous library experiences, either print or electronic, combined with a lifetime of skimming along the surface of the online world and accepting Facebook posts and Wikipedia entries as irrefutable truth. No wonder they think they know all about research. No wonder they show up at reference desks in a state of puzzlement or even panic, because they have literally tried everything else they know before consulting a librarian, and now they are out of time. (In the early days of the World Wide Web, a student showed up at our desk looking exhausted and said, "I've been on the Web for three days." We solved his problem within minutes.) Librarians have set up reference departments like clinics, but at certain times of the year they are actually more like emergency rooms. Too many students consult us about library assignments on the worst days of their lives, when they are clueless, upset, and afraid for their grades. This situation underscores the value of bringing a librarian into the assignment cycle (through instruction, faculty liaison, marketing the library to students, or whatever) before the students have reached the panic stage. When we see the distance that exists between student preparedness and faculty perception, we begin to understand the situation of the librarian.

RESEARCH ASSIGNMENTS AND THE LIBRARIAN: BETWEEN STUDENTS AND TEACHING FACULTY

Real learning begins when the student appears in the reference area, often clutching a handout and looking confused.—Biggs and Weber, 1979[39]

[T]he librarian must have limitless patience, sensitivity, a knack for clear and methodical explanation, and do nothing to confirm the . . . student's fear of appearing stupid. This is more difficult than one may think.—Biggs and Weber, 1979[40]

Research Assignments in Reference Work

It is generally acknowledged that librarians help people find information. Less recognized is the role of academic librarians in interpreting assignments and helping students acquire basic knowledge and strategies for fulfilling those assignments. McAdoo mentions two circumstances that place librarians—sometimes comfortably, sometimes uncomfortably—right in the middle of a teaching faculty–student dynamic: 1) "Students may feel uncomfortable asking their instructor questions about an assignment," and 2) "Students may not have the opportunity to provide feedback about their assignments."[41]

The librarian bias toward process is necessary but not sufficient to work effectively with research assignments.[42] The more we know about the subject matter *and* the more we know about research processes for different subjects, the better we do our jobs. As McAdoo puts it, "There is a direct relationship between librarians' familiarity with an assignment and their ability to provide effective and meaningful assistance."[43] He also states that, "Librarians need to wear different hats for different students."[44] The entire reference team is important because no one person can know all the relevant theories and approaches in every field. It is by sharing our specialist knowledge with one another that we can work with a variety of assignments as reference generalists.

Learning the right balance of content, process, and interpersonal communication for each student on each level is a never-ending challenge. Furthermore, technology keeps changing the communication channels, so we have to keep refining and reframing our responses to students to achieve mutual understanding. The interactions surrounding writing assignments can be the most complex.

Composition and Literature Papers

Dennis Isbell suggests not one but two useful frameworks for looking at the librarian's work with the college composition assignment: 1) Kuhlthau's information search process (ISP) from librarianship, and 2) the concept of rhetorical situation from composition theory.[45] Kuhlthau's work on the information search process (ISP) is familiar to many librarians. Stages of the ISP (in its 1988 version) include the following: 1) task initiation, 2) topic selection, 3) prefocus exploration, 4) focus formulation, 5) information collection, and 6) search closure.[46] Kuhlthau offers us not only insight into the process of research, with both its cognitive and affective aspects, but also a suggested scale of librarian intervention for different levels of inquiries. The results of the five zones of intervention can be summarized as follows: Z1) self-service (the librarian organizes material for use), Z2) single source, Z3) group of sources, Z4) sequence of sources, and Z5) process intervention. At times, working with student writers requires Z5 intervention, as well as accessing sources.[47] The ISP model helps both students and librarians understand the student's current stage of research; with this understanding, the librarian helps the student move through the process of prewriting, including topic development and exploration of information sources.

Isbell's second framework deals with rhetorical situation, a theory from the world of writing instruction. The Purdue Online Writing Laboratory describes rhetorical situation as the "position of your writing in relation to various elements that affect the content and comprehension of your words—the identity of the writer, the purpose, the audience, the topic, and the context for writing. Each of these factors plays an important role in the writing process."[48] Isbell explains that, "The rhetorical situation is simply the context and expectations for the writing (or speaking) assignment the student must complete."[49] Rhetorical situation is interesting within the context of work with research assignments (not just writing assignments), because it asks us to evaluate the situation in which the assignment is given and received, as well as the level of student readiness to complete the assignment.[50] By knowing something about the subject matter and level of the class, librarians can make an educated guess regarding the real and often unstated expectations for student performance. Although it is ideal to look at the syllabus and the assignment with the student, sometimes these are not available during the reference negotiation. Nevertheless, librarians can often make useful suggestions about both expectations and the process based upon previous experiences in the academic environment.

The more librarians know about the writing process, especially the writing process as advocated by their own writing department and taught by individual writing instructors on their own campus, the better they can help the students with composition papers requiring research. A useful approach is treating research/writing or writing/research as a single, intertwined process.[51] Given that your campus may have a writing center to help students with the writing itself, the librarian can help students with laying out research options, assist with initial research focus, and show how to use information sources, all of which Isbell labels as part of prewriting.[52] Using a database with a strong focus in mind saves time, but using the database as a way to find focus can also be successful. At the beginning of the writing process, the objective is to move the student toward the first draft.

Research for papers in composition or literature classes may involve either straight literature criticism or the exploration of outside topics, often in history or the social sciences, which have to be brought back to analysis of the text in question. Beginning students are often uncertain about which type of paper they have been asked to write, as well as how outside topics may be brought back to their text. Because the two kinds of papers require two different research strategies, the librarian can make a contribution during the prewriting phase in helping to clarify some of these issues.

Librarians can also reinforce the need for a thesis or research question for building an argument. This argument building is one of the biggest differences between high school and college writing, and many students fail to see how important an argument is to focusing their research and writing their papers. Sometimes the work is as easy as asking the student, "What do you want to say about this?" or "What is your attitude toward this?" In many cases, however, more questioning and context building on the part of the librarian are required to develop a research path. The beginning college student often has no idea how a really big subject cannot fit into a short paper without a clear research question or focused argument.

Research Papers in Other Subject Areas: Library and Web Sources

Research papers are often required of undergraduate students in classes other than English or composition. Here again, the librarian can provide guidance and help the student build context for the paper. Although the classic humanities paper might have included peer-reviewed sources, in addition to some primary text or texts, assignments in any subject may now require a blend of peer-reviewed sources with non-scholarly sources, news sources, case studies, reports from governments or nongovernmental organizations, or data from both library databases and the Web. Everything depends upon the aims and constraints of the assignment.

In applied disciplines what is happening in the field can be as important as any theoretical construct. Students need to learn how to use scholarly sources for models and theoretical frameworks to make sense of reports and data (often on the Web) and their own experience (work experience, surveys, interviews, experiments). As more useful sources of information move online, the librarian helps to demonstrate categories of information where the students may have no notion that such categories exist.[53] In some ways, the librarian is both a guide and a sort of systems/formats integrator, crossing platforms and categories to help students craft research strategies to make meaningful papers and projects.

Business assignments are a thing unto themselves, where theories of business and management may form one organizing principle, while the realities of the active business enterprise may form another. Business librarians spend many hours each week helping students find obscure data about companies, industries, and products. The student is responsible for weaving all of these data, other business knowledge, and a set of reasonable assumptions into a business paper or presentation. One professor described papers patched together from online sources without a solid business rationale as "surreal."[54]

Less Than a Full Research Paper: The Focused Writing Assignment

The student in a course other than English is often asked to examine some sources and write a brief analysis. McAdoo calls this kind of assignment a "content-based, writing from sources" assignment.[55] A successful writing assignment from one of our professors in biology goes something like this: Find a popular article on a biological research subject and then discover the research article behind it. Analyze the two articles and compare them. (A list of suggested science magazines for the general public is included.) This assignment leads students to recognize the differences between popular and scholarly publications, while polishing up their critical thinking, text analysis, and writing skills. The *General Science Full Text* database is ideal to get these students moving from popular to professional science literature.

Another (sometimes less successful) example is a common psychology assignment in which the student is asked to find some number of articles in psychology and analyze them.[56] In the variation we see most often at Dana, the student is given criteria appropriate for an empirical or experimental article. Sometimes the student understands that he or she is looking for an empirical article; other times, the student just asks for "an article in psychology." It is often up to the librarian to read the assignment carefully and translate the cues for the student.

Research Assignments in the Classroom

Collaboration and Integration

This is a librarian's dream of how classes and assignments can be: The students in a library class have read what they are supposed to read. They have chosen topics, and the professor has checked those topics and given feedback. The professor has assigned the students some writing, presentation, or class discussion about the topic before they walk into your library classroom. (Some of our best professors have done all three.) The writing prompts or research questions offered are comprehensible to this level of student, and the materials students need to complete the assignment are available in your library system. The professor is present in the classroom as an enthusiastic explainer, copresenter on certain points, and source of clarifications for the assignment expectations.

In a library class like this you can expect moderate to enthusiastic student engagement, just because the professor has laid all the groundwork. It is easy for a librarian to be a positive influence, providing information just at the moment it is required. Furthermore, this is an attainable goal, even though it is not always attained. For example, the writing program on my own campus has some great teachers who also mentor the next generation of writing instructors. The writing program director is an informed advocate of information literacy. Most writing instructors invite librarians into their classrooms. In some cases, we have even done grant-funded work together on writing/research or research/writing, the intertwined dance of process and content, so that students learn with a minimum of confusion and a maximum of successfully completed assignments.[57] Former writing center director and poet Patricia Bender and I have been teaching and writing together for more than a decade using research/writing or writing/research as our mantra.[58] Our collaboration began in an effort to give writing and research skills to transfer students in a remedial writing class, and it has gone on to include graduate students and faculty in activities related to both academic writing and grantsmanship.

Another grant-funded collaboration involved a standard writing course, English 102, which customarily has a research component. Writing instructor and creative writer Kevin Catalano and I began by meeting and analyzing the steps this master teacher planned to use to teach the academic writing process. The major steps are as follows: 1) topic approval; 2) research proposal; 3) exploratory research; 4) annotated bibliography (working bibliography, librarian-graded); 5) better thesis, more accurate argument; 6) outlining stage (detailed outline of thesis and each paragraph structured to show the topic sentence and supporting quotations from the text and outside sources); 7) typed first draft; 8) peer review; and 9) final draft (bibliography librarian-graded). I made a list of the kinds of library instruction and support that could be provided to his students, and together we negotiated where these pieces would appear in relationship to the teaching. (Interestingly, his perception of where things fit in the class was very different from mine, but we worked it out.) As a result, I attended his class six different times, sometimes simply as an observer, sometimes giving a presentation of as little as fifteen to twenty minutes, and twice using the entire class period in our hands-on computer lab at the library. Since the grant was part of a study on self-regulated learning (SRL), we did rigorous pretesting and posttesting and were able to show our positive impact on the students.[59]

Even without grant funding, and most often without multiple appearances in a class, my colleagues and I have worked with faculty members in multiple other subject areas who give thoughtful assignments and good support for students completing those assignments. It is the combination of a well-designed assignment and support system for the student that leads to success. What the best teachers do is to foster self-reliance and independent research, but they provide support while the students figure it all out. They introduce complex assignments in steps. They review each step and provide feedback to the student. They encourage class discussions, generally in small groups, with students reacting to the writing and research of other students in a constructive way. They prepare the students for each step of the process and make sure they are onboard. Most of them invite librarians in to provide appropriate instruction when it is optimal within the context of the course; for the rest, we prepare LibGuides tailored to their classroom needs.

Sometimes integration simply cannot work. If the professor has failed to give a meaningful or even comprehensible assignment, integration cannot work. If the students have not been properly prepared for the assignment, integration cannot work. If the librarians are accidentally or deliberately shut out, integration cannot work. And therefore, there are times when the librarian needs an assignment of his or her own.

Librarian-Graded or Librarian-Initiated Assignments

When I joined the Dana Library, we had a 1970s-style library curriculum based upon a workbook for our summer programs and expository writing classes. We structured worksheets and graded them ourselves. In its own way, the workbook approach was excellent, but, throughout time, the subject matter came to have less and less to do with the writing instructors' assignments as the "formats" approach came to have less and less to do with the realities of undergraduate research tools. The library assignment was just an extra burden on the students, and they came to resent it.

We found that one way to avoid this irrelevance is the guided generic assignment. This approach provides an introduction to the research process, so that the student's own research process can become more sophisticated. The content, however, is that of the class at hand. Instead of asking students to waste their time doing a library assignment they view as a burden, we simply facilitate the research process for their current, professor-given assignment. Throughout the years, I have built several of these for undergraduate composition classes to structure the library class time in a particular way or encourage undergraduates to think about authentic writing/research without being completely intimidated. (The "lists" assignment, developed with input from writing instructor Dale Howard of the Rutgers Newark Writing Program, appears in the appendix at the end of this chapter.) Generic assignments can also be useful when the professor has no assignment, or the preparation of students for the library class is inadequate. Some students and some classes really take to this approach, while others leave the forms lying about on the desks when they leave the library computer lab.

Another approach is the limited, but librarian-graded, library assignment strongly related to the course content. My colleagues, Ka-Neng Au and Wen-Hua Ren, and I have done these for business courses when we were invited to do so or proposed them ourselves to provide open-ended, transferable skills to the students. Three examples follow.

The first of these was constructed for an undergraduate business class in computer skills that featured the Microsoft Office suite. We built an in-class assignment asking the students to mine business databases for information that was displayed and manipulated in the Microsoft Office suite. The students practiced skills they needed to master for the current class while gaining knowledge of some important business databases that would help them complete assignments for future classes. The instructor gave us an entire class period, and we had the students e-mail their completed exercises to us in real time. When I taught my section, I projected my e-mail account up on the screen at the end of class. Students could see their assignments appear as they sent them to me, adding a touch of competition to the proceedings. Because we were present in the classroom during the exercise, we could provide assistance as needed. This assignment was designed to be completed during a single class period, which kept the students focused and did not burden them with extra homework. We graded these assignments ourselves and reported the results for each student and each section to the professor. She had us repeat the lesson for several semesters until she left the university.

A second librarian-built business assignment was part of Business Forum, an introductory class for undergraduate business majors with a total enrollment of about 1,000 in fall 2012. The class emphasized preparing for interviews, internships, and careers in business. We proposed a short online homework assignment using only three databases, offering activities inside each database. We estimated that students would require less than 30 minutes to complete the assignment. The purpose of the assignment was two-fold: 1) Prepare the undergraduates for interviews by highlighting each source's usefulness for getting quick company and industry information to impress potential employers, and 2) Make students familiar with a few basic business sources that they could use in other classes. We prepared a rubric for grading the assignments (five questions worth a total of fifteen points) and constructed a Google Docs form to receive the answers. We spent most of a classroom session for each section of the class introducing the databases and going over the homework assignment in great detail. Then we graded the assignment ourselves, reporting results to the classroom instructor in terms of points toward the final grade. The average grade for our 1,091 students was 12.58 points out of a possible 15. Since the point of the library assignment was to raise awareness of business sources, we were happy that so many students did well.

The third example was an in-class, extra-credit assignment, following the Business Forum classes, to be completed during a freestanding workshop in the library. Once again, we designed the assignment, created the Google Docs form, presented to the class, and graded the results. All sixteen students attending received their extra credit. This combination of clear purpose, integrated with the course, tight structure, librarian presentation/coaching, grading, and reporting back, appears to work well in a subject like business. The students are being exposed to content that is immediately relevant to their studies and, at the same time, are building some familiarity with business databases.

CONCLUSION: TOWARD BETTER RESEARCH ASSIGNMENTS

A "good" research assignment might have three different definitions, depending upon who you are: 1) A good assignment for the undergraduate student might be one that is successfully completed. 2) A good assignment for the teaching faculty might fulfill the goals of a course. 3) A good assignment for the librarian accomplishes 1 and 2, while paving the way for further independent learning in the future.

The assignment process begins with concept and design and continues through instructional and even institutional support. We have to admit that some of the basic problems in poor assignment outcomes can never be solved by librarians alone, as they are part of larger issues beyond our control. Taking a second look at McAdoo's assignment process model—development, distribution, completion, and evaluation—we see that the librarian's daily work with students and their assignments usually lies in the middle of the process.[60] This traditionally places the librarian in a sometimes uncomfortable, reactive stance between the student and the teaching faculty. This does not mean, however, that we give up trying to interpret assignments for students at the reference desk or assisting the teaching faculty in supporting better assignment outcomes.

Any positive actions librarians can take to influence research assignment development and evaluation, in addition to simple completion, move us toward preventing poor assignments and constructing assignments that help students learn better. These actions are well-known in academic library practice. They include the following: 1) talking with teaching faculty, department heads, and deans about their information needs and those of their students; 2) studying syllabi and curricula to find appropriate places for information literacy instruction; 3) volunteering to construct and grade research assignments inside other courses; and 4) designing and presenting our own workshops and classes. In short, seeking ever more useful ways to support the academic enterprise, however it is defined on our own campus, can lead to better assignments.

APPENDIX: DOING RESEARCH BY MAKING LISTS

One approach to research is to make lists and work with lists of sources. By working with lists, you never have to worry about a blank page or a blank mind while doing a paper or project.

1. Make a list of five possible topics or five aspects of one topic. Select the most promising one or two for preliminary research.
2. Make lists of what you know or questions you would like to ask about each topic. Make lists of relevant words and phrases for each topic as well.

3. Using library catalogs and databases, collect lists of sources that you think might be relevant to your research questions and send them to yourself via e-mail. Take full text at the same time if it is available. If the database will send references in the proper style (e.g., MLA format or APA format), make sure you take advantage of this feature to save time.

4. Evaluate your lists of sources ("working bibliography") and retrieve the items you need that you don't already have in full text.

5. Look at the resources you have consulted. Which ones appear to be of the best quality? The most relevant? The most complete? The most recent? The best introductions to your particular subject? The most cited by other experts?

6. Use the best of the best sources for your paper and document them in the text of your paper and in the List of Works Cited (MLA format).

Roberta Tipton and Dale Howard, 2006
Updated November 2012, RLT

NOTES

1. Office of Institutional Research and Academic Planning, Rutgers, the State University of New Jersey, "Headcount Enrollment by Campus, Full-Time/Part-Time Status, and Academic Level, Fall 2011," 2011. Available online at http://oirap.rutgers.edu/instchar/factpdf/enroll11.pdf (accessed December 22, 2012).

2. Carol Kuhlthau, "Developing a Model of the Library Search Process: Cognitive and Affective Aspects," *Reference Quarterly* 28, no. 2 (1988): 232–42; Carol Kuhlthau, *Seeking Meaning: A Process Approach to Library and Information Services*, 2nd ed. (Westport, CT: Libraries Unlimited, 2004).

3. Association of College and Research Libraries, "Information Literacy Competency Standards for Higher Education (Chicago: Association of College and Research Libraries, 2000). Available online at www.ala.org/ala/mgrps/divs/acrl/standards/informationliteracycompetency.cfm (accessed September 15, 2012).

4. Natalie Borisovets, personal conversation with the author, January 14, 2013.

5. Mary Mancuso Biggs and Mark Weber, *Course-Related and Personalized Library Instruction*, ED172724 (Washington, DC: ERIC Clearinghouse, 1979), 8, 10.

6. Nina McHale, "Eradicating the Rogue Assignment," *College and Research Libraries News* 69, no. 5 (May 2008): 254–57.

7. A review of library and some college teaching literature was conducted by searching for the terms *library assignment* and *research assignment* in *LISA*, the *Library Literature and Information Science* database, *LISTA* (Ebsco), *ERIC*, and *Education Full Text*. Some Google searches were done with the same terms.

8. A. Ehrhardt, J. D. Gerletti, and C. C. Crawford, "How Shall I Manage My College Library Assignments?" *Improving College and University Teaching* 2, no. 3 (1954): 44–47; A. Ehrhardt, J. D. Gerletti, and C. C. Crawford, "How Shall I Manage My College Library Assignments?" *Bookmark (Idaho)* 11 (September 1958): 9–12.

9. Ehrhardt, Gerletti, and Crawford, "How Shall I Manage My College Library Assignments?" (1954): 44–47.

10. Mara L. Houdyshell, "Navigating the Library." *College Teaching* 51, no. 2 (Spring 2003): 77–78.

11. Pixey Anne Mosley, "Creating a Library Assignment Workshop for University Faculty," *Journal of Academic Librarianship* 24, no. 1 (1998): 37.

12. Patricia Morris Donegan, *Creating Effective Library Assignments: A Workshop for Faculty*, ED329260 (Washington, DC: ERIC Clearinghouse, 1989), 25.

13. Necia Parker-Gibson, "Library Assignments: Challenges That Students Face and How to Help," *College Teaching* 49, no. 2 (Spring 2001): 65–70. DOI: 10.1080/87567550109595850.

14. Donna Miller, "Library Instruction and Information Literacy LibGuide," *Lebanon Valley College*, February 8, 2013. Available online at http://libguides.lvc.edu/content.php?pid=199082&sid=1664949 (accessed November 1, 2012).

15. Monty L. McAdoo, *Building Bridges: Connecting Faculty, Students, and the College Library* (Chicago: American Library Association, 2010), 29.

16. McAdoo, *Building Bridges*, 33–114.

17. Association of College and Research Libraries, "Information Literacy Competency Standards for Higher Education"; Benjamin S. Bloom, *Taxonomy of Educational Objectives: The Classification of Educational Goals* (New York: Longman, 1956); Lorin W. Anderson, David R. Krathwohl, and Benjamin Samuel Bloom, *A Taxonomy for Learning, Teaching, and Assessing: A Revision of Bloom's Taxonomy of Educational Objectives* (New York: Longman, 2001).

18. Evan Ira Farber, "Faculty–Librarian Cooperation: A Personal Retrospective," *Reference Services Review* 27, no. 3 (September 1999): 230. DOI: 10.1108/00907329910283151.

19. Biggs and Weber, *Course-Related and Personalized Library Instruction*.

20. Michael Mounce, "Working Together: Academic Librarians and Faculty Collaborating to Improve Students' Information Literacy Skills: A Literature Review, 2000–2009," *Reference Librarian* 51, no. 4 (October 2010): 300–320. DOI: 10.1080/02763877.2010.501420; Rubina Bhatti, "Teacher–Librarian Collaboration in University Libraries: A Selective Review," *Pakistan Library and Information Science Journal* 40, no. 2 (June 2009): 3–12; William B. Badke, "Can't Get No Respect: Helping Faculty to Understand the Educational Power of Information Literacy," *Reference Librarian* 43, no. 89/90 (2005): 63–80. DOI: 10.1300/J120v43n89_05; McAdoo, *Building Bridges*.

21. Larry L. Hardesty, *Faculty and the Library: The Undergraduate Experience* (Norwood, NJ: Ablex Publishing, 1991) and R. K. Baker, "Faculty Perceptions toward Student Library Use in a Large Urban Community College," *Journal of Academic Librarianship* 23, no. 3 (May 1997): 177–82, cited in Badke, "Can't Get No Respect," 63–80.

22. Badke, "Can't Get No Respect," 74.

23. Bhatti, "Teacher–Librarian Collaboration," 3–12.

24. Alicia B. Ellison, "Positive Faculty/Librarian Relationships for Productive Library Assignments," *Community and Junior College Libraries* 12, no. 2 (2004): 23–28.

25. Farber, "Faculty–Librarian Cooperation," 229–34; Bhatti, "Teacher–Librarian Collaboration," 3–12; Caroline Cason Barratt, Kristin Nielsen, Christy Desmet, and Ron Balthazor, "Collaboration Is Key: Librarians and Composition Instructors Analyze Student Research and Writing," *Portal* 9, no. 1 (January 2009): 37–56.

26. Badke, "Can't Get No Respect," 68.

27. Donegan, *Creating Effective Library Assignments*; Robert Miller, Edward O'Donnell, Neal Pomea, Joseph Rawson, Ryan Shepard, and Cynthia Thomes, "Library-Led Faculty Workshops: Helping Distance Educators Meet Information Literacy Goals in the Online Classroom," *Journal of Library Administration* 50, no. 7 (October 2010): 830–56. DOI: 10.1080/01930826.2010.488977; Mosley, "Creating a Library Assignment Workshop," 33–41; Ellison, "Positive Faculty/Librarian Relationships for Productive Library Assignments," 23–38; McHale, "Eradicating the Rogue Assignment," 254–57; Biggs and Weber, *Course-Related and Personalized Library Instruction*; Marsha Forys, "Library Buddies," *Research Strategies* 16, no. 3 (1998): 231–33. DOI: 10.1016/S0734-3310(00)80008-7.

28. Mosley, "Creating a Library Assignment Workshop for University Faculty," 33–41; Donegan, *Creating Effective Library Assignments*.

29. Daniel Brendle-Moczuk, "Encouraging Students' Lifelong Learning through Graded Information Literacy Assignments," *Reference Services Review* 34, no. 4 (November 2006): 498–508. DOI: 10.1108/00907320610716404; Nicole J. Auer and Ellen M. Krupar, "Librarians Grading: Giving A's, B's, C's, D's, and F's," *Reference Librarian* 43, no. 89 (2005): 39–61. DOI: 10.1300/J120v43n89_04.

30. McAdoo, *Building Bridges*, 14–18.

31. McAdoo, *Building Bridges*, 13–21.

32. Bloom, *Taxonomy of Educational Objectives*; Anderson, Krathwohl, and Bloom, *A Taxonomy for Learning, Teaching, and Assessing*.

33. Baker, "Faculty Perceptions toward Student Library Use in a Large Urban Community College," 177; McAdoo, *Building Bridges*, 14.

34. Ernest L. Boyer, *Scholarship Reconsidered: Priorities of the Professoriate* (Princeton, NJ: Carnegie Foundation for the Advancement of Teaching, 1990).

35. John Straus, personal conversation with the author, October 2, 2012.

36. Mosley, "Creating a Library Assignment Workshop for University Faculty," 35.

37. Lisa O'Connor and Julie VanHoose, "What They Didn't Tell Me in Library School Is That Students Don't Care about Learning to Use the Library," *Reference and User Services Quarterly* 52, no. 1 (Fall 2012): 26–27.

38. Constance A. Mellon, "Library Anxiety: A Grounded Theory and Its Development," *College and Research Libraries* 47, no. 2 (March 1986): 160–65; Edgar Bailey, "Constance Mellon Demonstrated That College Freshmen Are Afraid of Academic Libraries," *Evidence-Based Library and Information Practice* 3, no. 3 (October 2008): 94–97.

39. Biggs and Weber, *Course-Related and Personalized Library Instruction*, 19.

40. Biggs and Weber, *Course-Related and Personalized Library Instruction*, 20.

41. McAdoo, *Building Bridges*, 17.

42. Badke, "Can't Get No Respect," 63–80.

43. McAdoo, *Building Bridges*, 18.

44. McAdoo, *Building Bridges*, 18.

45. Dennis Isbell, "What Happens to Your Research Assignment at the Library?" *College Teaching* 56, no. 1 (December 2008): 3–6; Kuhlthau, *Seeking Meaning*; Lloyd F. Bitzer, "The Rhetorical Situation," *Philosophy and Rhetoric* 25, no. 1 (1992): 1–14.

46. Kuhlthau, "Developing a Model of the Library Search Process," 232–42.

47. Carol Kuhlthau, "Students and the Information Search Process: Zones of Intervention for Librarians," *Advances in Librarianship* 18 (1994): 57–72. Available online at www.gslis.utexas.edu/~vlibrary/edres/theory/kuhlthau.html (accessed November 14, 2012).

48. Purdue Online Writing Laboratory, "Rhetorical Situations," Purdue University, 2013. Available online at http://owl.english.purdue.edu/owl/resource/625/1/ (accessed November 14, 2012).

49. Isbell, "What Happens to Your Research Assignment at the Library?" 4.

50. Isbell, "What Happens to Your Research Assignment at the Library?"; Bitzer, "The Rhetorical Situation," 1–14; Purdue Online Writing Laboratory, "Rhetorical Situations."

51. Dennis Isbell and Dorothy Broaddus, "Teaching Writing and Research as Inseparable: A Faculty-Librarian Teaching Team," *Reference Services Review* 23, no. 4 (1995): 51–62; Deborah Huerta and Victoria E. McMillan, "Collaborative Instruction by Writing and Library Faculty: A Two-Tiered Approach to the Teaching of Scientific Writing," *Issues in Science and Technology Librarianship* 28 (Fall 2000). Available online at www.istl.org/00-fall/article1.html (accessed November 1, 2012).

52. Isbell, "What Happens to Your Research Assignment at the Library?" 3–6.

53. For this concept of missing categories, I am indebted to John Oliver of The College of New Jersey.

54. Robert Rothberg, personal conversation with the author, February 2000.

55. McAdoo, *Building Bridges*, 57–58.

56. McAdoo, *Building Bridges*, 57–58.

57. Isbell and Broaddus, "Teaching Writing and Research as Inseparable," 51–62; Huerta and McMillan, "Collaborative Instruction by Writing and Library Faculty."

58. Roberta Tipton and Patricia Bender, "From Failure to Success: Working with Underprepared Transfer Students," *Reference Services Review* 34, no. 3 (2006): 389–404; Roberta Tipton and Patricia Bender, "Teaching Alone and Together: A Narrative Inquiry," in *Using Qualitative Methods in Action Research: How Librarians Can Get to the Why of Data,* edited by Douglas Cook and Lesley J. Farmer, 35–46 (Chicago: Association of College and Research Libraries, 2011).

59. John Hudesman, Bert Flug, and Barry J. Zimmerman, "Dissemination of the Self-Regulated Learning (SRL) Model [Abstract]," *FIPSE Database,* August 31, 2010. Available online at http://fipsedatabase.ed.gov/fipse/grant-show.cfm?grantNumber=P116B060012 (accessed November 1, 2012); Barry J. Zimmerman, "Investigating Self-Regulation and Motivation: Historical Background, Methodological Developments, and Future Prospects," *American Educational Research Journal* 45, no. 1 (2008): 166–83. DOI: 10.3102/0002831207312909.

60. McAdoo, *Building Bridges,* 16.

FOUR

Toward the "Good" Research Assignment: An Academic Speaks

Williamjames Hull Hoffer

To start, introductions are in order. This chapter is written from the perspective of an associate professor of history at Seton Hall University in South Orange, New Jersey. These facts matter because teaching research methods begins with knowing your students and your subject matter. A research assignment proven successful at an elite private college may be a failure at a state university branch campus and vice versa. A research project that flies in a political science course may tank in a history course. Research projects for survey students will have different specifications and expectations from a research project for senior majors in the department. To be specific, a teacher of history, U.S. history to be more precise, at a midsized national research university has to construct as many different kinds of research assignments as there are kinds of classes. One rapidly discovers that there is no one-size-fits-all approach. Each assignment must match not only the type of class in which it appears, but also the purpose it is to serve.

The time-honored adage "The means must meet the ends" applies here as well. For the sake of this chapter, we will examine the three kinds of classes an academic instructor in history at a midsized national research university most likely faces and the kinds of research assignments that should appear in those classes, regardless of level, for there are both general rules to follow when constructing a research assignment and ones specific to the class and the purpose of that assignment.

But first, there are some discipline-centered ideas that affect every research assignment in history. Whether in an introductory survey class like U.S. History I or Senior Seminar—a capstone course in a history department for undergraduate majors—instructors teach students how to practice the craft of history. Please note the use of the word *craft* rather than *science* to describe history. Historians have long since rejected the so-called scientific history of the late nineteenth century that sought objective truths in laboratory-like seminar courses.[1]

Instead, modern methods themselves range from quantitative to literary, but all are based on a close reading of the primary sources, keeping an eye out for the important issues in the secondary literature. Primary sources are those items present or created during the time under study. Secondary sources are what other historians have written about the past. Students of history need both to collect and then analyze so they can formulate their own ideas.

Research is a vital part of what historians do. Fortunately, there are a number of resources an instructor can draw on for use in constructing a research assignment. These range from textbooks to manuals to even lighter guides.[2] The American Historical Association has provided a number of instructional guides for use in the classroom, both on its website and available for purchase.[3] Regardless of which book you assign or which batch of materials you prepare for your course, you cannot assume that students fully understand the process by which we do history until they have practiced it themselves. The historical method cannot be taught, but it can be learned. Every history teacher is merely a guide for the student.

In other words, the historical method entails both knowing how to find appropriate sources and how to evaluate those sources. The latter task is vital. Historians put their research findings into context, that is, the events, movements, ideas, and even the landscape around those findings. Both processes—locating and analyzing—must be embedded in every assignment, class session, and reading.

Educators have introduced the concept of the taxonomies of learning to give greater precision to the acquisition of such skills as the historical method. The most applicable of these taxonomies is a derivation of Benjamin Bloom's. One starts with the gathering of data (knowledge), then the evaluation of those data (analysis), and finally the synthesizing of that analysis into a new whole. Within the so-called "proficiencies" project, part of Seton Hall University's undergraduate core curriculum, this is classified as "critical thinking."

In the historical method's version of critical thinking, one must ask a series of questions at the analysis stage. They are as follows:

1. What is the provenance of this source? How authentic is it? Historians must be able to tell how the source reached them. Each medium, whether oral, written, or physical through which the source passed, alters the source in potentially important ways. The histo-

rian peels away or compensates for this translation to find the original.

2. Who created it and why? The creator of an artifact—an item from the past—was embedded in a time and place, subject to all of the influences of culture and society in his or her background, as well his or her place in that society and culture. To properly account for these factors, the historian must determine the creator's identity.

3. What is the context for this source? As noted earlier, context is everything. If formed during a war or other social calamity, the creator's perspective can change remarkably. If, by contrast, the source was created in a time of peace or relative harmony, it will reflect that context.

4. What is its significance? What does it tell us about its context and/ or its creator? Historians are not antiquarians, studying artifacts just to study artifacts. Historical scholarship is the search for meaning. To summarize, historians are concerned with reliability, bias, and the mediation of the historian's own cultural and social background on perception.[4]

A more impressionistic way to look at the historian's craft is to envision the historian as a detective attempting to solve a murder mystery. While great detectives like Sherlock Holmes, Hercule Poirot, Miss Marple, and Father Brown are creatures of Sir Arthur Conan Doyle, Agatha Christie, and G. K. Chesterton's imaginations, their powers of deductive and inductive reasoning, observation, and investigation are the tools of a good historian as well. I include this example in this chapter because it is also how many historians explain the historical method to their students. Everything is more fun when there is a mystery.

At this stage of the chapter, we need to pause, as an instructor would in class when giving a talk about the historical method. Almost all students will drop their pens or stop typing on their laptops when an instructor talks about the historical method. It is likely students do so when instructors in other fields talk about their discipline's rules. It is important for all instructors to remember that, while they are passionate about their disciplines and have long since figured out why they care about what they study, their students may never share that commitment.

This is why an instructor must explain why he or she chose his or her field, its importance to him or her, and, therefore, why it should matter to the students. Given the career-driven mindset of today's undergraduates, an instructor may have to go a bit further than just passion. The students have to know how what an instructor is teaching them applies to their everyday world. For example, studying history does not merely satisfy our insatiable itch to know the origins of everything, but it is a window into all of humanity. As a result, understanding history leads to the ability to better adapt to any situation in life with a maturity only a historical perspective can grant.

As previously noted, there are three kinds of history classes at the undergraduate level for our consideration: the introductory survey classes, the methods classes (titled "Introduction to Historical Research" in my department and the Senior Seminar capstone course), and the upper-level courses. Because each has its own particularities, it is necessary to describe them briefly. The introductory survey class can be either American History I, which covers all U.S. history from before Columbus to the end of Reconstruction in 1877, or American History II, the Civil War to the most recent past an instructor can fit into a fifteen-week semester. The survey's students range from experienced history majors to first-year students who take it to satisfy a requirement. Although almost all of them have had some kind of U.S. history before going to college, only a few have done and/or retained their knowledge of how to do historical research.

The Seton Hall University history department's Introduction to Historical Research and Senior Seminar semester-long courses are dedicated to the writing of a research paper, usually some fifteen pages in length, in a subject area the instructor has chosen at the outset. Topics may include the framing of the U.S. Constitution, U.S. government bureaucracies, U.S. political history, U.S. legal history, and U.S. local history. Such topics as Benjamin Franklin, nationalism, U.S. golden ages, and Leo Tolstoy's *Anna Karenina* may suit the instructor's preferences. Due to their length and dedication to a research project, these courses typically include multiple research assignments that progress from the initial stage of selecting a topic to completing a substantial project. Concomitantly, students should be learning about historiography—the study of the differences and similarities among historians on the same or similar topics—as well as proper formatting, whether it is the current *Chicago Manual of Style* or the slightly different (older editions named after Kate Turabian, the editor of the first versions).

An instructor must also dedicate a fair amount of time to teaching students how to avoid plagiarism, unfortunately an all too frequent occurrence in classes at any level or dealing with any subject.[5] Because plagiarism is such a plague on our college campuses, it is worth spending some time discussing it with reference to research assignments. Every course should initially include a talk about plagiarism. This discussion should not only spell out what plagiarism and its equivalent on exams—academic dishonesty—constitute, but it should also explain why it is of no educational value. Besides the penalties they incur, students are cheating themselves out of the very thing they are supposed to be learning. Detection always results from the teacher's cumulative knowledge of a student's writing, based on previous assignments, hence the ability to detect the obvious outlier of a plagiarized paper or assignment. One may also use the Blackboard provided system Safe Assign. It is more of a prophylactic than anything else, but, if students know you are keen to plagiarism, they are less likely to risk it.

Upper-level courses in a history department, composed mostly of history majors, tend to encompass more specialized topics, require a great deal more reading and writing than in lower-level courses, and usually have a research paper as one of the graded assignments. Breaking up the research paper into components due as the semester progresses is a good way to prevent student procrastination. The components can include topic, preliminary bibliography, outline, rough draft, and final draft. Although the final draft should be worth the most, at eighty-five percent or so of the research paper grade, breaking out the pieces, with each piece worth something, requires students to perform the research assignment in its proper stages. The research paper, as a whole, would be around thirty to thirty-five percent of their total grade, with exams and class participation making up the rest of a usual upper-level course.

Whatever the type of course, there are a few general rules about creating research assignments. The first is to break up the assignment's tasks into manageable steps or stages. For example, if an instructor wants a student to find history journal articles, he or she needs to break that process down into the following: 1) locating the appropriate searchable databases, 2) brainstorming search terms for those databases, 3) discussing how to configure a search for the largest number of manageable results, 4) discussing how to sift through a results list, and 5) discussing how to retain the results worth keeping.

The second general rule is that each step of the assignment must have an evaluative mechanism listing all of the important parts of the assignment, along with gradations of achievement. This is popularly known as a grading rubric. Students will not only know in advance what the instructor is grading, but he or she will have a transparent means of evaluation in the case of a grade dispute. More importantly, students will learn how to improve their performance in the future.

Third, the instructor needs to be clear and precise about the objectives of the assignment and how they relate to the overall goal of the course. While the tendency in graduate scholarship is sophisticated nuance, the writing and oral instructions for a research assignment for undergraduates must always be pitched at a basic level. This does not mean talking down to students. Condescension will turn them off. But do not assume they know about research, libraries, databases, or the elements of the college-level research method. Even if they have previously done a research project, everyone can benefit from a refresher course.

Fourth, the generations of college students in the average classroom are most likely different in significant ways from the instructor. Each year since 1998, professors at Beloit College have created the annual "Beloit College Mindset List."[6] It is a reminder that most first-year students were born seventeen or eighteen years before they stepped into our class-rooms. While the professor might remember using a payphone or listen-ing to Madonna's first hit on a CD, their students do not. At the time of this writing, the entering class of 2016 was born when the list started. The first president they remember is George W. Bush. Everything has always had an Internet site. The card catalogue has been out of use for more than fifteen years and there have always been on-line databases. It is a genera-tion that thinks the library is a place to be social.

For example, many libraries are transforming themselves into social spaces, a learning commons with coffee and other amenities available for purchase. Most of the incoming students will have had a cell phone or a smart phone since grade school. Computers are likely a constant compan-ion. They are likely adept at viewing, reading, and listening to *everything* on the Internet. If not, they soon will be. You must adapt to their way of viewing the world or you will be their dinosaur: entertaining to look at, but not relevant.

Last but not least, research assignments must build on one another so that the student's skills develop and the student can trace his or her development over the course of the semester. Most students will start with trepidation, lack of confidence, and a desire to put off the assign-ment. Once the student has performed an assignment, his or her confi-dence level will grow. This is both good and bad. Confidence eliminates the fear barrier to performing tasks in a timely manner, but it also leads to a false sense of security. The ability to overcome obstacles is directly related to one's realistic sense of the nature of research. Searches are hit and miss propositions. Often frustrating, the search for a particular item can exhaust even the most expert scholar. Only through a steady building of skills through ever more challenging assignments can a student gain the right amount of confidence.

One way of reinforcing all of these rules for constructing a good re-search assignment is to require students to take notes on everything they do in the course of fulfilling the assignment. A good way for them to do that is to keep a research journal—a log of everything they have done, including the adoption of search terms, websites visited, and sources they examined. One might be tempted to use the word lazy to describe stu-dents, but a more accurate way to refer to the phenomenon is the stu-dents' desire to be efficient. Call it conservation of energy. Regardless of terminology, students will resist taking notes, let alone detailed notes.

Therefore, you must require note-taking, and, like everything else, you must explain why it is necessary. For one thing, students will not have to do a search twice because they have forgotten the earlier one. For another, the act of writing it down helps us memorize what we are writ-ing. Last, but not least, the devil is in the details. A good research journal proves the student has done the research and records the bibliographic information needed for proper documentation in the research paper itself.

With that preliminary exposition out of the way, we can turn to the different types of research assignments: introductory, bibliographical, and archival. An introductory research assignment gives the student a particular item to find, either in the library or through databases. Instructors may elect to use a U.S. history survey textbook's resources or design their own series of assignments.[7]

An introduction to the library and online databases is a necessary first step. It may be helpful to have a member of the library faculty offer an instructional session or do the demonstration yourself at the library. Although it can lead to glazed over eyes in the classroom, a trip to the library is a good break in the routine. Repetition is the key to teaching someone how to perform a search, and that principle applies to learning where to look for resources.

The next step for an introductory research assignment is one that is necessary for all assignments: feedback. In the methods courses, it is a good practice to set aside time in class and during student-mandated visits to the instructor's office to go over their research methods. If necessary, one can do a search on the instructor's computer to reinforce good habits. Feedback demonstrates two things that are essential to student learning outcomes: First, it shows that the instructor cares about a student's progress. Students will perform better if they know the teacher is invested in their learning. Second, the authority as a teacher—why students should take what an instructor has to communicate seriously—comes from students respecting the professor's expertise in the subject matter. It is at least, in part, why it is a good idea to sprinkle stories from one's own scholarship experience into every class. Students have a finely tuned fakery detector. The teacher's expertise as a researcher is why they are there in his or her class. Instructors should use it. It will pay dividends.

It is also important for students not to be discouraged by poor marks in the early stages of an assignment. If there is promise for correcting their mistakes or simply doing a better job in the future, they will commit to the learning process. When feedback is minimal, students not only sense that the instructor is not invested in them, they will also be discouraged from making greater efforts. Again, rather than giving the student the lingering sense that the instructor just threw the papers down the stairs to sort them into grades, a well-designed grading rubric is of great help in diagnosing where the student can improve.

To render feedback, industry practice has turned from the more traditional hand-written comments on their printed-out papers to using the track changes function in Microsoft Word—the default word processing software at most institutions. This allows the instructor to provide corrections and comments, with the latter appearing in the margin's comment boxes. Although some may prefer using a less gruesome color than red, for example, purple, either electronically or on paper, one might choose to remain a traditionalist in that regard; however, the point remains that students need positive feedback regardless of the effort. Students can become easily discouraged with entirely negative feedback. When a teacher finds something good about the paper, he or she should let the author know. The student needs to be able to take some pride in his or her achievement despite the fact that there might still be a way to go before he or she produces top-quality work.

For introductory courses, it is often best to have several preparatory research assignments. Adhering to the general rule to make things simple, one should start with having survey students go into the library and find various sections, reference, circulation, microfilms, and fiche on a subject, if any, and so on. In another assignment, they will have to use one or more of the resources in this section and compare and contrast the entries on the same topic in those sources. For another, they have to use a database. Next, they have to find primary sources both online and in print. Finally, they should compare search engines. The instructor should give feedback on all of these assignments and go over them in class. When they hear what their peers are doing, the students will learn from one another, compete with one another, and begin to understand that they are in a shared enterprise.

Keeping the aforementioned points in mind, we should now turn to bibliographical and archival assignments. These assignments need to be tailored to the kind of course for which they are required. In the survey class at the introductory level, this means a search in the stacks, a set database, or resources online on an assigned topic. For an upper-level class or a methods course, this can be the first foray into the primary and secondary sources, so the student can find a topic for his or her paper. Even at the upper level, it is useful to suggest topics that would make for good research papers. Students thrive on examples. Although they may not use a single topic the instructor suggests, at least they know the kind of topics they can choose.

Good research is a combination of interlocking tasks. One has to locate the two kinds of sources, primary and secondary. One has to search through these sources once one has located them. One must discriminate among them. (Due to its association with bigotry, the word *discrimination* has fallen into disuse, but we need to rescue it from its cultural purgatory.) Historians have to be able to sort sources into valuable and not valuable. On more popular topics, one has to do this rather quickly or never emerge from the research stage of the project. Given the nature of most undergraduate topics, students are more likely to suffer from an overwhelming number of search results, or hits, than a dearth. They must learn how to discriminate.

A bibliography assignment is a good way for students to start learning this vital skill. For a history teacher's purposes, a bibliography (the more modern name is sources consulted or references) is a list in proper format of all of the sources the student can find on a topic. In the introductory survey, the teacher can give them the topic. For the methods courses, this is the first stage in finding a topic or demonstrating their progress in researching their topic. For the upper-level courses, it is a stage in their forced march toward a research paper. The instructor should require students to divide their bibliographies into primary and secondary sources and give them an example of what the bibliography should look like. Again, giving examples and being specific is better than vagueness for numerous reasons, foremost among them is to fight procrastination. Few things are more intimidating to a writer than a blank page.

The third major kind of research assignment is the archival. Archives are a storage location for primary sources—almost exclusively that of documents. These days they take two forms: physical and digital. The vast majority of historians swear by physical archives. On occasion, one can get the distinct impression that physical archive research is the only respectable kind of research. As a result, it is a good idea to include a trip to an archive, which may also be located in the library. Many students fall in love with archival research. They get to touch, albeit under special rules for handling historical documents, a part of history.

Others instructors take a different view. They do their archival research primarily on the Web. This reflects their love of technology; the demands on their time; and their fast food, Amazon, instant download mentality. Who would not succumb to this brave, new world more often than not? Who would not love being able to look up the exact date of the Monroe Doctrine almost instantaneously? When universities almost mandate the use of laptops, as well as smart phones and slates, it is almost malpractice not to encourage the use of Internet-based sources. One must take this into account when designing research assignments. Not only do students need to learn the how of what they often wrongly believe to be an intuitive process, they must also learn to use the same discriminatory powers for the Internet they are supposed to use for everything else.

This leads to the extraordinarily touchy issue of Wikipedia. Besides the fact that a lot of historians are practically luddites with regards to the Internet, Wikipedia represents an existential threat to academics in general. Wikipedia's sponsors, creators, and publicists have done themselves no favors in this regard by trumpeting their "open source" "power of the market" and "free and open" nature. It sounds very much like antiintellectualism, another in a long line of critiques of the so-called ivory tower. Many historians do not want to publicize or in any way condone the use of Wikipedia by their students.

However, academics in all settings must pay heed to this truth: Students already know about Wikipedia, or their search engine will quickly familiarize them with it. It is far better for instructors to recognize Wikipedia's power (and warn of its perils) than to behave like ostriches. One does not want to be like the dinosaur in the Gary Larson *The Far Side* cartoon strip. He addresses a conference of his fellow dinosaurs with the lament of how the Earth is cooling, the mammals are taking over, and they have brains the size of a walnut. One must adapt to this world or go the way of the dinosaurs. Teachers should encourage their students to bring their finely attuned skepticism of authority to a Wikipedia entry. They should then have those students look at the sources for the entry, question its reliability, and treat it as the tertiary source or reference work that it is. At least that way, students can use Wikipedia as a starting point rather than an end point.

Due to the place of this chapter in a book on what some universities have called the information fluency proficiency, there is no need to examine it here. Suffice it to say, information fluency in history courses is a version of the historical method, but history students would be ill-served if an instructor tried to teach information fluency instead of the historical method. As noted earlier, historians are practically obsessed with context. Although the ability to discriminate among sources is of use in other disciplines, historians have their own concerns; therefore, research assignments in upper-level and methods courses must help students think like historians.

The next level is to go beyond the accumulation of good sources and process those sources into a time and place and then tell the story of change over time. An instructor will spend a significant amount of the time with research assignments conveying how different what historians do is from the social sciences. The problem is one of presentism. Students want to relate everything to a present-day issue. To modify this notion, the teacher should explain that there are two ways to answer the "So what?" question, the question of the significance of what we are studying. First, the historical approach explains how we got here. Everyone loves an origins story. There is a reason why those movies are often the most successful ones in a franchise.

Second, the historical analysis gives us insight into the human condition. Despite the differences between us and the ones we study in the past, we are all human. Through the study of history we can get beyond the basic questions of who we are and what is our nature into the better questions of how we change and how we remain the same, as well as the whys of human events.

This is the reason the instructor should tell his or her students to start writing their account soon after their research has begun. Again, they may resist the extra work (they will change what they write as they learn more about the topic), but it is essential that they write at the same time they are researching. Writing helps us think. Putting words on the page, electronic or hard copy, forces us to structure our thoughts. As these inchoate ideas begin to take the form of prose, we start to see the outlines of arguments and holes in our knowledge, and the assignment becomes more manageable. Writing directs research, sending us in search of answers to questions the writing posed.

Although it is understandable why some want to proceed in stages, and many historians do not want to write a word until they know everything about their topic, this can easily turn into and, indeed, become a rationalization for, procrastination. It is something to which scholars and their students are very vulnerable, and it is a particularly dangerous disease for historians who can become lost in the sources. There is always another item to find, a newly published article or book to read.

To that tendency, graduate advisors often give their students two pieces of advice: The first is to start writing. The second is to stop. Instructors should give the same advice to their students in all fields at every level. It is never too early to start writing. Then, when the time comes, they must stop. The same applies to research.

It is time for an aside. While many historians and teachers in other disciplines turn loose on a given topic or assignment teams, committees, or work groups (or task forces), there are many of us who have an aversion to assigning group work. It is not just based on what they have learned from their historical studies about groups, although that probably has some influence on their thinking. It is simply that many have had bad experiences with group work: Either they always ended up doing most of the work—what economists call the free-rider problem—or that group effort resulted in a badly compromised outcome.

However, the results are in: Students do better when they work in groups. Apparently, humans are social animals conditioned from genetics or nurture or whatever to work together. If one wants to avoid the dissociative effects of isolated individuals, instructors should design some, if not all, of their research projects as group projects.

Whether organizing the work individually or by groups, there are several different active learning assignment types you can deploy in class when students have a break from their research.[8] These techniques give students a chance to demonstrate the maturing levels of skills they have attained. The first is an in-class discussion generating technique. One can break the class into groups of no more than four or five students and give them a question or task to write up and a certain amount of time in which to accomplish it. One member of the group has the task of reporting the result to the class. As the students interact in their groups, the instructor walks around the room to keep them on task, answer any questions they might have, and listen to their conversations. This is a graded assignment, so their group grade is based on what they are doing during that time period, as well as the result.

Another active learning method is to divide a class into groups and have them role play. A legal historian, for example, might have them play the roles of side A or side B and the justices of the U.S. Supreme Court. The roles one assigns need to reflect the historical figures in the controversy so the students can put themselves into the time period. Role playing assignments can be quite elaborate or of the next class variety, but always devote considerable attention to their structure, desired outcome, and purposes. One does not want a free-for-all when and if the students become overly involved in their roles. The instructor must reserve for him or herself the role of impartial moderator, ready to jump in should a student struggle, underperform, or miss an important point. This should be a graded exercise. Many students object to busy work or what they suspect is a way for a professor to not teach the class. The teacher's role needs to be recognized for the work that it is, not the least of which is that he or she is assigning students to debate something in which his or her expertise and research experience can be brought to bear.

While lecturing does not have to lead to passive learning by students, one cannot argue with the enthusiasm on display when students really become involved in a research project. The most successful research assignments are ones to which the students can easily relate, for example, local history. The students can dive into their hometowns, the nearest large, urban area, or their churches, combing through any record they could find. Students need to be able to gain a personal connection with the topic. The trick with designing a good assignment is, therefore, a matter of finding their connection with the topic.

One can do this in any number of ways. The instructor can personalize the historical figures involved. He or she can ask the students to put themselves into that time, place, and situation as a thought exercise. They then imagine their surroundings, thoughts, goals, and concerns. One should not allow students to write their histories from the first person. That violates their objectivity. But it can give them that personal connection to the material. One can also try having them write up their own circumstances and then have them compare those with the historical figures; however, the best way to have students connect to the assignment is to ask them to find a first-person account. Once they have immersed themselves in the primary sources, the only trouble an instructor will have is dampening their enthusiasm enough to dismiss the class.

CONCLUSION

There is no one best way to design a good research assignment. Even the rules listed in this chapter for constructing one are more like guidelines. As most teachers probably already know, the best teachers are usually the ones who adapt to their students, the dynamic of that particular class, and the needs of the time and place. Trying to avoid being a dinosaur is not easy, but preparation, investment, and creativity will pay dividends in students who emerge from class, if not ready to take on the world, at least better prepared for its challenges.

NOTES

1. For a good overview of developments in the history profession, see Mark T. Gilderhus, *History and Historians: A Historiographical Introduction*, 7th ed. (Upper Saddle River, NJ: Prentice Hall, 2010) and Peter Charles Hoffer, *The Historians' Paradox: The Study of History in Our Time* (New York: New York University Press, 2008).

2. Examples include Jacques Barzun and Henry F. Graff, *The Modern Researcher*, 6th ed. (Belmont, CA: Thomson Wadsworth, 2004); Jules R. Benjamin, *A Student's Guide to History*, 9th ed. (Boston: Bedford/St. Martin's, 2004); Anthony Brundage, *Going to the Sources: A Guide to Historical Research and Writing* (Wheeling, IL: Harlan Davidson, 2008); James West Davidson and Mark Hamilton Lytle, *After the Fact: The Art of Historical Detection*, 6th ed. (New York: McGraw-Hill, 2010); David E. Kyvig and Myron A. Marty, *Nearby History: Exploring the Past around You*, 2nd ed. (Lanham, MD: AltaMira Press, 2000); Jenny L. Presnell, *The Information-Literate Historian: A Guide to Research for History Students* (New York: Oxford University Press, 2007); Mary Lynn Rampolla, *A Pocket Guide to Writing in History*, 6th ed. (Boston: Bedford/St. Martin's, 2010); William Kelleher Storey, *Writing History: A Guide for Students*, 2nd ed. (New York: Oxford University Press, 2004); and Kate L. Turabian, *Student's Guide to Writing College Papers*, 4th ed., revised by Gregory G. Colomb, Joseph M. Williams, and the University of Chicago Press Editorial Staff (Chicago: University of Chicago Press, 2010).

3. American Historical Association, "Resources for Teachers at All Levels," *Historians.org*, October 13, 2011. Available online at www.historians.org/teaching/index.cfm#teachhistory (accessed July 11, 2012).

4. For a good example of the historical method in action, see Reference and User Services Association, a division of the American Libraries Association, "Using Primary Sources on the Web," *ALA.org*, January 10, 2008. Available online at www.ala.org/rusa/sections/history/resources/pubs/usingprimarysources (accessed July 14, 2012).

5. Again, the American Historical Association has a statement on plagiarism and some exercises for use in the classroom. See American Historical Association Professional Division, "Statement on Standards of Professional Conduct," *Historians.org*, October 13, 2011. Available online at www.historians.org/pubs/Free/ProfessionalStandards.cfm#Plagiarism (accessed July 11, 2012).

6. Ron Nief, "Beloit College Mindset List," 1998. Available online at www.beloit.edu/mindset/ (accessed July 16, 2012).

7. I have become the coauthor on the fourth and latest edition of this "worktext." Peter Charles Hoffer, William Stueck, and Williamjames Hull Hoffer, *Reading and Writing American History: An Introduction to the Historian's Craft*, 4th ed., Vols. I and II (Boston: Pearson Learning Solutions, 2012).

8. For some examples of active learning activities in a history classroom, see Peter J. Frederick, "Motivating Students by Active Learning in the History Classroom," *Perspectives*, October 1993. Available online at www.historians.org/perspectives/issues/1993/9310/9310TEC.cfm (accessed July 20, 2012). For a critical view of active learning, see Daniel D. Trifan, "Active Learning: A Critical Examination," *Perspectives*, March 1997. Available online at www.historians.org/perspectives/issues/1997/9703/9703tea1.cfm (accessed July 20, 2012).

FIVE

Teaching New Media as a Form of Writing: Explorations in Evolving Genres

James Elmborg

During the past decade, it has become increasingly common for students to be assigned multimedia projects as academic work. There are many perceived benefits to these assignments. It is generally assumed that students will be more engaged and excited about creating media projects and that their work will be more "authentic," and that skills they learn through such projects will be more useful in the "real" world. *Authenticity* and *engagement* are terms we often use in writing pedagogy. We want students to genuinely care about what they say and care about saying it well. Media projects certainly create new ways of communicating in many disciplines in the academy and many of the professions students might take up after graduation. Whether we define media projects modestly as PowerPoint presentations comprised of media content, or more ambitiously as digital projects that are entirely audio or video in design, the idea that students might compose in media has been emerging for at least the past decade. While a decade might seem a long time in media years, if we contrast the history of media production in academic contexts with the history of writing in academic contexts, we easily see how new and still unformed our conception of multimedia writing in the classroom is.

A tension runs through much of the approach to teaching multimodal composition in academic contexts. On one hand, theorists claim we can use multimedia to begin to teach habits of writing that will be transferable to traditional textual writing. In this argument, technology becomes a tool we use to teach the underlying skills of traditional writing, while the end goal is to teach students to write traditional academic texts. Karen Gocsik exemplifies this approach, arguing that the "multimedia assignment, properly designed, can enhance students' understanding of how to compose the traditional academic essay."[1] On the other hand, others argue that to truly write in multiple media, we need to completely reinvent composition to account for new modes of production. Cheryl Ball argues that if we "start with Word, we end with Word,"[2] which to me means that if we start with tools designed to produce traditional writing, we will end with products that resemble traditional writing. Perhaps we can best approach this tension by recognizing that we are in a prolonged period of transition. Students are still responsible for good "writing" in the textual sense; however, what we mean by "writing" is in flux, and it includes both traditional textual writing and writing in new media. We must make room for both. If we conceive of media as an emerging form of writing, one with legitimacy and power in its own right, then we need to be cautious in borrowing the past pedagogies of writing and imposing them on media. Multimedia writing is not an inferior form of composition, a form of "training wheels" for "real" writing. Multimedia authoring is a new form of authoring with new kinds of demands and affordances.

In teaching students to do multimedia projects, we can borrow certain concepts from the world of composition and rhetoric; however, we also need to be alert to the possibilities of new media as an emerging form. In trying to force media production into the writing framework, we might well miss the potential for new forms of expression in multimedia. This tension defines our efforts to bring multimedia into academic contexts. Multimedia composition involves the traditional aspects of writing. It involves a process of engagement during which time the student moves from the conception of a project through its execution. It involves an understanding of academic genres and how media produced for academic purposes might differ from media produced for other reasons. It involves the creation of an argument or a proof, some form of purposeful rhetorical engagement with an audience. It involves the selection of materials to support the argument or the proof. Finally, it involves the presentation and assessment of the media product. Each of these elements of media production has its own base of authority or credibility in the academy. Librarians, writing instructors, and faculty in the disciplines all have their roles in helping students understand how to produce academic media.

PEDAGOGY AND MEDIA WRITING

During the early years of the rhetoric and composition movement (through most of the 1970s), the pedagogical emphasis was on writing as a process. Prior to then, writing was taught largely through imitation of expert examples. Instructors would assign readings of sample essays, and students would read the essays. Class was generally devoted to close reading of the essays, with an eye toward how the writers' strategies served the ends of rhetoric (to intervene in some ongoing conversation). Students were then asked to write essays that followed these examples. There were problems with this pedagogy. Only the most accomplished student writers were capable of emulating professional essayists, of course, and this approach to teaching writing tended to have only one intervention into the student's work, the assigning of a grade at the end. The student was seen as a cognitive "black box." Some magic happened in the box, and a written product emerged.

In 1972, Donald M. Murray published a founding document of the writing process movement, "Teach Writing as a Process Not a Product."[3] Murray and others saw the writing process as a way of opening up that black box to create more productive ways for students to learn to write. Rather than disciplining students through grading finished essays, the writing process would guide students through the production process *before* the assigning of a grade and was intended to foreground the fact that writing emerged from rhetorical choices made by the writer. In this way, the student could be taught to produce a desirable, successful product, rather than having the teacher pronounce the paper successful or unsuccessful after the fact. Janet Emig's "Writing as a Mode of Learning" changed the discussion around writing.[4] Rather than simply writing to produce texts, students should be taught to write as a way of learning and mastering concepts. Generally speaking, the writing process involved four "stages." These were conceived as brainstorming (in which the student generated ideas and perspectives and tried to flesh out concepts and hierarchies in the relevant domain of ideas), drafting (when the student actually took a stab at putting the ideas down on the page in a coherent way), revising (when the student worked with the draft to make it more effective in achieving its purpose), and editing (when the student cleaned up flaws in punctuation, spelling, mechanics, etc.). Writing instruction was thus structured by process from the assignment to the due date, with the student being guided through the stages and taught how to work from general idea to completed paper.

Like writing, research skills prior to the 1970s were largely taught on the "black box" model. Students were shown tools (like bibliographies, catalogs, indexes, etc.) with the idea that something "magic" would happen once students knew such research resources existed. This was "bibliographic instruction." Carol Kuhlthau was largely responsible for bringing the concept of process to research pedagogy. Lagging somewhat behind the process movement in composition, Kuhlthau introduced process models to library and information science in her 1985 publication "A Process Approach to Library Skills Instruction."[5] Kuhlthau continued to develop her process models and ultimately identified a student information search process (ISP) comprised of six stages. Kulthau's process does not correlate to the writing process, even though it clearly situates itself within the writing process of a class assignment. The six stages in the ISP include "initiation" (when the assignment is given), "selection" (when the student chooses a topic), exploration (during which students begin to look for sources and materials to be used in their final paper), formulation (when the students focus their exploration and define their topic), collection (when the students begin to amass the final group of sources that will be used in their paper), and preparation (which involves shutting down the research process in preparation for writing).[6] Kuhlthau clarified and refined this understanding of the ISP through years of subsequent research.

Curiously, little has been done to try to align the writing process of brainstorming, drafting, revising, and editing with the research process of initiation, selection, exploration, formulation, collection, and preparation. It is outside the scope of this chapter to undertake such a synthesis, and perhaps the time for such an effort has passed; however, at this point we might greatly benefit from some general observations. Composition theory outgrew the writing process as its central theoretical construct largely because "process" became inadequate to do justice to the complexity of teaching writing. Writing is clearly not such a formally staged process, but rather a much more recursive, more fluid set of practices and activities influenced by powerful external forces. At the heart of the discontent with the process model, we can also discover a rejection of the research assumptions of the process models. To put it simply, the writing process model focuses on the autonomous writer working with content in cognitive isolation. Later developments in writing instruction shifted emphasis to social contexts that create expectations and provide structure for acceptable written products.

While clearly some process is involved in creating a written product, generally speaking, the rigidly conceived "stages" involved in the writing process or research process are not really naturally occurring phenomena, but largely the inventions of the theorists.[7] However—and this point is important—in academic writing it is clear that students really do move from a general understanding of their assignment toward clarification of what they themselves can say about it. Along the way, they also consult sources and organize the sources to fit into their writing. Some form of process clearly happens during a period of time, and any writing pedagogy (whether the writing is in traditional text or new media) needs to account for how students move through the process.

Whether the writing process as presented by process theorists was universal or accurate, we can safely say that process provided a powerful pedagogical structure for writing instruction, allowing the teachers to teach writing "as process" and construct syllabi and individual assignments around process. As a young writing instructor in the early 1980s, I learned to teach writing in freshman composition courses. I learned to facilitate free writing, clustering, and other brainstorming activities; assign drafts of essays; guide revision; and deal with editing as the final step in the process.

Clearly, multimedia (often called "multimodal") writing also involves process. In the same way and for the same reasons as the early days of the writing process, we cannot simply show students media and then ask them to "make things that look like that." In a class devoted entirely to learning media production, the instructor might productively structure process to help students produce various kinds of media. Each assignment can be taught through a guided "process" that roughly follows the writing/research process and guides students toward acceptable products. While that process might involve brainstorming, drafting, revising, and editing, we cannot assume (as we cannot assume in writing classes) that students actually *understand* what should be done in each of these steps with media or that these stages are rigid and sequential. While teaching process as a set of discrete steps misses the reality of writing, writing is ultimately a process that takes place throughout time. And, ultimately, we still need to open up the black cognitive box to make sure students understand what qualities we value in writing and how they can produce texts that we value.

The first theorists to create a framework for understanding media as a new form of communication with new techniques came from the New London Group, a group of literacy theorists who began to work in the early 1990s to create ways of thinking about literacy in new times without reference to print. One of the earliest publications from the New London Group articulates a framework for thinking about how new literacies function to create new realities and new ways of understanding through new ways of reading and writing. In contrast to process-based approaches to literacy, which emphasize the linear and progressive, the new "pedagogy of multiliteracies" builds from a sense of simultaneity. To teach students to do projects that involve words, sounds, and images (both still and moving), we need to teach them to think simultaneously about a number of issues. In my own teaching of multimedia production, I have come to the opinion that (unlike the more rigidly conceived writing process) the order of instruction does not matter much; however, each of the following concepts (derived directly from the New London Group's "pedagogies of multiliteracies") should be conveyed to the students when they are asked to produce media in academic contexts.

Situated Practice: The work of the students needs to be situated in some context. Are we asking students to explore something from their own world? From a social sphere they explore as an outsider? If the media they are to produce has to adhere to conventions unique to academia, then these conventions should be understood in relation to the students' situated understandings. In other words, students new to the academy have a different situated practice than graduate students or faculty with long periods of accommodation to the academic world. To produce media, students have to "come from somewhere." Media needs to evolve from where the students are.

Overt Instruction: When students are assigned media projects, they need to use software. Software is itself complex and simultaneous, and students need to be explicitly taught how to use it. If students are assigned a film, they should receive overt instruction in how the editing software works. They should be taught about the relationship between image and sound, about how to trim clips and how to combine clips. If they are being taught to produce audio for podcasts or sound track to images, they need to be taught how audio editing software and microphones work. We can easily assume that students know all about software since they are "born digital." My experience in teaching students to produce media has taught me that their training is often random and that they welcome explicit instruction in how to use software.

Critical Framing: To produce media in academic contexts, students need to be able to take a critical stance toward their subjects. Academic projects imply learning to think and analyze with tools for thinking. For centuries, textual writing has been the technology we use to critique, analyze, and derive meaning from our subjects. While media production introduces new forms of rhetoric, we should still strive to understand, analyze, and critique our subjects, rather than simply present what we see with beautiful sound and image. Students need to learn to think and express themselves critically using the tools for multimodal thought.

Transformed Practice: As students produce new media, they should be challenged to think about how this media production can continue to shape what they are doing and becoming. If new literacies are embodied in new practices, then new ways of thinking and doing can and should emerge from these practices. At the outset of a project, students are situated somewhere along a spectrum from novice to expert and along a spectrum of not knowing and knowing. Through the process of media production, students transform their expertise, belonging, and knowledge. This process forms an important part of the pedagogy of media production.[8]

In traditional college work, instructors can generally assume that students have been writing papers for school for their entire educational lives. The conventions of written prose have been nurtured, taught, and enforced. To introduce multimedia writing into the classroom means that instruction needs to more directly address fundamental questions about what academic work should accomplish. The production of media needs to become more a part of the course. In his landmark essay "Writing the University," David Bartholomae argues that when beginning writers sit down to compose for academic audiences, they need to invent the discourse that is valued in such settings.[9] They need to learn what writers in academia produce and why they produce it that way. Such understanding is profoundly important and can be an exciting way to cut through cynicism and generate new and fresh conversations about why we do what we do. The argument resonates even more powerfully with media production in academic contexts. What does academic media look like? In what ways does it differ from other media students might encounter in their lives? How does it put its values on display for understanding and interpretation? While the questions are as old as academia, they take on fresh and new qualities in the context of new media.

ACADEMIC GENRES AND MULTIMEDIA

Following the writing process movement, a new socially situated understanding of student work began to emerge. Focus shifted from understanding of the lone student working through a cognitive process of composition toward an understanding that the student works within a complex social framework. Students are novice academics. Much of what they need to know is not in their minds or bodies, but is instead "out there" in the world of the academy that judges their success. Teaching students to write became part of the larger project of teaching them about higher education. Retention rates became more a cause for concern as students recruited for college could not succeed no matter how hard they worked. Writers like James Paul Gee (part of the New London Group) began to explore how language from one's home community (one's "lifeworld") prepared the student to function in the linguistic world of the academy. Clearly, some homes (especially upper-middle class and Caucasian) prepared students admirably for the language world of college. Other kinds of homes did not. Writing instruction increasingly developed a pedagogy designed to facilitate the transition from "lifeworld" to academic world, with writing being one key component of that transition.[10]

In 1993, Carol Berkenkotter and Thomas N. Huckin published their highly influential article, "Rethinking Genre from a Sociocognitive Perspective." They argue that in their academic work, students were being asked to write academic "genres" unique to academia. Without explicit instruction on how to write such genres, students were left to their own devices to figure out what academic writing looks like and why certain things (like citations) seem to matter so much. They propose that academic genres have a series of functions that students need to understand to write well in college. Among other things, they claim that genres are a kind of situated activity, "embedded in communicative activities of daily and professional life."[11] They also suggest that genres include both form and content, creating implicit "rules" for what can and cannot be produced in a given discipline. To use a genre effectively, students need to reproduce a version of the genre; however, the genre is not a formula, but rather a structure that allows for improvisation and creativity within its bounds. Finally, they claim that genre conventions "signal a discourse community norms, epistemology, ideology, and social ontology."[12] Taken in totality, genres put on display the various norms and expectations of a discipline. To be able to effectively produce a piece of writing that "fits" within a discipline is to ultimately be an insider to the discipline. As long as students are still struggling to produce writing that is recognizable as an academic genre, they are still not part of the academic community.

Academic genres present significant challenges for teachers. On one hand, we can recognize the existence of genres, and it makes sense to teach students about the forms they are supposed to write; however, as Ann M. Johns persuasively argues, understanding of genre as a theoretical concept does not easily translate into a straightforward pedagogy. Framing the challenge as a question, Johns asks, "How can we apply 'genre,' the most socially constructivist of literacy concepts, to novice academic classroom[s]?"[13] Johns's identification of academic genre as the "most socially constructivist of literacy concepts" signals the complexity. Genres are "constructed" by academic communities as part of the process of moving the discourse in disciplines forward, but genres only exist in examples, none of which perfectly illustrates the form. Johns suggests that we need to present genres as "theoretically sound and sufficiently coherent," and we need to "take into consideration the complexity of genres and their varied realizations." We also need to "promote rhetorical flexibility and genre awareness" so students can "adapt and/or negotiate a genre to a situation."[14]

The conventions of writing, its genres, have evolved, but the genres function to control the rate of improvisation allowed to writers, especially novice writers, whose primary job is to show that they have mastered the genre (not that they can improvise on its boundaries). Traditionally, the vast majority of rules that govern the production of academic genres remain unspoken, a procrustean bed of expectations laid down during years of instruction about how to write for school. A number of questions arise when we begin to think about allowing students to perform academically in nontextural genres. Given the ubiquitous media in modern life, students tend to be savvy media consumers; however, genre theory tells us that academic media will take different forms than consumer media. Students need explicit instruction to help them understand what kinds of genres will qualify as "academic." In what ways, for example, is a PBS documentary an academic genre? A TED talk? A *60 Minutes* episode? What other kinds of academic forms are available to structure academic media? Should the academic media product argue for a thesis? Should it attempt to prove a hypothesis? What kinds of evidence will be acceptable to support the argument or proof?

These questions lie at the heart of assigning media in the classroom. There are no easy answers, but these questions are not new, either. *Kairos: A Journal of Rhetoric, Technology, and Pedagogy* has been publishing "webtexts" since its inception in 1996. The journal was founded specifically to explore the ways that texts might evolve if freed from the constraints of word processing and the linear essay. The instructions to authors say that, "*Kairos* publishes 'webtexts,' which means projects developed with specific attention to the World Wide Web as a publishing medium. We do not suggest an ideal standard; rather we invite each author or collaborative writing team to think carefully about what unique opportunities the Web offers."[15] The instructions to authors go on to recommend several award-winning webtexts for authors to study as examples. Examples of similar webtexts, video and image projects, podcasts, and collages exist in abundance online, but in directing students to examples of academic genres, we need to avoid a return to the cognitive black boxes of preconstructivist pedagogies. Students need examples of media that illustrate appropriate genres, but they also need to understand why some such texts succeed, while others do not.

Indeed, the challenge is not in finding examples of media to emulate. The challenge is in beginning to define appropriate genre conventions for *academic* media. In the blur of media one can access through the search engine of choice, how do we begin to tease out the qualities and forms we want to promote for academic media? In my experience teaching media, I think the best approach is to adopt the *Kairos* model. We should identify media that we think convey academic approaches to thinking about a given subject. We should make that media part of our explicit framing of the academic assignment by showing the students the media and discussing it with them. The primary challenge is to define what we mean by "academic." Students are immersed in media. They see newscasts, YouTube videos, and Facebook and Twitter feeds with media embedded. They have naturally absorbed the conventions of such media. Just as we need to teach students about the academic forms of writing through exposure to academic genres, we need to acknowledge the need to help them understand how media might function to do academic work.

There are tentative efforts to define academic genres for multimedia emerging. Gocsik describes what she sees as emerging academic forms for student work. She suggests that one such genre might be videos and short films. In the short film genre, she claims that the video genre can encourage students to structure arguments in new ways, helping them to "think about ways to construct their films so that the thesis is implied," or to "craft a film that posits several theses." She goes on to note that, "students must think about how to represent their argument verbally and visually" and how the "play of visual and textual evidence" and how "these two levels of argument intersect." She notes that students will engage a number of questions relevant to academic writing, including the "film's point of view, its multimedia 'voice,'" and through the process, "they will gain a new understanding of authorship."[16] These are rich and interesting challenges presented by new media composition.

Gocsik also suggests that students be asked to compose websites. Unlike traditional composition, a website "allows the reader to move horizontally and vertically through its argument, encouraging the writer to think about the many ways that a reader might enter, navigate, and exit their argument, and to manage information accordingly." She suggests that the blog might be a type of academic genre, one that "can give budding writers the chance to work the kinks out of their evolving voices," and that writing publicly for a "real" audience is a "serious time commitment." Gocsik closes by suggesting we might have students create podcasts. She notes that they tend to come in three categories, which include "monologues, interviews, or NPR-style stories." She contends that the monologues help students "learn a great deal about voice: As they hear themselves reading what they've written, they come to hear the strengths and weaknesses of their prose" and "they stand to learn a lot about style." In doing the NPR-style stories, she states that students "must learn how to compose good interview questions." They also have to learn to think "on the spot" for "interesting threads in their subjects' remarks." In editing, students "face ethical considerations; have they taken something out of context that might alter the meaning of a speaker's response?" She claims that these questions "raise students' information literacy (in helping them to understand the context and credibility of sources)," and ultimately that in academia, they have to "edit these many voices into a coherent argument." They learn that "scholarship represents a polyphony of voices . . . coming together to explore new ground and create new arguments."[17]

At this point in time, no discussion of multimodal genres can pretend to be exhaustive. I have had students do photographic essays, in which they arrange photos to create a central statement. I have also had students do an assignment I call "PowerPoint without Words." This assignment, conceived as a way for students to use a familiar linear software as a media platform, bridges what they know how to do (compose in PowerPoint) with a new challenge (media design). They are not allowed to speak during the presentation, and they are only allowed to put words on the first screen as a title. My point here is that genre is an extremely fluid concept in media production these days, and instructors have great latitude in structuring genre for pedagogical purposes. The assignments described by Gocsik are notable for the salient questions they raise about how questions of authorship, audience, evidence, and voice translate into new media contexts. These elements are crucial to the idea of genre, and it makes good sense to think about how these new forms require academic habits of mind to be successful.

In thinking about academic genres and new media, we need to recognize how exploratory and tenuous the state of academic media production remains. Academia is deeply invested in traditional forms of writing. There are various levels of acceptance of nonprint media as valid for academic work. Many faculty might welcome alternative production models in theory, but, ultimately, prose remains the coin of the realm for serious academic work. This position provides a brake on runaway media production and an "anything goes" acceptance of multimodal media for the conveying of academic work. To move the multimodal project forward in academic contexts, we need to consistently revisit the core values of academic writing and begin to translate these core values into multimodal texts. We need to ask what an academic text does that makes it different from an advertisement text, a personal missive, or an opinion text on talk radio. These definitions will take disciplinary shape and, to some extent, will be shaped by the academic instructor's understanding of what the student, the subject, and the audience need and expect.

Does the multimodal text being assigned need to prove a hypothesis or report the findings of an experiment? Does it need to make an argument based on a thesis? Academic writing has long been marked by the presence of citation. What kinds of sources are credible in an academic multimodal text? How can these sources be introduced and cited in a multimodal environment? These are all questions that must be addressed in a public and direct way during class instruction about the conventions of writing multimodal texts. There are no right answers here, only ways of appropriately beginning the long process of adapting multimodal authorship to the traditional expectations of academic work. As the call for submissions to *Kairos* notes, "we invite each author or collaborative writing team to think carefully about what unique opportunities the Web offers." [18] In beginning to form appropriate academic genres for multimodal texts, we need to be self-conscious about the need to forge new genres that do the work of the academy, while taking full advantage of possibilities of composing in new media. There is great freedom and responsibility in this new instructional role.

ASSESSMENT

Assessment is a complex challenge for any instructor. While students clearly and rightly expect grades for their academic work, most instructors dislike grading and prefer not to spend too much time thinking about grading or discussing how they do it. Grading is intimately tied up with expectations, however, and the less clear the expectations, the more important it is to be explicit and see the continuum from expectation to assessment. An overarching theme of this chapter is that multimodal/ multimedia authorship is only now emerging as a valid way of communicating student work to an academic audience. As a fledgling activity, multimodal composition can be seen as a cognate to more traditional writing; however, we always need to see multimodal composition as inherently different from textual prose. Along the spectrum from process to genre to assessment, we need to help students understand what they are being asked to do, and we need to give them the tools to be successful. These demands connect across the instructional process. As we describe the assignment, as we teach students to do it, as we move to assessing it, we need to be careful at each stage to make our expectations explicit and consistent and our instruction coherent.

Ball has written persuasively about the need for clarity in assessing scholarly multimedia. Drawing largely on her editorial work at *Kairos*, she describes her approach to teaching undergraduates to produce *Kairos*-style webtexts with special focus on the creation of rubrics for assessment. Ball is quick to tell us that no "one-size-fits-all" rubric can be offered as a way to assess what she calls "scholarly multimedia."[19] What matters is that there is a rubric and that the rubric is designed to assess the specifics of the assignment as the students have been given it. Ball suggests that we develop the rubric in consultation with the students, but this may not be practical for all situations. Ball teaches a semester-long class in scholarly multimedia production. A series of assignments allows her and her students to explore the dimensions of this work, including adopting the rubric the class will use to assess its products. Other classes that incorporate media in different ways (perhaps as part of a more traditional "content" class) will probably have different rubrics.

Ball's proposed rubric for assessing scholarly multimedia derives from a framework first established by Virginia Kuhn and others at the Institute for Multimedia Literacy at the University of Southern California. In this honors program, students produce a multimedia senior thesis. They have developed a rubric for assessing the thesis, one that relates in fairly obvious ways to a rubric one might use in a standard writing course. In the introduction to the thesis parameters, the authors note that, "students are given these criteria early on." They also claim that the parameters are "flexible enough to allow students innovation, but rigorous enough to ensure academic excellence."[20] Kuhn's framework (as presented by Ball), involves four main criteria. First, each project must have a "conceptual core." This "core" relates to the thesis of an essay or the main idea, and it must "effectively engage with the primary issues of the subject area into which it is intervening." Second, the project needs a "research component." It must "use a variety of credible sources and cite them appropriately." Third, "form and content" of the project "must serve the conceptual core" and "must be deliberate, controlled, and defensible." Finally, the project is judged on "creative realization." The project needs to engage the core concept with a creative or innovative approach, and it "must achieve significant goals that could not be realized on paper."[21] These assessment metrics seem highly sensible and appropriate; however, they also seem much more appropriate for some assignments than others. The analogy to prose writing also seems clear in that these criteria could also form an assessment rubric for a traditional written essay with almost no modification.

In my classes, I have developed a rubric that I adapt to various pedagogical purposes. The research component of the project in my class is much less important than for students to learn to use media to perform a professional role. Students are asked to use a media project to introduce and teach a core concept, or to develop a video that documents the literacy practices in a subculture of the student's choosing. I have three primary categories in the assessment rubric. The first is "conceptual core," which is much like the core in Ball's rubric. I look for a main concept or idea to control the content of the project. The second is "design execution." The project should have a look and feel that is appropriate for the conceptual core. The project should be aesthetically effective. These criteria are obviously subjective but also important. Multimedia projects comprised of sound, image, and movement bring into play a series of questions about effective design. This category seems no more problematic on that level than to grade an essay based on "style." The final category in the assessment rubric I use is "technical mastery." I want students to display advanced technical skills that result from prolonged engagement with the software and hardware. I want to see evidence of sustained work to create a professionally polished project. In addition to these criteria, I also ask students to produce an "artist's statement." This statement needs to summarize the vision of the project and clarify what the student hoped to achieve in doing it. The statement also allows students to reflect on challenges they had in completing the project. I was convinced to include the required artist's statement by the students themselves based on their desire to contextualize their work in their own learning.

Whatever the rubric (and part of my goal here is to suggest that no magic rubric exists, as long as the rubric reflects the stated goals of the assignment), I find it crucial to the learning process to have students publicly present their work and involve them in the assessment activity. This process begins when they are assigned the project. As part of each class, I ask students for their permission to use their projects as examples for future classes, and I ask current classes to assess the work of past students by using the rubric that will be used to assess their work. I find that generally speaking, students are much harder graders than I am. They are quick to see imperfections in technical execution, and they are tough critics when it comes to aesthetics. The discussion of assessment is ongoing until students present their work. At that point, the opinion of the grader (their formal instructor, i.e., me) often matters much less than the collective opinion of the class. Students tend to enjoy seeing the work of other students, and they enjoy doing work that allows them to share part of their personality with their peers. Presentations take on a high-stakes quality as students strive to create high-quality multimedia for their peers. In this sense, the "authenticity" of media production and the potential to speak to a "real" audience via media reaches fruition. This authenticity and reality does not derive from some inherent superiority in the communication possibilities of media overwriting, but rather from the fact that the project itself is accessible to the entire class simultaneously as one experience, and also later, online, for reviewing. The actual grades students receive often feel like an afterthought to the importance of showing their projects to one another in class.

CONCLUSION

The guidelines in this chapter are not offered as canonical, definitive, or even "best practices." They represent theories and practices that I have found effective to think about and implement academic projects using new media. A tremendous amount has been written about new media, technology and teaching, and new pedagogies for new times. This chapter has not aimed toward a comprehensive presentation of this scholarship. As an educator who has been working in new media and new media writing for twenty years, I have instead tried to provide a coherent analysis of what has worked for me and what ideas I have found useful in shaping my thinking. In closing, I want to emphasize a few themes that have emerged and reflect on the concepts and practices I describe in this overview.

First and foremost, teaching multimedia authoring presents fundamental challenges to the teacher's classroom authority. A number of factors combine to create this situation. First, the lack of clear expectations means that the instructor must create context and define genres. No handbook of acceptable multimedia genres exists for students and teachers to consult. Everything is open to negotiation. In addition, the technologies are complex, and technologies are embedded in other technologies. Even a simple video editing tool (like Apple's iMovie) is both conceptually and technically complex, and to make effective films, students also need to edit audio and images using an audio editor and image editor, both of which are also complex. Students have varying degrees of expertise with these technologies, and in most classes there are a few students with more expertise (at least in one or two areas) than the instructor. Given this complexity, few instructors can have mastery over every possible technical challenge. For an instructor to be successful in teaching media writing, he or she needs to develop specific and overt strategies for dealing with these issues of authority. Given the situation, however, students do have a right to believe their teachers know their subjects. Every teacher who expects students to take on the learning curve of producing media needs to make the commitment to take on that learning curve for himself or herself.

The writing process originally aimed to give control to the student to honor the student's creative processes, which constituted a kind of transfer of authority from teacher to student. In pedagogical practice, the writing process sometimes became something the teacher knew and taught, a new basis of authority. Students who produce academic multimedia need time and space to explore, but they also need structure to avoid muddling around and wasting time. This delicate balance between playing and wasting time needs to be explicitly addressed in a collaborative and constructive way. In my classes, I try to enact structures to help students think about the media they are producing. I try to intentionally structure classes and experiences so that students focus their energies on productive strategies. Having said that, I also recognize that the students I have taught throughout the years who are best with media tend to be obsessive about details. They may spend hours getting a particular transition just right, or seeing how fast they can make images flash in PowerPoint. Some students would consider this "wasting time." The end products, however, achieve a level of excellence because they reflect such attention to detail. The class must be structured to both move students through a process (without becoming dogmatic about it) and provide space for activities that require time and attention to detail.

An assignment in one of my classes might go something like this: On the day I assign a media project, I will demonstrate the basic framework of the necessary technologies to students. Students are in a technology lab with access to the software I am demonstrating. I walk students through the interface, and I quickly build a basic example of the final project they are required to produce. I am not interested in producing a polished version of the project or showing off my advanced techniques, a strategy that would establish my authority and expertise. I often include nonsense footage of myself walking my dog or cleaning the house. I want students to get the big picture of the assignment, and I want them to see that I am willing to take the same personal risks (of looking foolish on camera) as I am asking them to take. My finished product for this class will be very basic, but I will have taught them the framework of the software. I have scaffolded the project.

In the next session, we will look at prior student work. I will introduce the rubric, or, if the class has used the rubric before, we will apply it to the new assignment. I will foreground technical challenges, and we will discuss where student effort should go in making sure the final project is technically polished. I will compare the media project with more traditional academic work by reminding them that they would never submit a first draft of an essay for a final grade, so they shouldn't submit a first draft of a media project. I use the writing process analogy to signal that media production is serious academic work with the same expectations of rigor as writing. We will discuss core controlling concepts and how the concepts fit the assignment given. We will look at ways that students produced surprising and interesting effects and discuss which projects deserve special credit in the aesthetic category for artistic polish. Through this session, we should begin to define the genre of the project and explore the ways that prior students used the genre to make something new and original. We will also begin the process of critical framing. We will discuss how the projects present content in rigorous, thoughtful ways and which ones take a naïve or innocent perspective.

In the next class period, we will have a workshop. Students will be given time to work on their projects and will be expected to bring their problems with production to class for solving. In this session, I am most interested in modeling my own willingness to keep learning. I teach a lot of technologies, and I have more control over some than others. With all technologies, however, I need to have faith that I can recognize and solve problems using research online, trying the tools in the software, and ultimately collaborating with the student to share conversation (in the best Vygotskian sense of conversation as learning). On this day, I also invite students who have demonstrated advanced skills with these technologies to assist me in the lab. In this way, I acknowledge their expertise and encourage them to assume the role of instructor and coconstructor of knowledge with their peers. I may also ask one or two students to teach a particular subskill to the class. Audio editing is deceptively difficult, and audio quality is often a major factor in the success of a project. I regularly ask a student to demonstrate ways of cleaning up audio to remove hiss or background noise and how to control volume for distortion. One goal of this class is to gauge their progress toward completion. Each class is different. Some are quick to pick up new technologies, and some struggle. Some are anxious about performance, and others are unconcerned. I tend to build padding into the schedule to accommodate the need for more time if the class needs it.

Throughout this process, I aim to create a continuous conversation with students about what they have been asked to do, a conversation centered on their work and progress toward its successful completion.

The media-writing process, the understanding of genre conventions, the social environment of class as constructive and supportive while still challenging, and the ultimate assessment rubric: All these aspects of the instruction are derived from the theories discussed in this chapter and are intended to work together among all members of the class. Many students are not confident when they begin to compose in new media, and the class only succeeds if each student can succeed. My job is to establish challenging but achievable goals for the students and provide the context necessary for them to succeed. Some students have amazing talent, strong technical skills, and a strong critical education. These students do great work. Other students lack some part of this package, and their work is missing the dimensions it might have. All students can do these assignments, however, and all can make gratifying, rapid gains in skill and conceptual understanding through their efforts.

Writing pedagogy ultimately provides the most promising conceptual framework for how we might teach students to compose academic work in new media. As a new form of composition in the academy, new media is both "like writing" and "different." While we have yet to answer all the questions raised by the introduction of multimedia authorship as an academic practice, composition and rhetoric theory gives us not just a model for thinking about writing, but also a lively community that has been willing to challenge its own assumptions and evolve rapidly in its thinking about what writing is and how it should be taught. Rather than focus on the multimedia product itself or the technologies that we use to compose, writing theory connects directly to both student learning and pedagogy in practice. This dual emphasis provides powerful grounding for understanding what is different about doing media in academia, different from using media in other contexts, and different from prior work with traditional writing. Unlike approaches that emphasize corporate training or information technology training models, composition and rhetoric allows us to understand media composition in the context of academic work of teaching and learning. As we move forward with teaching and learning and writing with new technologies, we will sort through important questions about what we expect from student writing and what role new media plays in helping us shape student learning. It is imperative that we do this work in the spirit of academic traditions and values and with a willingness and openness to make it new.

NOTES

1. Karen Gocsik, "Digital Discourse: Composing with Media in the Writing Classroom," *Perspectives on Writing and Rhetoric*, Dartmouth Institute for Writing and Rhetoric. Available online at www.dartmouth.edu/~writ8/index.php/perspectives-on-writing-aamp-rhetoric/digital-discourse (accessed January 9, 2013).

2. Cheryl Ball, "Assessing Scholarly Multimedia: A Rhetorical Genre Studies Approach," *Technical Communication Quarterly* 21, no. 1 (2012): 72.

3. Donald M. Murray, "Teaching Writing as a Process Not a Product," in *Cross-Talk in Comp Theory: A Reader*, edited by Victor Villanueva and Kristin L. Arola (Urbana, IL: National Council of Teachers of English, 2003), 3–6.

4. Janet Emig, "Writing as a Mode of Learning," in *Cross-Talk in Comp Theory: A Reader*, edited by Victor Villanueva and Kristin L. Arola (Urbana, IL: National Council of Teachers of English, 2003), 7–15.

5. Carol Kuhlthau, "A Process Approach to Library Skills Instruction," *School Media Quarterly* 13, no. 1 (1985): 35–40.

6. Carol Kuhlthau, *Seeking Meaning: A Process Approach to Library and Information Services* (Norwood, NJ: Ablex Publishing, 1993), 45–51.

7. Paul Prior, *Resituating the Discourse Community: A Sociohistoric Account of Literate Activity in the Academy* (Mahwah, NJ: Lawrence Erlbaum, 1998), 6.

8. New London Group, "A Pedagogy of Multiliteracies: Designing Social Futures," in *Multiliteracies: Literacy Learning and the Design of Social Futures*, edited by Bill Cope and Mary Kalantzis (London: Routledge, 2000), 33–35.

9. Donald Bartholomae, "Inventing the University," in *Cross-Talk in Comp Theory: A Reader*, edited by Victor Villanueva and Kristin L. Arola (Urbana, IL: National Council of Teachers of English, 2003), 524.

10. James Paul Gee, "What Is Literacy?" in *Literacy: A Critical Sourcebook*, edited by Ellen Cushman, Eugene R. Kintgen, Barry M. Kroll, and Mike Rose (New York: Bedford/St. Martin's, 2001), 542–43.

11. Carol Berkenkotter and Thomas N. Huckin, "Rethinking Genre from a Sociocognitive Perspective," *Written Communication* 10, no. 1 (October 1993): 478.

12. Berkenkotter and Huckin, "Rethinking Genre from a Sociocognitive Perspective," 478.

13. Ann M. Johns, "Genre Awareness for the Novice Academic Student: An Ongoing Quest," *Language Teaching* 41, no. 2 (2008): 238.

14. Johns, "Genre Awareness for the Novice Academic Student," 238.

15. "About Kairos," *Kairos.technorhetoric.net*, 2013. Available online at http://kairos.technorhetoric.net/about.html (accessed January 9, 2013).

16. Gocsik, "Digital Discourse."

17. Gocsik, "Digital Discourse."

18. "Submissions," *Kairos.technorhetoric.net*, 2013. Available online at http://kairos.technorhetoric.net/redesign/submissions.html (accessed January 9, 2013).

19. Ball, "Assessing Scholarly Multimedia," 62.

20. Virginia Kuhn, "Speaking with Students: Profiles in Digital Pedagogy," *Kairos: A Journal of Rhetoric, Technology, and Pedagogy* 14, no. 2 (Spring 2010): 1–3. Available online at http://kairos.technorhetoric.net/14.2/interviews/kuhn/index.html (accessed January 9, 2012).

21. Ball, "Assessing Scholarly Multimedia," 66.

SIX

From Punitive Policing to Proactive Prevention: Approaches to Teaching Information Ethics in the College Classroom

Maria T. Accardi

The *Online Dictionary for Library and Information Science* defines information ethics as "The branch of ethics that focuses on the relationship between the creation, organization, dissemination, and use of information, and the ethical standards and moral codes governing human conduct in society."[1] In the context of the college classroom, information ethics is an issue that concerns classroom teachers and librarians alike. While there are many issues to consider when it comes to information ethics, one thing is clear: Students need help navigating these thorny, problematic matters, and teachers and librarians have an obligation to transform moments of ethical conflict into teachable moments and learning opportunities.

TROUBLED STUDENTS, TROUBLING SITUATIONS

A distraught student approached the director of her campus writing center. She had been accused of plagiarism, and she honestly did not understand what she had done wrong. Her teacher wouldn't talk to her about it, except to assume that the plagiarism was deliberate and inform her that it was one of the worst cases of plagiarism he had ever seen. It was not clear why this teacher considered it the worst case, given that he would not speak to the student about the situation. Not knowing where else to turn, the student appealed to the writing center, asking, "What did I do wrong?" The writing center director was able to spot the error right away. It was a matter of not citing a source properly, a matter both simple and complex at the same time. The writing center director explained to the student where she went wrong and how to avoid such missteps in the future. The student ended up failing the course due to this instance of plagiarism, and her transcript was permanently marked with an academic misconduct notation.

Another equally distressed student attended an educational workshop on plagiarism prevention. He informed the workshop leaders that while he had been called before the vice chancellor for Student Affairs and sanctioned for plagiarism, he still didn't understand what he had done wrong. He and his girlfriend, both in the same highly competitive, prestigious academic program, used the same sources for their papers in a similar way, so parts of their papers were identical, as indicated by the plagiarism detection software program used by his teacher. The workshop leaders tried to explain what probably went wrong in his situation, but the student remained unconvinced of the nature of his misdemeanor. Having been thrown out of the academic program as a result of this instance of plagiarism, he still puzzled over what had gone wrong and why he was in this situation.

And yet another troubled student was called before the vice chancellor for Student Affairs for plagiarism at the same institution. This student, it seemed, had used and failed to cite Wikipedia as a source. Wikipedia is a free encyclopedia where content can be created and edited by anyone with access to a Web browser and keyboard. Thus, the student considered Wikipedia a source of "common knowledge," and when something is common knowledge, she had learned, you do not need to cite it. (Aside from the problematic aspect of using Wikipedia as a valid academic source, the student's confusion was not all that mysterious.)

While I have changed a few identifying details, these scenarios actually happened. For whatever reason, the first student was unfamiliar with the secret handshake that signifies full citizenship in the academy: the conventions of ethical academic research writing. For her, citing was a complicated mystery cloaked in fog, uncertainty, and byzantine rules, and, as a result, it was inevitable that she would make mistakes. But what should not have been inevitable were the negative consequences of her error. Her teacher could have treated this as a teachable moment about plagiarism prevention and the conventions of citing instead of proclaiming "gotcha!" and refusing to talk to the student about the problem. Her teacher could also have given the student the benefit of the doubt instead of assuming that the student deliberately plagiarized.

The second student came from a culture and environment that privileges and values collaborative information sharing and knowledge building, so to be confronted with an environment that appeared to reject those values he had come to believe were valid was perplexing, confusing, and distressing. That is, collaboration was such a huge part of his learning environment that it seemed bewildering when collaboration was suddenly considered to be an academic misconduct violation. It also did not help that he was the victim of the ineffective use of plagiarism detection software, which was used to police, but not teach about or prevent, plagiarism in student writers. When used as a proactive, preventative tool, plagiarism prevention software can be useful and effective, but not in the way it was used in his case.

And in the final student scenario, we see echoes of the information ethics issues presented in the previous scenario: How can students be expected to know who is in charge of information and what is authoritative and what is common knowledge when the information age has flattened hierarchies and made everyone an expert? That is, our information culture has become ever more Wikipedian, in which ordinary people share ideas and knowledge with the world without going through the rigors of the traditional publishing or peer-review process.

When it comes to plagiarism and other problems concerning the ethical use of information, teachers have an obligation to resist the policing, punitive impulse and instead focus on the learning opportunities ethical problems present. Dealing with information ethics requires more than corrective homilies and academic sanctions. As Lea Calvert Evering and Gary Moorman observe, "Students need to be engaged in instruction that clarifies the origins and importance of honesty in intellectual pursuits. . . . Refocusing on higher-order goals can persuade students that plagiarism and other forms of academic dishonesty are not in their long-term best interests."[2]

Teaching college students about information ethics and academic integrity is a complex and important duty that academic librarians and other college instructors share. From copyright to intellectual property, to plagiarism prevention, and to scholarly communication, college instructors grapple with translating these concepts in ways that are easy to understand. Individual approaches to information ethics instruction vary, but the one common underlying principle is that information ethics is too complex a concept to be addressed in a single instruction session or solved by a software program:

> Given the nuances of citation and their entanglement with issues of educational goals, originality, intertextuality, selfhood, and individuality, it is clear that students cannot simply be handed a brochure and be expected to get it. The message has to be broadcast over and over, by many sincere people who have given it much thought.[3]

This chapter's goal is to provide theoretical background and specific strategies for those sincere people involved in teaching students about the ethical use of information.

THEORETICAL FRAMEWORKS FOR INFORMATION ETHICS
TEACHING AND LEARNING

A number of useful theories help provide frameworks for the pedagogy of information ethics, critical pedagogy, constructivist theory, and student development teaching. Critical pedagogy theory seeks to transform society through emancipatory, egalitarian educational practices. By de-centering the authority of the teacher, privileging student voices, and raising awareness of the various forms of oppression that have a strangle-hold on society, for instance, classism, racism, sexism, and homophobia, critical pedagogical tactics seek to empower learners to bring about societal change through ending these forms of oppression. By applying critical pedagogy to the teaching of information ethics to student researchers, teachers can enrich their teaching strategies. Teachers can also gain a new perspective on which teaching methods are ineffective.

For example, college instructors might employ plagiarism detection software programs like Turnitin.com or Safeassign.com in teaching the prevention of the persistent and prevalent problem of plagiarism. These plagiarism detection tools compare student work against a proprietary database of previously published work, including submitted student work, and produce originality analyses of student work. Instructors can use such software to identify instances of undocumented, unoriginal writing.

In this way, Turnitin.com reflects the "typical way in which plagiarism discussions are focused on detection and outcomes, rather than on holistic considerations of prevention in the context of writing instruction and student written work."[4] That is, while Turnitin.com sells itself as ostensibly a prevention tool, it is, in reality, used as a detection tool. In other words, the problem with tools like Turnitin.com is that they can be used as policing surveillance tools employed to catch plagiarism in action. While students can use the tool to get originality reports on their own writing during the writing process, these reports are not useful unless there has been proactive instruction in accurate and complete citing for the purposes of plagiarism prevention. There is also some evidence that using plagiarism detection software does not actually deter or prevent plagiarism.[5]

Another problematic aspect of Turnitin.com is that it charges thousands of dollars for institutional access, while using student work to populate its databases. Turnitin.com thus benefits from student work but does not compensate students for providing this content. While a court decision ruled that use of student work in this manner falls under the fair use provision of copyright law,[6] students should have the right to dictate what is done with their work. Moreover, plagiarism detection software can foster a culture of wary suspicion, as the following example illustrates.

Pedagogically, software surveillance becomes an altogether ineffective strategy in the teaching of plagiarism prevention.

> [W]riting is a process through which students, with the assistance of a trusted teacher, can explore and critique dominant social processes, particularly those in which students—and perhaps teachers, too— would otherwise participate unawares. Conversely, plagiarism detection treats writing as a product, grounds the student-teacher relationship in mistrust, and requires students to actively comply with a system that marks them as untrustworthy.[7]

Critical pedagogy resists policing tools like Turnitin.com and transforms a hierarchical, suspicious relationship between teacher and student into a more trusting, egalitarian one.

This egalitarian environment fostered by critical pedagogy means that teachers have to rethink teaching beyond traditional models. Those traditional models no longer hold significance in the critical classroom.

> With the trend toward increasingly less authoritative and traditional interaction between professors and students, it has become incumbent upon universities to identify the means by which students may engage in classroom behaviors that are in keeping with new standards of engagement—those that reflect traditional values for learning, as well as postmodern values for autonomy.[8]

Thus, those concerned with teaching information ethics have to keep in mind that hierarchical, authoritative, punitive models of teaching are no longer relevant in today's classroom.

Similarly, teachers might adopt a critical pedagogical approach to teaching college students about copyright and intellectual property. In this digital age, where it is easy to conduct a Google image search and copy and paste that image into a research paper, it is imperative that students understand that images are intellectual property and subject to copyright law. Introducing students to the notion of the Creative Commons and such open access websites as Flickr.com is one way of teaching students about copyright, while also challenging the strict laws and power structures that govern it. The Creative Commons is a collection of licenses that work with, not as a replacement for, copyright, to allow copyright holders to share and modify creative content.[9]

This was a hard lesson for my campus student-edited journal to learn. The journal had accepted a student paper about body modification, and the paper was illustrated with several striking photographs of tattoos and piercings. In the editorial process, however, the student editors learned that the writer had obtained the images through a Google image search and had not sought permission to use those images. After consulting with their faculty advisor, the student editors realized that they could not print those images without risking copyright infringement. They reluctantly removed the images from the paper and published the article without the powerful illustrations; however, this would have been the perfect opportunity to introduce students to the freely available, copyright-free images available on photo sharing site Flickr.com that are available for use and reuse.

Social constructivism is another theoretical lens through which we can examine the teaching and learning of information ethics. "This approach centers on the ways in which power, the economy, and political and social factors affect the ways in which groups of people form understandings and formal knowledge about their world."[10] In a constructivist model, the concept of plagiarism is "incompatible with the concept of ownership of ideas and knowledge."[11] Furthermore, "learning is a constructive activity that the students themselves have to carry out. From this point of view, then, the task of the educator is not to dispense knowledge but to provide students with opportunities and incentives to build it up."[12] In the constructivist worldview, ideas have a social history, and knowledge is collectively developed throughout history via language, which is used to construct common understandings.[13]

If knowledge is collectively and collaboratively constructed, as this theory contends, then it is no wonder that students struggle with the concept that words, ideas, images, and concepts can belong to individuals rather than to everyone. In the plagiarism prevention workshops that I regularly coteach with the director of the campus writing center, I inform students that the root of the word *plagiarism* comes from the Latin word meaning "kidnapper."[14] This vivid etymological lesson illustrates more concretely what plagiarism is and what it entails. It renders more black and white what seems like a gray area, these subtle gradations between borrowing and copying, paraphrasing and quoting, copying and pasting.

These nuances are unclear in a constructivist information culture that privileges collaboration and cooperation. For example, consider the following scenario: In a writing class, the instructor has students work in groups to brainstorm ideas for individual papers. When students submit their papers, the instructor finds that two papers from students in the same group contain very similar ideas. The instructor immediately assumes that plagiarism occurred and fails both students for the assignment. The students are puzzled and shocked because they were instructed to work together to brainstorm, so of course they are going to have similar ideas. This seems normal to them in their context, where knowledge is collectively developed and collaboratively shared and created. In this case, the teacher fostered a constructivist environment by having students work in groups, but then simultaneously denied and repudiated the effects of the constructivist environment by failing students for thriving in the environment she created. This example is useful for instructors to keep in mind; if we want students to have the benefit of working in groups, learning from one another, and collectively creating knowledge, we have to face the reality that students are not always going to produce original, unique work.

Finally, another useful theory to consider is the student development theory. When we encounter traditionally aged college students in the classroom, we only see a mere glimpse of the complex cluster of psychosocial changes that college students are undergoing as they develop a sense of identity and emerge into adulthood. In a sense, the student is a mystery; we see the outward exterior, but we are not privy to what is going on inside. The literature on student development attempts to reveal the mystery of a student's inner workings. Arthur W. Chickering's 1969 theory of the psychosocial development of college students was originally conceptualized as a process that continues in a mostly sequential path along seven vectors, which include 1) developing competence, 2) managing emotions, 3) moving through autonomy toward interdependence, 4) developing mature interpersonal relationships, 5) establishing identity, 6) developing purpose, and 7) developing integrity.[15] Chickering's original research was primarily based on traditional students between seventeen and twenty-two years of age at small liberal arts colleges, but, even with this limitation, the seven vectors are still viewed as foundational to the field of student development theory. And, in 1993, Chickering and Reisser revised and updated the theory of the seven vectors in *Education and Identity*, which incorporates new research and redefinition of the seven vectors.

Understanding the developmental processes most students undergo while in college can have an impact on how college instructors conceive of information ethics instruction. If student development and student learning are inextricably connected, as these theories contend, then shouldn't our learning outcomes take into consideration Chickering's model for student development? For example, the final vector of Chickering's psychosocial development model involves developing integrity. College students develop core values and beliefs, which are foundational to self-respect and informing how one acts. These values include humanizing values, personalizing values, and developing congruence between values and behavior.[16] The theory posits that student learning and success in the college classroom leads to self-esteem and self-respect, both of which aid in developing integrity. I argue that integrity is also developed through academic honesty, which instructors can address through information ethics and plagiarism instruction as well.

The application of student development theory can help instructors be more patient and less punitive when students commit information ethics violations. That is, it is helpful to be tolerant and recall that students are not fully wired yet; they are still forming the vital psychosocial connections that transform a student into an active and ethical participant in the information age.

PRACTICAL STRATEGIES FOR TEACHING
INFORMATION ETHICS

The aforementioned theoretical frameworks provide a useful point of view for conceiving of practical tactics for teaching information ethics and academic integrity in the college classroom. These tactics include instruction on copyright, the various forms of citing, and methods of documenting the research process. I argue that teachers who spend less time enumerating the terrible things that will happen if a student is caught plagiarizing or committing other academically unethical acts have more time to focus on education and prevention.

Copyright and intellectual property are important concepts for college students conducting research. According to one study, students' conceptions of copyright law indicated that students believed that the "Internet content is all open for the public to use, the Internet is always free, and all educational use is fair use."[17] It is therefore imperative that instructors "guide their students to take advantage of the Internet to enhance their learning and productivity, but at same time know how to avoid possible copyright infringement."[18]

One student research paper does not stand alone in a vacuum; it takes up space in the rich and varied history of intellectual property. Teaching students about intellectual property will contextualize for them the conventions of academic writing and where they, as students, have a place in that framework. A lesson on the history of intellectual property and copyright, starting with, perhaps, the Statute of Anne of 1710, and extending into today's relevant law, the Digital Millennium Copyright Act of 1998, can give students an idea of what is at stake when dealing with intellectual property issues and how they, as student writers, come into play in this situation.

Plagiarism is perhaps the most common information ethics issue that college instructors encounter in the classroom. A study by Ronald W. Belter and Athena du Pré indicates that most plagiarism results from insufficient knowledge about the conventions of quotation and citation. Belter and du Pré write that, "Our findings suggest that an effective way to reduce unintentional plagiarism is to explicitly teach students how to properly quote and cite sources and to test their understanding of this information."[19] Instructors should narrow their focus to this knowledge gap, rather than take a castigatory, surveillance approach. In short, students need to learn about the differences between citing, quoting, paraphrasing, and just plain borrowing. Teachers can demonstrate that there are different conventions in different contexts, and that "Just as we distinguish between tasting a grape at the supermarket and stealing a car, we don't want to lump together all infractions of academic citation norms."[20] Taking someone else's paper and turning it in as one's own is quite different from a less than ideal paraphrase or forgetting to put quotation marks around a direct quote.

Another study offers a teaching approach that emphasizes the process of information gathering: the i-Map, an assessment technique that requires students to document their research process using visual communication strategies. The i-Map is a student-centered approach to focusing on some of the triggers of plagiarism. It emphasizes information gathering, information evaluation, the development of argument, and the editing process.[21] While no tactic is a perfect panacea, this intervention is valuable in scenarios where a lack of knowledge leads to plagiarism.

A similar process-oriented strategy concerns a note-taking method that helps students organize their ideas and sources. Using a two-column format, students place their main ideas in the left column, while placing their citations and supporting materials in the right column.[22] This emphasis on process highlights the importance of prevention and preemption, of stopping plagiarism before it has the chance to start.

These practical tactics are closely aligned with the theories outlined earlier in this chapter. In particular, the process approach favored by the i-Map and the two-column note-taking method are consistent with the pedagogical approaches espoused by critical and constructivist theories, as well as the student development theory.

ENVISIONING THE IDEAL CLASSROOM

I close this chapter by telling yet another story. In this scenario, a student wrote a research paper for her education class. The following semester, she had an assignment in her research writing class, and she decided to reuse the same paper. After all, she had written it, it was her paper, and she had carefully documented all of her sources. It did not occur to her that there could be a problem with her action until the plagiarism detection software her teacher used flagged her paper as 100 percent unoriginal. Since she had already submitted it once, and her previous teacher used Turnitin.com in that first instance, her paper now lives inside Turnitin.com's database forever. The student had two issues with this situation: She did not understand how it was possible for someone to plagiarize oneself, and she also did not think it was fair that her work now resides in this database without her permission. This unfortunate situation could probably have been prevented if she had had adequate instruction in plagiarism prevention, information ethics, and academic integrity.

In my vision of the ideal college classroom, plagiarism prevention instruction is the norm. The importance of information ethics is a vital part of the curriculum. Students receive instruction from both their classroom teachers and librarians on how to locate, evaluate, and ethically use information. This student-centered emphasis is on learning and prevention, rather than policing, surveillance, and punitive measures. This is not to suggest that students ought not be sanctioned for violations of information ethics. Rather, I am arguing that when students encounter an information ethics issue, there exists a teachable moment, and the onus is on teachers and librarians to seize that moment and help students learn how to make the right choice. These teachable moments can be rendered more visible and palpable when the theoretical underpinnings of pedagogy and student development are laid bare on the examination table.

NOTES

1. Joan M. Reitz, "Information Ethics," *ODLIS: Online Dictionary for Library and Information Science.* Westport, CT: Libraries Unlimited, 1996. Available online at www.abc-clio.com/ODLIS/odlis_A.aspx (accessed November 9, 2012).

2. Lea Calvert Evering and Gary Moorman, "Rethinking Plagiarism in the Digital Age," *Journal of Adolescent and Adult Literacy* 56, no. 1 (September 2012): 41.

3. Susan D. Blum, "Academic Integrity and Student Plagiarism: A Question of Education, Not Ethics," *Chronicle of Higher Education* 55, no. 24 (February 2009): A35.

4. Kelly Ritter, "Buying in, Selling Short: A Pedagogy against the Rhetoric of Online Paper Mills," *Pedagogy* 6, no. 1 (Winter 2006): 27.

5. Robert J. Youmans, "Does the Adoption of Plagiarism-Detection Software in Higher Education Reduce Plagiarism?" *Studies in Higher Education* 36, no. 7 (November 2011): 749–61.

6. Jeffrey R. Young, "Judge Rules Plagiarism-Detection Tool Falls under 'Fair Use,'" *Chronicle of Higher Education* 54, no. 30 (April 4, 2008): A13.

7. Sean Zwagerman, "The Scarlet P: Plagiarism, Panopticism, and the Rhetoric of Academic Integrity," *College Composition and Communication* 59, no. 4 (June 2008): 692.

8. Emma R. Gross, "Clashing Values: Contemporary Views about Cheating and Plagiarism Compared to Traditional Beliefs and Practices," *Education* 132, no. 2 (Winter 2011): 439.

9. "About Creative Commons," Creative Commons. Available online at http://creativecommons.org/about (accessed November 9, 2012).

10. Virginia Richardson, "Constructivist Pedagogy," *Teachers College Record* 105, no. 9 (December 2003): 1,624.

11. Evering and Moorman, "Rethinking Plagiarism in the Digital Age," 36.

12. Ernst von Glasersfeld, "Introduction: Aspects of Constructivism," in *Constructivism: Theory, Perspectives, and Practice,* edited by Catherine Twomey Fosnot (New York: Teachers College Press, 2005), 7.

13. Evering and Moorman, "Rethinking Plagiarism in the Digital Age," 36.

14. Merriam-Webster's Dictionary of Law, s.v. "plagiarize," cited in Lilly M. Lancaster, ed., *Palmetto Business and Law Review 2010* (Spartanburg: George Dean Johnson Jr. College of Business and Economics, University of South Carolina Upstate, 2010). Available online at www.credoreference.com/entry/mwdlaw/plagiarize (accessed October 27, 2012).

15. Arthur W. Chickering and Linda Reisser, *Education and Identity* (San Francisco, CA: Jossey-Bass, 1993), 45.

16. Chickering and Reisser, *Education and Identity*, 51.

17. Chou Chien, Chan Pei-Shan, and Wu Huan-Chueh, "Using a Two-Tier Test to Assess Students' Understanding and Alternative Conceptions of Cyber Copyright Laws," *British Journal of Educational Technology* 38, no. 6 (November 2007): 1,079.

18. Chien, Pei-Shan, and Huan-Chueh, "Using a Two-Tier Test to Assess Students' Understanding and Alternative Conceptions of Cyber Copyright Laws," 1,073.

19. Ronald W. Belter and Athena du Pré, "A Strategy to Reduce Plagiarism in an Undergraduate Course," *Teaching of Psychology* 36, no. 4 (November 2009): 260.

20. Blum, "Academic Integrity and Student Plagiarism," A35.

21. Kim Walden and Alan Peacock, "The i-Map: A Process-Centered Response to Plagiarism," *Assessment and Evaluation in Higher Education* 31, no. 2 (April 2006): 212.

22. Evering and Moorman, "Rethinking Plagiarism in the Digital Age," 40.

SEVEN

Assessing the Information Research Process

Stephanie Sterling Brasley

Assessment is a process that focuses on student learning, a process that involves reviewing and reflecting on practice as academics have always done, but in a more planned and careful way. —Catherine Palomba and Trudy W. Banta[1]

WHY ASSESS?

Seminal and contemporary works on assessment underscore the importance and value of carefully and purposefully linking assessment and learning. At its core, assessment seeks to measure student learning, answering the questions: What have students learned? What do they know? What are they able to do as a result of instruction? What have they gained from self-reflection on their learning? Notably, several contemporary authors cast assessment within a robust learning framework, namely that of learner-centered teaching and student learning outcomes. Linda Suskie and Trudy W. Banta juxtapose contemporary and traditional ideas regarding assessment, noting that the contemporary approach is "carefully aligned with goals . . . focused on thinking and performance skills . . . used to improve teaching and learning, as well as to evaluate and assign grades to individual students" versus the traditional approaches, which are "planned and implemented without consideration of learning goals . . . often focused on memorized knowledge, used only to evaluate individual students, with decisions about changes to curricula and pedagogies often based on hunch and anecdote."[2] Lorna Earl contrasts "assessment of learning," "assessment for learning," and "assessment as learning," stating that there are advantages to all three approaches; however, she asserts that "assessment for learning" "offers an alternative perspective to traditional assessment . . . [it] shifts the emphasis from summative to formative assessment, from making judgments to creating descriptions that can be used in the service of the next stage of learning."[3] Megan Oakleaf, also a proponent of "assessment for learning," affirms the work of Grant Wiggins, who states that "good teaching is inseparable from good assessing."[4] In a later article, Oakleaf cites additional expert assessment theorist Mark Battersby, as well as Esther S. Grassian and Joan R. Kaplowitz, who are also clear proponents of the idea that learning and assessment should be inextricably linked and that these two concepts improve not only student learning, but also the instructional practice of teachers.[5] Elizabeth F. Avery concurs with research in this area, declaring that assessment "is now the means for learning, not just the method of evaluation."[6] Earl furthers this conversation, positing that this is the most powerful form of formative learning, with the student being the link. In this third approach, "students, as active, engaged, and critical assessors, can make sense of information, relate it to prior knowledge, and master the skills involved." Ultimately, "students are their own best assessors."[7] These are empowering ideas for librarians, since most engage in formative rather than summative assessment activities. It is clear that there is ample support from assessment experts for learner-centered assessment.

The transition to a learner-centered approach was likely fueled by the accountability movement. The public and state legislatures were calling for K–16 public education to demonstrate its value with respect to public funding[8] by a move toward more performance-based curricula; increased pressure from accrediting agencies to frame and assess learning in terms of outcomes;[9] the "Continuous Improvement Movement," in which "colleges and universities pursued continuous improvement because of competition for students"; the "need to reduce costs and improve quality of services"; and the "desire to enhance learning."[10] In addition, the burgeoning emphasis on student-centered learning and teaching methodologies (including active and cooperative/collaborative inquiry; project-, problem-, and resource-based learning; student engagement; and motivation and reflective practice to improve student learning and teaching effectiveness) also acted as catalysts in this sea change. Kathleen Dunn underscores this mandate, noting that "Assessment is a necessary byproduct of the current emphasis in higher education on accountability and outcomes."[11] Furthermore, libraries are being asked to prove their value concretely, and librarian-instructors are increasingly being pressured to demonstrate positive connections between their work in information literacy and successful outcomes in student learning.[12]

Framing this discourse within a learning context, this chapter provides a primer on assessment (definitions, methods, levels, domains, and types) and student learning outcomes; discusses the relationship between the information research process, information literacy, and assessment; and outlines various types of assessment tools, with emphasis on those most effective for assessing the information research process. This chapter does not attempt to present a comprehensive review of the information literacy assessment literature; rather, it examines representative literature that enables librarian-instructors to engage in fruitful assessment endeavors to improve students' mastery of the information research process. Note that the assessment strategies discussed may be molded and employed at multiple levels, including in the classroom and at the program or institutional levels.

INFORMATION LITERACY, THE INFORMATION RESEARCH PROCESS, AND ASSESSMENT

During the last fifteen years, library and information science (LIS) scholarship has contributed greatly to the body of literature on assessment and is replete with books and articles on the topic. This is due, in large part, to the proliferation of works dealing with information literacy. Defining the term *information literacy* has been challenging.[13] Apart from the controversy over definitions, the one developed by the American Library Association (ALA) has been widely accepted. It states that individuals should attain skills to "recognize when information is needed and have the ability to locate, evaluate, and use effectively the needed information."[14] The controversy over the myriad definitions of information literacy has not deterred librarian-instructors from exploring various assessment methods to measure the efficacy of information literacy and research skills.

Writing in 1999, a year prior to the publication of the IL Standards, Patricia Iannuzzi offers guidance on how libraries and librarians should position information literacy within academic institutions to contribute fully to student learning. This requires looking at the "teaching library" model as an effective one for promoting information literacy and establishing assessment approaches that emphasize performance and outcomes measures for student learning. Information literacy can be integrated into the fabric of the academic at "four levels": "within the library, in the classroom, on campus, and beyond the campus."[15] Iannuzzi proffers suggestions for assessment approaches at each of level. Most librarians have worked primarily within the library setting, creating measures that are within their control, including "in-class assignments . . . self-directed learning tutorials such as workbooks or Web-based modules, and competency tests or self-assessments administered as pretests or posttests."[16] Once librarians move outside of the library, collaboration becomes a key component; librarians and faculty can partner on assignment design and evaluation of "bibliographies, reviews of assignments that underscore the research process, and the use of portfolios or journals . . . [enabling a] meaningful transfer [of information literacy outcomes] to other learning environments."[17] More complex, yet more impactful, are assessment strategies at the campus level and beyond. The former requires programmatic buy-in from senior library and campus administrators and a "library culture for information literacy strong enough to influence a campus culture."[18] Transference and application of information literacy skills in the professional arena are the ultimate barometers of effectiveness.

The Association of College and Research Libraries' (ACRL) "Information Literacy Competency Standards for Higher Education,"[19] hereafter referred to as IL Standards, have been the leading "assessment guidelines"[20] for information literacy programs in the United States. Published a year after Iannuzzi's vision piece, the IL Standards provide needed performance and outcome measures; they are categorized into five broad areas of information literacy proficiency, accompanied by twenty-two performance indicators, along with outcomes that guide construction of assessments to measure performance. The IL Standards are framed in terms of what a student will be able to do. The five standards state that the "information literate student" does the following:

1. Defines and articulates the need for information;
2. Accesses needed information effectively and efficiently;
3. Evaluates information and its sources critically and incorporates selected information into his or her knowledge base and value system;
4. Individually or as a member of a group, uses information effectively to accomplish a specific purpose; and
5. Understands many of the economic, legal, and social issues surrounding the use of information and accesses and uses information ethically and legally.[21]

The IL Standards have become the benchmark for information literacy assessment activities. These standards endorse the "assessment for learning" theories, which propose that teaching activities may also be used to measure learning.

Discipline faculty and librarian-instructors may view assessment with mixed emotions, approaching this concept with equal feelings of trepidation, hesitance, and resentment. These reactions are understandable; some faculty and librarian-instructors are unfamiliar with assessment methods beyond the traditional research paper, criterion-referenced tests,[22] or affective surveys. Assessment is generally perceived as being labor- and time-intensive. The typical instruction activity for a librarian-instructor is the single-session library instruction session (i.e., "One-Shot or Multiple Shots"), which may impede the implementation of certain types of assessment and cause tension as content and assessment goals collide when both need to be completed in a short time frame.

In addition, in some instances, despite continual accountability requirements, the environment of the institution is not supportive of assessment efforts. Trudy W. Banta and colleagues outline nine principles of effective student learning. They added a tenth after further feedback from the academic community that affirmed the following idea: "Assessment is most effective when undertaken in an environment that is receptive, supportive, and enabling."[23] I find this principle particularly compelling. Assessment efforts, large or small, may be thwarted by an environment that is dismissive of the positive impacts assessment engenders; however, regardless of the climate at an institution, at the very least, a discipline faculty member or librarian-instructor has control over individual and classroom assessment efforts that can improve student learning. It is hoped that the following primer on assessment methods will dispel, or at least diminish, negative thoughts or misconceptions about conducting assessments to improve the information research process.

ASSESSMENT OVERVIEW

Definitions of assessment abound in the literature, with some individuals suggesting that each institution develop its own, based on its mission and learning goals.[24] These definitions will facilitate understanding of the hallmarks of effective assessment. Suskie summarizes Thomas A. Angelo and K. Patricia Cross's definition of assessment as "the ongoing process of establishing clear, measurable, expected outcomes of student learning; ensuring that students have sufficient opportunities to achieve those outcomes; [and] systematically gathering, analyzing, and interpreting evidence to determine how well student learning matches our expectations, using the resulting information to understand and improve learning."[25]

As understood by Mary E. Huba and Jann E. Freed, assessment is "the process of gathering and discussing information from multiple and diverse sources in order to develop a deep understanding of what students know, understand, and can do with their knowledge as a result of their educational experiences; the process culminates when assessment results are used to improve subsequent learning."[26] These authors' definitions and that of Palomba and Banta at the beginning of this chapter reveal the following commonalities concerning assessment: process, student learning, data collection, and reflection. All talk about assessment as a process. It is not episodic; rather, it is continual, involving planning and forethought. In this way, the assessment process is similar to the information research process in that both are cyclical rather than linear and both warrant attention to multiple steps to reach the desired goal. Assessment also involves the compilation of data that should then be utilized to inform a learning improvement cycle. Suskie and Banta and Huba and Freed proffer similar assessment processes, each comprising four elements.[27] As table 7.1 demonstrates, both cycles begin with determining the learning goals or outcomes and end with using the results to improve student learning. The two models deviate slightly with the order for developing learning experiences and assessments to measure learning. Notwithstanding the order in which these elements are implemented, the authors agree that these are the essential elements. As we delve into effective practices for assessing the information research process, these elements will undergird the foundation for planning.

Student Learning Outcomes and Learning Domains

Student learning outcomes (SLOs), intended learning outcomes, expected learning outcomes, student learning objectives, and learning goals are frequently used interchangeably to describe what learners should know, understand, believe, and be able to do as a result of instructional activities. SLOs are the cornerstone of any assessment endeavor, and they produce benefits for students, faculty, the institution, and the public.[28] Assessment is conducted at three different levels: course, program, and institutional, with SLOs guiding the formulation of curricula and other instructional interventions to help students understand what is expected of them.[29] Writing SLO statements usually begin with the phrase, "Students will . . ." or "Students will be able to . . . ," followed by an action verb describing the learning domain (i.e., affective, cognitive, and psychomotor). When creating SLOs, it is best to use verbs from Bloom's taxonomy (1956), a seminal work that classifies learning objectives into three domains: cognitive (knowing/knowledge), affective (feelings, attitudes, opinions), and psychomotor (actions/behaviors). It also includes a hierarchical list of verbs to describe the attainment of skills, knowledge, and abilities of the learner.[30]

Table 7.1.   Suskie and Banta's and Huba and Freed's Assessment Processes

Suskie/Banta's Teaching, Learning, and Assessment Cycle	Huba/Freed's Assessment Process
Establish learning goals	Formulate statements of intended learning outcomes
Provide learning opportunities	Develop or select assessment measures
Assess student learning	Create experiences leading to outcomes
Use the results	Discuss and use assessment results to improve learning

As stated earlier, learning and assessment are inextricably linked. It is for this reason that assessment scholars emphasize the importance of planning learning activities and assessments simultaneously. At times, an assessment may influence a revision of the learning activity, and, at other times, a learning activity can also be an assessment tool. Such is the case with in-class exercises, among others.

Assessment Types and Tools

Any plan for assessment must begin with an understanding of methods or types employed to measure learning at the three levels. We will examine informal and formal assessment; diagnostic, formative, and summative assessment; and direct and indirect assessment. These forms of assessment are accompanied by examples of tools that can be used during various learning activities.

Informal Assessment

Observation, inquiry, and reflective practices form the basis of this assessment technique. It is spontaneous, quick, provides immediate feedback,[31] and best-suited to individuals with flexible teaching styles and a certain level of comfort with revising teaching strategies in the moment. During an instructional activity, instructors are able to question students and observe nonverbal cues to elicit feedback on comprehension of content. Subsequently, based on information gleaned from observation, inquiry, and quick reflection, instructors have the opportunity to change course to enhance the instructional experience. Additional classroom activities that may inform assessment include peer teaching (student pairs explain a concept immediately after it has been taught), the five-minute quiz (students respond to one or two questions covering a previous lecture), or other classroom assessment techniques (CATs), which are discussed later in this chapter. Informal assessments lend themselves to formative, low-stakes forms of measurement that guide improvements in teaching and learning. Kari D. Weaver and Penni M. Pier successfully used observation as one of several assessment strategies within an oral communications course in which librarians collaborated with discipline faculty fully ito ntegrate information literacy.[32] The observations of the team in conversations about one iteration of the course guided revisions that improved students' speeches in a subsequent course.

Formal Assessment

Put simply, formal and informal assessments are distinguished by grades. Formal assessments are graded and "undertaken for accountability purposes."[33] Direct assessment measures (e.g., research papers, fixed-choice or essay exams, portfolios, presentations, quizzes, graded exercises, standardized tests, products that use rubrics, etc.) are components of formal assessment. Observation is generally used as an informal assessment but may also be utilized as a formal assessment. Andrew Walsh reports on two studies that used observation for a specific purpose. One involved librarians who wanted to find out whether their instruction had revised students' search strategy in the library catalog. They had students think aloud as they performed their searches.[34] In another example, Dunn reports on an excellent study conducted within the California State University system to assess information literacy. They used a combination of close observations of students in two scenarios, one in which students were shadowed and behaviors noted, and another in which librarians examined screen shots of students' searching behaviors.[35]

Diagnostic Assessment

Diagnostic assessments (also called preassessments) generally take place prior to instruction, and they enable instructors to determine students' knowledge levels, strengths, gaps, and points of remediation.[36] This information helps instructors plan lesson outlines and also offer a baseline for the amount of learning that has occurred after an instructional activity. Although some authors consider diagnostic assessment a component of formative assessment, others consider it a distinct type of measurement.[37] Champions of constructivism believe that students do not present to a learning environment as empty vessels; rather, they bring with them prior knowledge, experiences, beliefs, skills, and attitudes. This form of measurement enables instructors to tailor instruction to the needs of students. Diagnostic assessment can be used informally in the form of guided questions issued verbally at the beginning of instruction or via the use of such CATs as the Background Knowledge Probe (a simple questionnaire that can be administered at the beginning of a unit of instruction) or the Misconception/Preconception Check (which identifies incorrect knowledge). Librarian-instructors can distribute a pretest prior to an information research instruction session to ascertain students' levels of knowledge and identify gaps.

Formative Assessment

Formative assessment is a measurement process that helps instructors and students gauge progress of learning throughout an instructional activity; it also gives instructors feedback on the effectiveness of their instruction. This measurement benefits instructors and students alike. It tends to be informal in nature, allowing instructors to observe students and make any necessary adjustments to their pedagogy.[38] Students benefit from these "on-the-spot corrections" as learning occurs.[39] The advantage, then, of formative exercises is that they provide immediate feedback to both students and instructors. Do note that they also serve as a drawback for librarian-instructors who are new to teaching or are not yet comfortable enough in a spontaneous teaching situation to revise content to respond immediately to the learning needs of students. Librarian-instructors need not be dissuaded, however. Continue using this assessment, and your comfort level and confidence will increase in time. Formative assessment takes place throughout the learning process. Consequently, exercises, quizzes, CATs, reflective essays, research process logs, graphic organizers like concept maps, and KWL (What I *Know*, What I *Want* to Know, What I've *Learned*) charts are all examples of formative assessment activities that can be used effectively in learning activities.

Summative Assessment

As its name implies, this form of assessment occurs at the end of an instructional unit or course and is used to determine whether learners have met the learning outcome.[40] Standardized tests, fixed-choice or essay exams, research papers, and capstone projects are examples of this type of assessment.

Direct Assessment

"Direct methods of evaluating student learning are those that provide evidence of whether . . . a student has command of a specific subject or content area, can perform a certain task, exhibits a particular skill, demonstrates a certain quality in his or her work (e.g., creativity, analysis, synthesis, or objectivity), or holds a particular value."[41] Well-designed direct methods should answer the following critical questions: "What did students learn as a result of an educational experience? To what degree did students learn? What did students *not* learn?"[42] Performance or authentic assessments are direct forms of measurement. Examples include standardized tests (developed either commercially or locally); embedded assignments (like oral presentations), poster projects, and class exercises; and such capstone experiences as portfolios, research papers, and other culminating activities.[43]

Indirect Assessment

"Indirect methods of evaluating student learning involve data that are *related to* the act of learning, such as factors that predict or mediate learning or perceptions about learning but do not reflect learning itself."[44] These assessments deal with students' perceptions of their attainment or mastery of SLOs. Examples include surveys, focus groups, interviews, and questionnaires. Reflective assignments (e.g., some CATs, journals, and essays) may also be considered as an indirect form of assessment, as they record students' subjective ideas and opinions.

Direct and indirect methods both have limitations. Specifically, "direct assessments of student learning, while providing evidence of *what* the student has learned, provide no evidence as to why the student has learned or *why* he or she has not learned."[45] With respect to indirect assessments, "they do not evaluate student learning per se, and therefore should not be the only means of assessing outcomes."[46] When planning assessments, it is best to include a balance of direct and indirect measures so that you are provided with both *what* the student has learned and *why* learning occurs.

Levels of Assessment

The level and domain should guide the planning of assessments to measure competency with the research process. Much of the scholarship on assessment references three major levels. As previously outlined, these are course, programmatic, and institutional. Assessment performed at the course level seeks to measure students' mastery of content at a specific level. SLOs are developed to measure student learning during the course or several class sessions. Programmatic assessment, the next level up, examines a series of courses in a discipline or program to ascertain whether the content is fulfilling the program's learning goals. The third level, institutional assessment, looks more broadly at assessment than at the other two levels; measures are tied to the mission, accreditation requirements, and overarching educational goals.[47]

ASSESSMENT PLANNING CONSIDERATIONS

Planning for the assessment of the information research process requires forethought into the types of assessments that will be used and at which levels. This will necessitate examination of the library's and institution's views on assessment and information literacy. For example, at large research one-level institutions, primary emphasis in the library may reside in collection building and maintenance rather than in instruction. Conversely, at institutions with strong traditions of teaching excellence or within libraries that have adopted a "teaching library" model, instruction about and assessment of the information research process will likely thrive. It is also prudent to examine your institution's perceptions of assessment. If assessment is viewed in a pejorative light or if it has not been embraced as a valuable component of the instructional process, then classroom, program, and institutional assessment is a distant goal; first, the groundwork needs to be laid, with individual efforts by librarians during workshops or one-shots.

Another factor is the library's current library instruction or information literacy program. Where the program is in terms of its developmental stages[48] will determine the insights that come about regarding the point at which assessment can be incorporated. Relationships with discipline faculty should be factored in, as those relationships will have an impact on the types of assessments you are able to implement. For example, if strong relationships around basic library instruction have not been forged within departments or with individual faculty, it will impact your ability to plan for classroom, programmatic, or institutional assessment initiatives. It may be prudent to build relationships and partnerships before moving on to other levels. If strong partnerships have already been solidified and several instructional models are in place (e.g., course-integrated, workshops, and credit courses), then the environment is ripe for larger-scale assessments of the information research process.

Within the library, personnel issues also need to be addressed. Answers to these questions will add valuable information to the decision-making process: How many librarians are currently involved in instruction and assessment? What additional resources would be needed? If planning for large-scale assessments, will reassignment of librarian-instructors be warranted? What are the professional development needs surrounding information literacy, the research process, and assessment? If necessary, what training mechanism needs to be put in place? What are the costs associated with building or ramping up assessment activities? The aforementioned environmental scan and data-gathering activities will be useful in planning for assessment of the information research process.[49]

DESIGNING ASSESSMENT: TOOLS FOR THE INFORMATION RESEARCH PROCESS[50]

Now that the foundation for assessment has been laid with a primer and planning guidance, the design of assessment of the information research process can proceed effectively. Ideally, a blend of assessment strategies that incorporate direct and indirect, and formal and informal, measures provides the librarian-instructor with richer data from multiple dimensions of the learning process. In summary, assessment of the information research process can be undertaken at the institutional, programmatic, and course levels. Furthermore, assessments can be designed to measure affective, cognitive, and psycho-motor or behavioral learning goals. Finally, there are a variety of direct and indirect techniques at our disposal to design effective learning activities for teaching information literacy and the information research process. We will explore strategies to assess learning and teaching effectiveness that may be employed before, during, and after activities for teaching the information research process. Some techniques can be used during multiple stages of the instruction process.

Knowledge Tests

"Knowledge tests focus on what students know, rather than on their skills, behaviors, attitudes, or opinions."[51] Fixed-choice tests, essays, and standardized tests fall into this category. Standardized tests are direct forms of assessment that may be developed locally or purchased commercially. Literature on locally developed fixed-choice tests dominate in the information literacy and library research skills assessment arena.[52] Interested in discovering information literacy assessments that provide "illustrative examples of reliability and validity,"[53] Walsh conducted a rigorous search for relevant peer-reviewed articles. He found thirty-one articles on multiple-choice questionnaires and fourteen articles on "quiz/test" projects. Surprisingly, he found little discussion of the rationale for this assessment choice. A few authors cited "ease of use, speed, and convenience" as justification.[54]

However, Oakleaf's 2008 article on information literacy assessment approaches aptly delineates the benefits and limitations of fixed-choice tests. Among the advantages, they "measure acquisition of facts, are easy and inexpensive to score, provide data in numerical form, can be made highly reliable."[55] They can also "be used to compare pretest and posttest results . . . [and] people believe in them."[56] But she cautions that they do little to measure higher-order thinking skills, "complex behavior," or "authentic performances," and they don't lend themselves to "assessment for learning" strategies.[57] Oakleaf further states that a "major limitation of fixed-choice tests is that they are indirect assessments"[58] (however, some assessment theorists categorize these as direct assessments). Nevertheless, Oakleaf cites newer research by education scholars in this area, who assert that these tests "lack authenticity" and are "fallible, limited measures of learning goals."[59] Librarian-instructors interested in fixed-choice assessment would benefit from reading this section in its entirety. Walsh's study also found substantial variety in the development of multiple-choice tests; some tests had as little as eight questions testing skills acquisition, and others had sixty.[60] This collection of various types of multiple-choice tests can provide a jumping-off point for librarian-instructors electing to create a locally developed test or shorter pretests/posttests.[61]

The value of information and information and communication technology (ICT) literacy has increased in the last decade, as exemplified by such accrediting agencies as the Middle States Commission on Higher Education (MSCHE), which have included information literacy in its standards. The MSCHE published *Developing Research and Communication Skills: Guidelines for Information Literacy in the Curriculum.*[62] This has resulted in increased interest in standardized tests to evaluate these skills. The iSkills™ test,[63] the Standardized Assessment of Information Literacy Skills (SAILS),[64] and James Madison University's Information Literacy

Test (ILT)[65] are three prominent standardized, professional examinations that test information literacy or ICT literacy competency and are based on the ACRL "Information Literacy Competency Standards for Higher Education." ICT literacy is "the ability to use digital technology, communication tools, and networks appropriately to solve problems in order to function in an information society."[66] iSkills™ is an outcome and scenario-based test of ICT literacy skills developed by the Educational Testing Service (ETS). It tests seven proficiency areas, which include "define, access, evaluate, manage, integrate, create, and communicate."[67] ETS currently markets iSkills™ as a measure of the "ability to think critically in a digital environment through a range of real-world tasks."[68] Note that the scenario-based questions that comprise the iSkills™ assessment can be viewed as a form of performance assessment, which is discussed later in this chapter.

According to its website, "Project SAILS is a knowledge test with multiple-choice questions targeting a variety of information literacy skills." Brian Lym and associates provide a good overview of the administration and use of SAILS, along with insights into its benefits and limitations.[69] Similar in format to the SAILS test, the ILT, developed at James Madison University, is a multiple-choice exam assessing students' mastery of information literacy concepts. Lynn Cameron and colleagues give a detailed account of the process for developing and validating the ILT, which should prove useful for librarians desiring to use a standardized test to measure information literacy skills.[70] Any of these assessments are able to provide information to advance information literacy goals, at either the institutional or program levels. These tests may be used as diagnostic tools to identify gaps in students' knowledge, to provide data for accountability purposes, and for curricular improvements.

Alternatively, colleges or universities may develop local tests. Administering standardized tests to all students can be a costly proposition; implementing a testing project within a discipline program can provide focused data about the information research process. These tests are able to be administered at a testing center or within courses; therefore, partnerships and collaborations are particularly beneficial when initiating or advancing information research process projects. Knowledge tests may be administered at any point in an assessment initiative, in the middle to assess whether milestones have been reached, and as a summative assessment at the completion of a major, as a posttest, or as part of other culminating activities.

Indirect measures that tap into the affective domain also provide valuable qualitative information to complement direct measures. For example, surveys or focus groups inquiring about students' perceptions of their information literacy or information research skills can inform the development or selection of standardized or locally developed tests and provide useful information to structure a learning experience.

Classroom Assessment and CATs

Inherent in the notion of classroom assessment is feedback. K. Patricia Cross and Mimi H. Steadman define classroom assessment as "small-scale assessments conducted continually in college classrooms . . . to determine what students are learning in that class.[71] They contend that its purpose is to "make both teachers and students more aware of the learning that is taking place—or perhaps not taking place in the classroom—it is an assessment of learning in process, during the semester, in a given classroom."[72] These formative measures quickly inform instructors about what students have learned and where they might have misconceptions regarding content. Moreover, they enable students to reflect on their learning in a nonthreatening way. Classroom Assessment Techniques (CATs), which hone in on learners' misconceptions, exhibit the following characteristics: "learner-centered, teacher-directed, mutually beneficial, formative, context specific, ongoing, and rooted in good teaching practice."[73] Furthermore, they are simple to administer and are low stakes. Constructivist learning theory states that new knowledge is self-constructed and that learners construct this new knowledge through analysis, sense-making, and synthesis of new information into prior knowledge. Thus, tapping into what students already know can be a powerful tool.

Librarian-instructors teach in a variety of learning situations; they are increasingly teaching credit courses, either solo or in collaboration with faculty from other disciplines. More typical, however, are the single or double information research sessions taught as a component of a credit course. CATs are ideal tools for librarian-instructors, as they enable librarians to engage in an effective form of assessment that yields useful feedback to help both instructors and learners. Librarian-instructors desiring to try this simple, yet powerful, tool would benefit from starting with the following CATs: the 1-Minute Paper, the Muddiest Point, the Background Knowledge Probe, the One Sentence Summary, and Directed Paraphrasing or 3-2-1. I have used all of these successfully in "one-shot" sessions, as well as in a credit-bearing course. These CATs were hosted online so that students could select the name of the librarian teaching the information research session. Students were asked to complete the CAT during the last five minutes of the session. The results immediately were sent to librarians, enabling them to close the assessment loop by analyzing and reporting findings to students and the discipline instructor.

I also developed an online survey that was a twist on the Background Knowledge Probe with a colleague. It was a short, online survey that was developed using Survey Monkey to provide librarians with information on students' prior information skills knowledge and experience, as well as perceptions and attitudes toward conducting library research. Discipline instructors were asked to distribute the URL for the survey upon requesting a session (typically two weeks in advance). Students answered the online survey, and librarians were able to access a summary of the results. This provided insight to help librarians better prepare lesson outlines that targeted students' learning needs to a greater extent.

Michelle K. Dunaway and Michael T. Orblych employed a similar preassessment tactic in their study, which reports on teaching information skills to MBA students enrolled in an organizational behavior course. Their paper pretest was administered to students by the discipline faculty member two weeks prior to the instruction session to identify their current level of information literacy competency and gain information on knowledge gaps to guide what the librarian would teach during the session.[74] They asked students the following: "A teacher in your graduate program has assigned a research paper that requires high-quality sources. In your own words, what features do you look for to identify high-quality sources?" You have been asked to find a high quality source on this specific topic: "How to improve creativity in teams." Please describe, in detail, the specific steps you would follow to find a high-quality source on this topic, and complete the process you described in number 2 to identify a high-quality source on improving a team's creative problem-solving ability and give the citation of the best source you've identified."[75] These open-ended questions are phrased well to measure higher-order thinking skills. If time doesn't allow for open-ended questions, similar fixed-choice questions may be developed to elicit comparable information. Librarian-instructors might experiment with modifying these questions to work with undergraduates and in other disciplines as well.

Using a multifaceted assessment approach with the MBA students, Dunaway and Orblych also utilized an in-class assessment in which students responded to three multiple-choice questions using classroom response system devices (i.e., clickers). The questions were designed to determine the extent to which students had mastered the information literacy concepts posed in the preassessment. Unique to this assessment activity was the use of technology—the clickers—to allow the librarian-instructors to adjust the session content to address misconceptions or gaps in knowledge.

Visual Organizers

Graphic organizers (e.g., concept maps, mind maps, and KWL charts) are visual tools that represent knowledge in graphical form. They enable students to construct and structure knowledge in a visual manner.[76] Concept maps are typically characterized by a hierarchical structure; however, Radcliff and colleagues endorse the use of flat concept maps, particularly for "process-oriented information literacy skills."[77] Concepts are generally framed in a word or brief phrase and situated within nodes with lines connecting them. Demonstration of interrelationships is facilitated by "linking words or linking phrases" that identify the type of relationship; "includes," "leads to," "involves," and "based on" are examples.[78] The ability of organizers to help students demonstrate these interrelationships is their primary advantage.[79] Marjorie L. Pappas further specifies that, "organizers allow learners to deconstruct concepts and visually demonstrate relationships."[80] Joseph D. Novak and Alberto J. Cañas suggest/assert that creating good concept maps requires a context or domain; therefore, identifying a "focus question, that is, a question that clearly specifies the problem or issue the concept map is trying to resolve," is an effective starting point for creating a concept map.[81]

The underpinnings of concept mapping can be traced to learning theories surrounding meaningful and rote learning in cognitive psychology. Specifically, Novak's work is based upon the assimilation learning theory of David Ausubel, who contends that learning occurs by the "assimilation of new concepts and propositions into existing concept and propositional frameworks held by the learner."[82] Assimilation learning theory directly supports constructivist notions of knowledge construction. Concept maps can then complement CATs as assessment measures.[83]

Uses of Visual Organizers for Information Literacy

Concept maps are flexible tools that can be used in a wide array of information literacy sessions relating to the research process. They may be used to tap into prior knowledge about an information literacy topic or as a summative tool to evaluate mastery of a concept related to the information research process; hence, they work well as visual pretests and posttests. Radcliff and associates suggest that they are "best used to evaluate the effectiveness of information literacy instruction focusing on such concepts as research strategy, publication cycle, types of information sources for specific disciplines, and evaluation of information resources for authority and applicability to a research paper."[84] They go on to note that concept maps could be utilized to evaluate attainment of Information Literacy Standard Three, "Evaluation of Information Sources." Concept maps and mind maps are well-suited for tapping into the learning style of visual learners. April Colosimo and Megan Fitzgibbons present an excellent overview of the literature concerning the use of concepts maps in libraries for teaching, learning, planning, and organizing, in addition to assessment.[85]

Similar to concept maps, mind maps help students organize their learning. They facilitate brainstorming for idea generation and articulating in a visual form, a learner's thought patterns. Mind maps may be used during one-shot sessions to formulate a research question or assess what students know prior to an instructional session.

KWL charts are assessment tools that are used throughout the learning process. The "K" stands for what learners already know, the "W" is what learners want to know, and the "L" captures what students have learned. Although these charts are more commonly used in the K–12 arena, KWL is an excellent tool for capturing the elements of the research process, and the charts are easy to use. For example, when teaching a one-shot session, distribute the chart just prior to an instructional segment on any aspect of the information research process. If you are teaching students how to do effective searches in a particular database, give them a few moments to write bulleted items of what they already know about conducting an online search and what they might expect to learn from your information research instruction. Ask students to share from both of these columns. After the instruction concludes, students may write down what was meaningful (i.e., what they learned). If time permits, capture the last piece of information; if not, the instructor may allow students to complete it during the next class period and return it to you. It is important to "close the assessment loop" or collect and analyze data to plan for improvements in student learning; therefore, if the opportunity presents itself to analyze the KWL charts and provide feedback to students and the instructor—verbally or in writing—this will provide learning insights to students, the instructor, and you.

Performance Assessments

Performance assessments elicit information about what students are able to do as a result of learning activities. When constructed well, they are valuable tools to help students apply their knowledge, thus accessing multiple learning domains (psychomotor, affective, and cognitive). Some assessment practitioners refer to these as authentic assessments because a student's ability to apply the knowledge to a real-world situation can be observed or gleaned from an end product. In addition, these tools facilitate identification of gaps in knowledge or misconceptions. Although Walsh reports that 34 percent of the assessments he reviewed were multiple-choice questionnaires, making them the single most popular measurement tool choice, in actuality, performance assessments (e.g., bibliographies,[86] essays, portfolios, observations, self-assessments, and simulations) accounted for 48 percent of those he examined.[87] This demonstrates a shift from the traditional fact-based assessments to those that document what students know, feel, and can do. Radcliff and colleagues offer a useful list of sample assignments that can be utilized to assess the information research process. They include "bibliographies, essays, evaluation reports, portfolios, presentations, research journals, research reports, speeches, student self-reflections, study guides (student produced), term papers, and websites (student produced)."[88]

The advantages of performance assessments are significant, a major one being the ability to assess higher-order skills, including analyzing, evaluating, and creating.[89] Oakleaf also outlines several others, including the following: "1) close connection between instruction and assessment; 2) contextualization of assessment that leads to transfer of knowledge, greater equitability, and increased validity; and (3) ability to use results to improve instruction and programs."[90] Drawing a stark contrast between performance assessments and traditional summative assessment, Huba and Freed argue that, "traditional assessments provide little information to enhance student learning . . . [and] test scores and grades help professors and students *monitor* learning, but they do little to *promote* learning."[91] These compelling advantages and arguments from assessment experts should motivate librarian-instructors to utilize a variety of assessments (formative and summative, direct and indirect) to promote student learning and, ultimately, student success.

Despite the compelling advantages, these assessments have a few drawbacks, which include a hefty time commitment and use of people resources,[92] along with cost considerations for their development and administration.[93] I believe that the learning benefits associated with performance assessments outweigh any disadvantages; however, these types of assessments lend themselves to long-term/credit courses. Consequently, partnerships will often be a crucial component when using this measurement. Librarian-practitioners whose information literacy program's repertoire primarily consists of one-shots should consider collaborating with a classroom faculty member or partnering with a department to integrate information research process assignments within larger performance assessments. That said, there are instances when this tool may be used within single or multiple class sessions.

I have used this technique as learning and assessment in a one-hour-and-fifty-minute class session for English composition students. The instruction session took place in one of the library's lab classrooms. There were approximately twenty-five students and twenty computers available for use. The English instructor provided a fairly specific writing prompt. The learning objectives for the session entailed having students select keywords or phrases and synonyms to be combined in a Boolean search to perform searches in prescribed databases and, after reviewing and evaluating results, select two sources relevant to the prompt. For approximately thirty minutes, I presented basic research strategies for choosing keywords, searching for articles in a database, and evaluating criteria for selection of materials. I also covered instructions for the project and answered clarifying questions. Afterward, students were placed into groups of four or five and directed to select a spokesperson and a scribe for the reporting segment to take place later on. Groups were given forty to forty-five minutes to work on the assignment. The class then reconvened to present their findings, with each group being allotted five to seven minutes. It was during the presentation segment that I, along with the faculty member, was able to gauge areas of learning that were strong and identify gaps and misconceptions. The remaining ten minutes of class was spent addressing areas of the information research process that needed further explanation. This formative assessment experience provided feedback to students and instructors alike and engaged students in their own learning process.

Reflective Assessments

The importance and value of reflection in assessment have been explored throughout this chapter. Merriam-Webster defines reflection as "a thought, idea, or opinion formed or a remark made as a result of meditation."[94] Students extend their knowledge base by means of deep and meaningful meditation on their learning processes. Pamela A. McKinney and Barbara A. Sen, citing D. Schön, an expert on reflective practice, extend our understanding of reflection, defining it in the following manner: "Reflection provides an active and structured way of thinking and of facilitating professional development." "This classic definition of reflection introduces the idea that reflection is not just an abstract concept, it is dynamic and gives framework for professional change and development."[95] Schön describes two types of reflective practice: "reflection in action," or that which takes place "during an experience or event," and "reflection on action," in which an individual reflects on a "past experience or event."[96]

Depending upon how reflective pieces (e.g., essays and journals) are designed, they can tap into affective and cognitive learning domains. Reflective components of this type of assessment must be carefully constructed. Librarian-instructors must prepare students well, equipping them with the definition, purpose, and benefits of reflective assignments. The LIS literature provides several examples of reflection assignments that access multiple learning domains and equip students with requisite information to make their self-reflection a successful experience. For example, as part of the design of their multifaceted information literacy assessment project, McKinney and Sen incorporated a workshop component on reflective assessments in which they provided definitions, examples of effective and ineffective essays, tools to help students think more deeply about their learning, and discussions about the value and benefit of reflective practice.[97] This 800-word reflective essay revealing their progress on information literacy skills complemented a group project and another reflective concerning the group experience. The multifaceted approach to assessment proved valuable in assessing learning. In similar fashion, Claire McGuinness and Michelle Brien utilized pretests and learning journals to document students' research process.[98] At SUNY Brockport, Jennifer Nutefall and colleagues cotaught a communication and information literacy course. In addition to multiple-choice questions about the research process embedded into the midterm and final, they developed the "Paper Trail" assignment, which consisted of a reflective component in which students documented what went well, missteps, and ideas for change.[99]

Rubrics

Put simply, rubrics are " scoring rules."[100] Elucidating this concept, citing John C. Hafner, Oakleaf adds that, "rubrics . . . provide descriptive levels of performance on a particular task and are used to assess outcomes in a variety of performance-based tasks."[101] Rubrics set the standard for what is expected of student performance at different levels or degrees. They provide information on what the student should "strive to emulate,"[102] and these rules or standards provide a road map of the learning process.

As an authentic assessment tool, rubrics have a number of advantages for students and instructors alike. Rubrics provide clear guidelines for students,[103] thus "mak[ing] rankings, ratings, and grades more meaningful."[104] They motivate students to reach goals set for the assignment, enable them to receive "direct feedback about current and future learning," and promote reflective practice and "self-evaluation."[105] In contrast, the limitations are few but bear examination: "Design flaws that impact data quality," and the heavy time demands for developing them, need to be factored into decisions about whether to move forward with this type of tool.[106] Huba and Freed offer six guiding questions for designing good rubrics that result in a finished product. The questions are accompanied by "actions" that facilitate creation of a rating scale. (Follow the actions to complete a scale.):

1. What criteria or essential elements must be present in the student's work to ensure that it is high in quality? Action: Include these as rows in your rubric.
2. How many levels of achievement do I wish to illustrate for students? Action: Include these as columns in your rubric and label them.
3. For each criterion or essential element of quality, what is a clear description of performance at each achievement level? Action: Include descriptions in the appropriate cells of the rubric.
4. What are the consequences of performing at each level of quality? Action: Add descriptions of consequences to the commentaries in the rubric.
5. What rating scheme will I use in the rubric? Action: Add this to the rubric in a way that fits in with your grading philosophy.
6. When I use the rubric, what aspects work well and what aspects need improvement? Action: Revise the rubric accordingly.[107]

Good design cannot be overemphasized. Oakleaf discusses the need for "rigorous approaches to methodology" for rubric development, advocating for an Interrater Reliability approach.[108] Articles about use of rubrics for information literacy projects are not prevalent in the literature; however, Oakleaf and Britt A. Fagerheim and Flora G. Shrode provide representative examples that can be used as either models or strategies for implementing this tool. Oakleaf and Fagerheim and Shrode write about their use of rubrics within two discipline courses. The distinguishing features of their project involve collaboration with faculty from a chemistry and psychology course, the use of discipline benchmarks to establish goals and objectives, and the employment of this strategy in an undergraduate capstone course.[109] Librarian-teachers thinking about this assessment option can find free applications by using the search terms "rubric builders" in a search engine.

Portfolios

Ina Fourie and Daleen van Niekerk quote F. Leon Paulson, Pearl R. Paulson, and Carol A. Meyer's definition of portfolios as follows:

> A portfolio is a purposeful collection of student work that exhibits the student's efforts, progress, and achievements in one or more areas. The collection must include student participation in selecting contents, the criteria for selection, the criteria for judging merit, and evidence of student self-reflection. A portfolio . . . provides a complex and comprehensive view of student performance in context. It is a portfolio when the student is a participant in, rather than the object of, assessment . . . it provides a forum that encourages students to develop the abilities needed to become independent, self-directed learners.[110]

Educators are able to hone in on what students are actually able to do in this form of assessment, enabling a truly authentic experience for students.[111] This measurement "stresses the learning process, improvement, and growth, and not only the final product."[112] For portfolios to move beyond a collection of student work to an assessment necessitates written reflective assignments by students on their learning process, whether at the course or program level.[113] Portfolios can be used as both a formative and summative assessment tool.

There are two types of portfolios: all-inclusive and selection. In the former, students submit the totality of their work in a course or program; in the latter, instructors, sometimes informed by student input, select the goal for the portfolio. In either case, students are apprised of the goal prior to beginning the collection phase.[114] Librarian-instructors may have the opportunity to use either type of portfolio depending on the instructional situation. Of course, if the librarian is teaching a credit course, he or she may elect to use either type. In the case where librarian-instructors are collaborating with faculty in other courses, the selection portfolio might work best to capture the work products and student reflections from focused aspects of the information research process. For example,

Fourie and van Niekerk's use of a selection portfolio in a module in research information skills provides useful insights into the benefits of this measurement for mastery of information research process skills. Their essay details their process and offers examples of the rubric, with criteria used to assess the portfolio products. As with rubrics, the time intensity and staffing resources needed might pose barriers to implementing this type of assessment; however, these limitations aren't insurmountable.

Critical to success is careful planning to include some of the following important elements:

> The development of a common language about portfolios;
> The development of states of portfolio progress (working portfolio/ draft revisions/finished product);
> The selection of appropriate components to be incorporated;
> The development of clear guidelines for performance criteria, grading, and assessment; and
> The development of approaches for students to conduct self-assessment and reflection.[115]

Following planning, effective implementation components include the following:

> A careful review with students of all elements and processes;
> Instructions on development and presentation; and
> Clear understandings of the mechanism for feedback.[116]

The advantages of portfolios as a performance assessment option are clear; however, Loanne A. Snavely and Carol A. Wright offer further persuasive rationale for the use of portfolios in documenting students' research processes, proclaiming that their power lies in "using the . . . structure . . . it provides in developing a template for the present and future information gathering aspects of their research." They go on to say that having a progression of the students' work products in one place allows for a "framework [for students] to see the connectedness of work."[117] These authors provide more detail on their implementation process, which may provide guidance for librarians desiring to implement this in a credit course. Davida Scharf and colleagues describe a rigorous portfolio assessment project in which they collaborated with humanities instructors to assess information literacy using writing portfolios from graduating seniors enrolled in a capstone course. Their essay contains a robust design and analysis, as well as examples of their criteria and rating scales.[118]

PUTTING IT ALL TOGETHER: EXAMPLES

As previously mentioned, the last decade has seen a proliferation of articles about assessment of library instruction, the information research process, and information literacy skills. In addition to examples cited throughout this chapter, the following are some other examples of assessment projects that use either a multidimensional approach or focus on a specific level or learning environment.

Institutional/Large-Scale

> Penny M. Beile's essay on assessing an institutional information fluency program.[119] Following a campus-wide call for quality enhancement program proposals, the library's Information Fluency Quality Enhancement Program was chosen. Beile's essay details the collaboration from a broad spectrum of stakeholders throughout the university in developing an assessment and implementation plan.
>
> Shaun Jackson, Carol Hansen, and Lauren Fowler's essay on using selected assessment data to inform information literacy program planning.[120] Jackson, Hansen, and Fowler describe institutional efforts at Weber State University to gather information literacy assessment data to distribute to education campus partners about their efforts.
>
> Paula McMillen and Anne-Marie Deitering's essay on using information on information literacy assessment to build momentum for the idea of a Teaching Library.[121] McMillen and Deitering used focus groups, individual meetings with campus stakeholders, rubrics, and the SAILS assessment test.

Credit Courses

> Nancy Goebel, Paul Neff, and Angie Mandeville's essay chronicling activities related to teaching and assessing their discipline-based information literacy courses.[122] Assessments include pretests and posttests and discussion of an in-house Web-based assessment tool.

Programmatic

> Sue Samson and Merinda McLure's essay providing a unique approach to information literacy in their 360-degree planning approach for their library instruction plan.[123] Samson and McClure present a programmatic and individual plan based on Angelo and Cross's cycle of assessment.

Multiple Methods

> Kornelia Tancheva, Camille Andrews, and Gail Steinhart's essay about three formative and summative assessments that they piloted at a large research library: attitudinal, outcomes-based, and gap-measure.[124]

Literature Reviews on Information Literacy/Library Instruction Assessment

> Yvonne N. Meulemans's useful historical overview, which covers the essential concepts and activities that shaped information literacy assessment.[125]
> Marjorie M. Warmkessel's essay providing summaries of what she calls "Best of the Literature" in information literacy assessment.[126]

CONCLUSION

Assessment and learning are powerfully intertwined concepts for advancing student success. Good assessment planning considers learner-centered assessment theories. Assessment of the information research process requires an understanding of assessment methods, strategies, and techniques. The LIS literature contains valuable examples of various types of assessment that may be utilized at the individual, classroom, program, and institutional levels. Assessment of the information research process is beneficial for both students and instructors. When librarian-instructors engage in assessment, they add value to student learning, engagement, and success.

NOTES

1. Catherine Palomba and Trudy W. Banta, *Assessment Essentials: Planning, Implementing, and Improving Assessment in Higher Education* (San Francisco, CA: Jossey-Bass, 1999), 1.

2. Linda Suskie and Trudy W. Banta, *Assessing Student Learning: A Common Sense Guide,* 2nd ed. (San Francisco, CA: Jossey-Bass, 2009), 4.

3. Lorna Earl, "Assessment of Learning, for Learning, and as Learning," reprinted from *Assessment as Learning: Using Classroom Assessment to Maximise Student Learning* (Thousand Oaks, CA: Corwin Press, 2003), 4.

4. Grant Wiggins, "Creating Tests Worth Taking," in *A Handbook for Student Performance in an Era of Restructuring,* edited by Robert E. Blum and Judith A. Arter (Alexandria, VA: Association for Supervision and Curriculum Development, 1996), cited in Megan Oakleaf, "Dangers and Opportunities: A Conceptual Map of Information Literacy Assessment Approaches," *Portal: Libraries and the Academy* 8, no. 3 (2008). DOI: 10.1353/pla.0.0011. 241.

5. Esther S. Grassian and Joan R. Kaplowitz, *Information Literacy Instruction: Theory and Practice,* 2nd ed. (New York: Neal-Schuman, 2009), cited in Megan Oakleaf, "The Information Literacy Instruction Assessment Cycle: A Guide for Increasing Student

Learning and Improving Librarian Instruction Skills, *Journal of Documentation* 65, no. 4 (2009): 540.

6. Elizabeth F. Avery, *Assessing Student Learning Outcomes for Information Literacy Instruction in Academic Institutions* (Chicago: Association of College and Research Libraries, 2003), 2.

7. Earl, "Assessment of Learning, for Learning, and as Learning," 4.

8. Claire McGuinness and Michelle Brien, "Using Reflective Journals to Assess the Research Process," *Reference Services Review* 35, no. 1 (2007): 21. DOI: http://dx.doi.org/10.1108/00907320710729346; Lois M. Pausch and Mary Pagliero Popp, "Assessment of Information Literacy: Lessons from the Higher Instruction Assessment Movement," paper presented at the 1997 Association of College and Research Libraries National Conference, Nashville, TN. Available online at www.ala.org/acrl/publications/whitepapers/nashville/pauschpopp (accessed November 5, 2012); Stephanie Sterling Brasley, "From an Initiative to a Program," *Public Services Quarterly* 3, no. 1/2 (2007): 112. DOI: http://dx.doi.org/10.1300/J295v03n01_06.

9. Mary E. Huba and Jann E. Freed, *Learner-Centered Assessment on College Campuses: Shifting the Focus from Teaching to Learning* (Boston: Allyn and Bacon, 2000), 17; Carolyn J. Radcliff, Mary Lee Jensen, Joseph A. Salem, Kenneth J. Burhanna, and Julie A. Gedeon, *A Practical Guide to Information Literacy Assessment for Academic Librarians* (Westport, CT: Libraries Unlimited, 2007), 7.

10. Huba and Freed, *Learner-Centered Assessment on College Campuses*, 17.

11. Kathleen Dunn, "Assessing Information Literacy Skills in the California State University: A Progress Report," *Journal of Academic Librarianship* 28, no. 1/2 (2002): 26.

12. Pausch and Popp, "Assessment of Information Literacy."

13. Catherine Haras and Stephanie Sterling Brasley, "Is Information Literacy a Public Concern? A Practice in Search of a Policy," *Library Trends* 60, no. 2 (2011): 366–67.

14. American Library Association, "Presidential Committee on Information Literacy: Final Report," *ALA.org*, January 10, 1989. Available online at www.ala.org/acrl/publications/whitepapers/presidential (accessed November 5, 2012).

15. Patricia Iannuzzi, "We Are Teaching, but Are They Learning? Accountability, Productivity, and Assessment," *Journal of Academic Librarianship* 25, no. 4 (1999): 304.

16. Iannuzzi, "We Are Teaching, but Are They Learning?" 304.

17. Iannuzzi, "We Are Teaching, but Are They Learning?" 305.

18. Iannuzzi, "We Are Teaching, but Are They Learning?" 305.

19. Association of College and Research Libraries, "Information Literacy Competency Standards for Higher Education" (Chicago: Association of College and Research Libraries, 2000). Available online at www.ala.org/ala/acrl/acrlstandards/informationliteracy-competency.htm (accessed November 5, 2012).

20. McGuinness and Brien, "Using Reflective Journals to Assess the Research Process," 21.

21. Association of College and Research Libraries, "Information Literacy Competency Standards for Higher Education."

22. Robert L. Linn and Norman E. Gronlund (2000) define criterion-referenced assessments as "a test or other type of assessment designed to provide a measure of performance that is interpretable in terms of a clearly defined and delimited domain of learning tasks" (42). Furthermore, they "include items that are directly relevant to the learning outcomes to be measured. . . ." (43). See Robert L. Linn and Norman E. Gronlund, *Measurement and Assessment in Teaching*, 8th ed. (Upper Saddle River, NJ: Merrill, 2000).

23. Trudy W. Banta, Jon P. Lund, Karen E. Black, and Frances W. Oblander, *Assessment in Practice: Putting Principles to Work on College Campuses* (San Francisco, CA: Jossey-Bass, 1996), 62.

24. Palomba and Banta, *Assessment Essentials*, 3.

25. Thomas A. Angelo and K. Patricia Cross, *Classroom Assessment Techniques: A Handbook for College Teachers* (San Francisco, CA: Jossey-Bass, 1993), cited in Suskie and Banta, *Assessing Student Learning*, 4.

26. Huba and Freed, *Learner-Centered Assessment on College Campuses*, 8.

27. Suskie and Banta, *Assessing Student Learning*; Huba and Freed, *Learner-Centered Assessment on College Campuses*.

28. Middle States Commission on Higher Education, *Student Learning Assessment: Options and Resources* (Philadelphia, PA: Middle States Commission on Higher Education, 2003), 10–11.

29. Huba and Freed, *Learner-Centered Assessment on College Campuses*, 94.

30. Benjamin S. Bloom, Gordon V. Anderson, Ruth Churchill, Max D. Engelhart, Edward J. Furst, Walker H. Hill, David R. Krathwohl, and Bertram B. Masia, *Taxonomy of Educational Objectives: The Classification of Educational Goals* (New York: David McKay Co.), 1956.

31. Radcliff, Jensen, Salem, Burhanna, and Gedeon, *A Practical Guide to Information Literacy Assessment for Academic Librarians*, 25–26.

32. Kari D. Weaver and Penni M. Pier, "Embedded Information Literacy in the Basic Oral Communication Course: From Conception through Assessment," *Public Services Quarterly* 6, no. 2/3 (2010): 259–70. DOI: http://dx.doi.org/10.1080/15228959.2010.497455.

33. Grassian and Kaplowitz, *Information Literacy Instruction*, 210.

34. Andrew Walsh, "Information Literacy Assessment: Where Do We Start?" *Journal of Librarianship and Information Science* 41, no. 1 (2009): 19–28. DOI: 10.1177/0961000608099896.

35. Dunn, "Assessing Information Literacy Skills in the California State University," 24.

36. Richard Swearingen, "A Primer: Diagnostic, Formative, and Summative Assessment," Heritage University, 2002. Available online at http://slackernet.org/assessment.htm (accessed November 5, 2012).

37. Richard D. Kellough and Noreen G. Kellough, *Secondary School Teaching: A Guide to Methods and Resources* (Upper Saddle River, NJ: Prentice Hall, 1999) and J. H. McMillan, *Classroom Assessment: Principles and Practice for Effective Instruction*. Pearson Technology Group, 2000. Available online at www.pearsonptg.com/book_detail/0,3771,020529751X,00.html (accessed November 5, 2012), cited in Swearingen, "A Primer."

38. Grassian and Kaplowitz, *Information Literacy Instruction*; Swearingen, "A Primer."

39. Grassian and Kaplowitz, *Information Literacy Instruction*, 210.

40. Grassian and Kaplowitz, *Information Literacy Instruction*, 210.

41. Middle States Commission on Higher Education, *Student Learning Assessment*, 30.

42. Middle States Commission on Higher Education, *Student Learning Assessment*, 31.

43. The Middle States Commission on Higher Education has a detailed list of direct and indirect examples on page 29 of *Student Learning Assessment*, and also Linda Suskie in the second edition of *Assessing Student Learning*, in which she provides examples of evidence of student learning.

44. Middle States Commission on Higher Education, *Student Learning Assessment*, 32.

45. Middle States Commission on Higher Education, *Student Learning Assessment*, 31.

46. Middle States Commission on Higher Education, *Student Learning Assessment*, 33.

47. Radcliff, Jensen, Salem, Burhanna, and Gedeon, *A Practical Guide to Information Literacy Assessment for Academic Librarians*, 11–13.

48. For guidance on where your information literacy program stands, see Association of College and Research Libraries, "Characteristics of Programs of Information Literacy That Illustrate Best Practices: A Guideline" (Chicago: Association of College

and Research Libraries, 2012). Available online at www.ala.org/acrl/standards/characteristics (accessed November 5, 2012).

49. There are several good sources that guide librarians through the process of assessing information literacy. One example is Megan Oakleaf and Neal Kaske, "Guiding Questions for Assessing Information Literacy in Higher Education," *Portal: Libraries and the Academy* 9, no. 2 (2009): 273–86. For information on a full information literacy program and aspects of assessment, see Eleanor Mitchell, "Readiness and Rhythm: Timing for Information Literacy," in *Proven Strategies for Building an Information Literacy Program*, edited by Susan Curzon and Lynn Lampert, 77–93 (New York: Neal-Schuman, 2007).

50. For detailed explanations of some of the assessment techniques discussed, consult Radcliff, Jensen, Salem, Burhanna, and Gedeon, *A Practical Guide to Information Literacy Assessment for Academic Librarians*.

51. Radcliff, Jensen, Salem, Burhanna, and Gedeon, *A Practical Guide to Information Literacy Assessment for Academic Librarians*, 90.

52. Walsh, "Information Literacy Assessment," 21.

53. Walsh, "Information Literacy Assessment," 19.

54. Walsh, "Information Literacy Assessment," 21.

55. Oakleaf, "Dangers and Opportunities," 236.

56. Oakleaf, "Dangers and Opportunities," 235.

57. Oakleaf, "Dangers and Opportunities," 236.

58. Oakleaf, "Dangers and Opportunities," 237.

59. Lorrie A. Shepard and Katherine A. Ryan, eds., *The Future of Test-Based Educational Accountability* (New York: Routledge, 2008), cited in Oakleaf, "Dangers and Opportunities," 237.

60. Walsh, "Information Literacy Assessment," 21.

61. For specific examples of these exams, consult Walsh "Information Literacy Assessment," 19–28, and Bonnie Gratch-Lindauer and Amelie Brown, "Developing a Tool to Assess Community College Students," in *Integrating Information Literacy into the Higher Education Curriculum: Practical Models for Transformation*, edited by Ilene F. Rockman, 165–206 (San Francisco, CA: Jossey-Bass, 2004). Also in this edited work is Lynn Cameron "Assessing Information Literacy," 207–36.

62. Middle States Commission on Higher Education, *Developing Research and Communication Skills: Guidelines for Information Literacy in the Curriculum, Executive Summary* (Philadelphia, PA: Middle States Commission on Higher Education, 2002).

63. Educational Testing Service, "The iSkills™ Assessment from ETS," *ETS.org*, 2013. Available online at www.ets.org/iskills/about (accessed November 5, 2012).

64. Kent State University, "Standardized Assessment of Information Literacy Skills (SAILS)," 2013. Available online at www.projectsails.org/ (accessed November 5, 2012).

65. Madison Assessment, "Information Literacy Test," James Madison University, 2013. Available online at www.madisonassessment.com/assessment-testing/information-literacy-test/ (accessed November 5, 2012).

66. Educational Testing Service, "2006 ICT Literacy Assessment: Preliminary Findings," *ETS.org*, 2006, 3. Available online at www.ets.org/Media/Products/ICT_Literacy/pdf/2006_Preliminary_Findings.pdf (accessed November 5, 2012).

67. Educational Testing Service, "2006 ICT Literacy Assessment," 4.

68. For a comprehensive overview of iSkills™ consult Irvin R. Katz, "Testing Information Literacy in Digital Environments: The ETS iSkills™ Assessment," *Information Technology and Libraries* 26, no. 3 (2007): 2–13. For application of iSkills™ at a university, consult Mary M. Somerville, Gordon W. Smith, and Alexius Smith Macklin, "The ETS iSkills™ Assessment: A Digital Age Tool," *Electronic Library* 26, no. 2 (2008): 158–71.

69. Brian Lym, Hal Grossman, Lauren Yannotta, and Makram Talih, "Assessing the Assessment: How Institutions Administrated, Interpreted, and Used SAILS," *Reference Services Review* 38, no. 1 (2010): 168–86. DOI: 10.1108/00907321011020806.

70. Lynn Cameron, Steven L. Wise, and Susan M. Lottridge, "The Development and Validation of the Information Literacy Test," *College and Research Libraries* 68, no. 3 (2007): 229–36.

71. K. Patricia Cross and Mimi H. Steadman, *Classroom Research: Implementing the Scholarship of Teaching* (San Francisco, CA: Jossey-Bass, 1996), 8.

72. Cross and Steadman, *Classroom Research*, xviii.

73. Thomas A. Angelo and K. Patricia Cross, *Classroom Assessment Techniques: A Handbook for College Teachers*, 2nd ed., San Francisco: Jossey-Bass, 1993, p. 4.

74. Michelle K. Dunaway and Michael T. Orblych, "Formative Assessment: Transforming Information Literacy Instruction," *Reference Services Review* 39, no. 1 (2011): 27.

75. Dunaway and Orblych, "Formative Assessment," 28.

76. April Colosimo and Megan Fitzgibbons, "Teaching, Designing, and Organizing: Concept Mapping for Librarians," *Partnership: The Canadian Journal of Library and Information Practice and Research* 7, no. 1 (2012): 1; Joseph D. Novak and Alberto J. Cañas, "The Theory Underlying Concept Maps and How to Construct and Use Them," Technical Report IHMC CmapTools 2006-01 Rev 01-2008. Florida Institute for Human and Machine Cognition, 2008, 1. Available online at http://cmap.ihmc.us/Publications/ResearchPapers/TheoryUnderlyingConceptMaps.pdf (accessed November 5, 2012); Marjorie L. Pappas, "Tools for the Assessment of Learning," *School Library Media Activities Monthly* 23, no. 9 (2007): 22; Radcliff, Jensen, Salem, Burhanna, and Gedeon, *A Practical Guide to Information Literacy Assessment for Academic Librarians*, 107.

77. Radcliff, Jensen, Salem, Burhanna, and Gedeon, *A Practical Guide to Information Literacy Assessment for Academic Librarians*, 109.

78. Novak and Cañas, "The Theory Underlying Concept Maps and How to Construct and Use Them," 1.

79. Pappas, "Tools for the Assessment of Learning," 22.

80. Pappas, "Tools for the Assessment of Learning," 22.

81. Novak and Cañas, "The Theory Underlying Concept Maps and How to Construct and Use Them," 11.

82. Cited in Novak and Cañas, "The Theory Underlying Concept Maps and How to Construct and Use Them," 11; Eric Plotnik, "A Graphical System for Understanding the Relationship between Concepts." *Teacher Librarian* 28, no. 4 (2001): 42.

83. For additional information about this theory and concept mapping's contribution to "meaningful learning," see Novak and Cañas, "The Theory Underlying Concept Maps and How to Construct and Use Them."

84. Radcliff, Jensen, Salem, Burhanna, and Gedeon, *A Practical Guide to Information Literacy Assessment for Academic Librarians*, 107.

85. Colosimo and Fitzgibbons, "Teaching, Designing, and Organizing."

86. Annotated bibliographies are another popular choice for librarians. For examples of this assessment tool from peer-reviewed articles, see Walsh, "Information Literacy Assessment."

87. Walsh, "Information Literacy Assessment," 21.

88. Radcliff, Jensen, Salem, Burhanna, and Gedeon, *A Practical Guide to Information Literacy Assessment for Academic Librarians*, 116.

89. Oakleaf, "Dangers and Opportunities," 242; Radcliff, Jensen, Salem, Burhanna, and Gedeon, *A Practical Guide to Information Literacy Assessment for Academic Librarians*, 116.

90. Oakleaf, "Dangers and Opportunities," 242.

91. Huba and Freed, *Learner-Centered Assessment on College Campuses*, 153.

92. Radcliff, Jensen, Salem, Burhanna, and Gedeon, *A Practical Guide to Information Literacy Assessment for Academic Librarians*, 116.

93. Oakleaf, "Dangers and Opportunities," 244.

94. *Merriam-Webster's Collegiate Dictionary*, 11th ed. (Springfield, MA: Merriam-Webster, 1998).

95. D. Schön, *The Reflective Practitioner* (New York: Basic Books, 1983), cited in Pamela A. McKinney and Barbara A. Sen, "Reflection for Learning: Understanding the

Value of Reflective Writing for Information Literacy Development," *Journal of Information Literacy* 6, no. 2 (2012): 111. Available online at http://ojs.lboro.ac.uk/ojs/index.php/JIL/article/view/ LLC-V6-I2-2012-5 (accessed November 5, 2012).

96. Schön, cited in McKinney and Sen, "Reflection for Learning," 113.

97. McKinney and Sen, "Reflection for Learning," 111.

98. McGuinness and Brien, "Using Reflective Journals to Assess the Research Process."

99. Jennifer Nutefall, "Paper Trail: One Method of Information Literacy Assessment," *Research Strategies* 20, no. 1/2 (2005): 93. McKinney and Sen list a number of information literacy assessment projects containing reflection pieces in "Reflection for Learning," 115.

100. Huba and Freed, *Learner-Centered Assessment on College Campuses*, 155.

101. John C. Hafner, "Quantitative Analysis of the Rubric as an Assessment Tool: An Empirical Study of the Student Peer-Group Rating," *International Journal of Science Education* 25, no. 12 (2003): 1,509–28, cited in Oakleaf, "Dangers and Opportunities," 245.

102. Oakleaf, "Dangers and Opportunities," 168.

103. Oakleaf, "Dangers and Opportunities," 245.

104. Oakleaf "Using Rubrics to Assess Information Literacy," 969.

105. Oakleaf, "Dangers and Opportunities," 245.

106. Oakleaf, "Dangers and Opportunities," 248.

107. Huba and Freed, *Learner-Centered Assessment on College Campuses*, 178.

108. Oakleaf "Using Rubrics to Assess Information Literacy," 969.

109. Oakleaf, "Dangers and Opportunities," 168; Britt A. Fagerheim and Flora G. Shrode, "Information Literacy Rubrics within the Disciplines," *Communications in Information Literacy* 3, no. 2 (2009): 158–70. Available online at www.comminfolit.org/index.php?journal=cil&page=article&op=viewFile&path[]=Vol3-2009AR8&path[]=104 (accessed November 5, 2012).

110. F. Leon Paulson, Pearl R. Paulson, and Carol A. Meyer, "What Makes a Portfolio a Portfolio? Eight Thoughtful Guidelines to Help Educators Encourage Self-Directed Learning," *Educational Leadership* 48, no. 5 (1991): 60–63, cited in Ina Fourie and Daleen van Niekerk, "Using Portfolio Assessment in a Module in Research Information Skills," *Education for Information* 17, no. 4 (1999): 335.

111. Huba and Freed, *Learner-Centered Assessment on College Campuses*, 234.

112. Fourie and van Niekerk, "Using Portfolio Assessment in a Module in Research Information Skills," 337.

113. Huba and Freed, *Learner-Centered Assessment on College Campuses*, 234.

114. Huba and Freed, *Learner-Centered Assessment on College Campuses*, 235–36.

115. Snavely and Wright, "Research Portfolio Use in Undergraduate Honors Education," 300–301.

116. Snavely and Wright, "Research Portfolio Use in Undergraduate Honors Education," 300.

117. Snavely and Wright, "Research Portfolio Use in Undergraduate Honors Education," 301.

118. Davida Scharf, Norbert Elliot, Heather A. Huey, Vladimir Briller, and Kamal Joshi, "Direct Assessment of Information Literacy Using Writing Portfolios," *Journal of Academic Librarianship* 33, no. 4 (2007): 462–78.

119. Penny M. Beile, "Assessing an Institution-Wide Information Fluency Program," *Public Services Quarterly* 3, no. 1/2 (2007): 127–46. DOI: http://dx.doi.org/10.1300/J295v03n01_07.

120. Shaun Jackson, Carol Hansen, and Lauren Fowler, "Using Selected Assessment Data to Inform Information Literacy Program Planning with Campus Partners," *Research Strategies* 20, no. 1/2 (2005): 44–56.

121. Paula McMillen and Anne-Marie Deitering, "Complex Questions, Evolving Answers," *Public Services Quarterly* 3, no. 1/2 (2007): 57–82. DOI: http://dx.doi.org/10.1300/J295v03n01_04.

122. Nancy Goebel, Paul Neff, and Angie Mandeville, "Assessment within the Augustana Model of Undergraduate Discipline-Specific Information Literacy Credit Courses," *Public Services Quarterly* 3, no. 1/2 (2007): 165–89.

123. Sue Samson and Merinda McLure, "Library Instruction Assessment through 360°," *Public Services Quarterly* 3, no. 1/2 (2007): 9–28.

124. Kornelia Tancheva, Camille Andrews, and Gail Steinhart, "Library Instruction Assessment in Academic Libraries," *Public Services Quarterly* 3, no. 1/2 (2007): 29–56. DOI: http://dx.doi.org/10.1300/J295v03n01.

125. Yvonne N. Meulemans, "Assessment City," *College and Undergraduate Libraries* 9, no. 2 (2002): 61–74. DOI: http://dx.doi.org/10.1300/J106v09n02_07.

126. Marjorie M. Warmkessel, "Information Literacy Assessment," *Public Services Quarterly* 3, no. 1/2 (2007): 243–50. DOI: http://dx.doi.org/10.1300/J295v03n01_22.

II

The Strategies in Action: Four Ideas That Work

EIGHT

Sources before Search: A Scaffolded Approach to Teaching Research

Stephanie N. Otis

Librarians and instructors are often confronted with a frustrating puzzle: Students complain that they already know how to use the library, but we continue to suspect that they do not know how to do research. Are we missing the mark altogether, or simply focusing on the wrong aspects of research? Many times, when students are asked to do a research project, they are surprised and overwhelmed by the expectation that they do something new with the sources they find. Summarizing, synthesizing, comparing, and evaluating information sources is difficult for students, but instructors and librarians can help prepare them to do this work. This chapter includes specific activities instructors and librarians can use to show students how to work with sources before they are expected to use them in a larger research project. These activities will provide scaffolded learning for students and an opportunity for librarians and instructors to collaborate on meaningful, content-based research instruction.

SCAFFOLDED RESEARCH INSTRUCTION

Many college-level research assignments ask students to undertake the process of locating, evaluating, and incorporating information sources as one uninterrupted endeavor they face on their own. The anxiety that accompanies such assignments may not be so much about students' inability to find sources, but a lack of direction and support in what they should do with those sources to successfully complete a research project. Drawing on educational theory related to scaffolded learning and library applications of this concept,[1] the activities in this chapter allow students to add to their experiences with information sources to support their success at performing more complex and sophisticated research activities. To address the unwieldy research project and students' anxiety and unpreparedness, the activities and suggestions in this chapter provide a scaffolded or tiered approach to guiding students through the research process. The activities are specifically designed to help students grapple with information sources in a critical way before they are asked to take on the entire process alone.

David Wood, Jerome S. Bruner, and Gail Ross originally defined scaffolding as a process in which a knowledgeable person provides a student or novice with specific, just-in-time support and guidance to move forward with a task that would otherwise be beyond the student's ability. The knowledgeable person is both expert and facilitator and supports the student's learning in several ways: recruiting the student's interest, simplifying the task, maintaining direction, highlighting the critical task features, controlling frustration, and demonstrating ideal paths to a solution.[2] Each of these supports will resonate with librarians and instructors; the potential for providing this support in the research process has led to specific discussions of scaffolding in the context of research instruction.

We ask students to find and use multiple sources of information early in their introduction to the research process. Exploring sources, connections, and meanings initially gives them more knowledge to call upon in their subsequent research endeavors. A traditional approach asks that students accomplish the selection, evaluation, and synthesizing of information sources as steps in the process—only asking that they do it, not showing and supporting them first. Scaffolding, on the other hand, provides support to "build knowledge/skills until learners can stand on their own."[3] Providing scaffolded support for learning the research process also helps students understand and invest in the outcome they are expected to accomplish.

A simple iteration of this approach is to ask students to summarize and evaluate single sources on a topic that may contribute to a more extensive exploration of that topic. As a starting point, the instructor or librarian can provide students with an initial source and structure in groups or whole-class work to answer the questions and build the summary/evaluation. Once students have seen how the process of summarizing and evaluating works, they can apply the questions to additional sources, either instructor provided or student selected.

* * *

SOURCE SUMMARY AND EVALUATION

Answer the following questions about your information source:

1. Where was this information published? How does its format and origin contribute to the relevance and usefulness of this source?
2. What is the main topic of this source? In a few sentences, how would you summarize the information in the source for someone new to the topic? What specific information or perspective would this source offer to someone who already knew something about the topic?
3. What information is most interesting or surprising in this source?
4. What information about the topic is missing from this source?
5. What information or perspective makes this source useful and important for this topic?

* * *

Giving students experience with sources in isolation will strengthen their ability to construct meaning in the research process while they are seeking information. Encouraging synthesis of information gives students experience with confronting information sources. Slowing down and voicing their thinking also leads them to generate new insights, and the process helps pair their evaluative thinking with explorations of content more cohesively and with more meaning than checking off a list of criteria.

In addition to providing students with guidance and support, this approach of scaffolding learning around the research process prepares students to think about information in more abstract, flexible, and independent ways. These activities disrupt the linear and sometimes mechanical approach to teaching the research process and introduce critical thinking into the instruction. The ability to question connects critical thinking to the research process. The activities here model and require such questioning before students enter into longer-term research.

While increasing students' interest and investment in the tasks that make up the research process, activities like these also position this learning as constructive: Students use their experiences with research sources to construct their own understanding, rather than have understanding delivered to them. These source activities should create "situations in which students can interpret information to create meaning for themselves."[4]

Another activity for tiered research instruction at a more advanced level would ask students to use an instructor-provided source to trace the authors' use of sources and other research in their work. Students are often asked to enter into an academic or professional conversation with their research projects, but they may not have a clear understanding of what that conversation involves. Keeping in mind the goals of scaffolding instruction, instructors or librarians using this activity provide their students guidance in understanding research conversations and give them the opportunity to build their own knowledge of this element of research.

* * *

TRACING RESEARCH "CONVERSATIONS": USES OF INFORMATION SOURCES IN RESEARCH WRITING

When researchers and scholars seek to answer their research questions, they consult other sources that give background or context, important insights, previous studies, and other information on related and relevant topics. By exploring the referenced sources and information for a given source, we can see how each new source relies on and adds to an existing conversation about that topic or issue. With the source provided, answer the following questions to explore the relationships or conversation between this source and the sources its authors reference and use in their work.

1. What is the question or issue this source addresses?
2. Looking at the source itself or the bibliography, what are some topics of the sources referenced by these authors?
3. List one or two sources that these authors use to provide background information on their issue or question.
4. What new information or perspective is this source adding to the conversation?
5. Which sources from the bibliography would be most important to read to fully understand this question or topic?

* * *

These activities accomplish Jean Donham and Mariah Steele's goal of "providing a coordinated system of support that extends beyond locating and accessing information sources."[5] By integrating conversations like these into instruction session or course design, we better articulate and support the steps in the research process that we expect students to accomplish. With scaffolding, modeling and support are both essential and accomplished by offering earlier and more meaningful work around information sources. Rolf Norgaard challenges us to "make the research process visible, a subject of explicit and ongoing discussion, and not some mysterious process that occurs behind the scenes. . . . And offer activities that encourage engaged conversation with the other voices that they might invite into their own work."[6] This scaffolded approach of putting source work ahead of search builds upon and complements this goal.

SOURCES BEFORE SEARCH

Librarians and instructors often lament students' reliance on Wikipedia as an information source. Their preference, however, may be less about the ease of search and access, and more about the comfortable familiarity of general, overview sources and web-based text. Wikipedia entries are not just easier to find, they are easier to read. The current generation of college students may be technically savvy, but not necessarily source savvy. Donham and Steele find that "today's college students enjoy more confidence than their predecessors in their technical knowledge, but continue to approach college research assignments with anxiety."[7] They are accustomed to a world where information is ever-present and available in myriad formats. The Internet provides text on a page but doesn't ask students to consider where the information came from, how it got there, or what to do with it. College research assignments, on the other hand, ask students to find specific types of information from particular sources and, at their best, expect that students will synthesize those sources to create their own meaning. Many library instruction sessions focus on search, which may actually be the strength of our students, and do not confront students' discomfort and lack of experience with the rich variety of information sources. If students see all information as equal and readily available, they will have difficulty making connections, conclusions, and comparisons and fall back on a tendency to cut and paste from familiar and similar sources. If research instruction only teaches students how to search, it is leaving out an important step, and one that may do the most to ensure student success and meaningful research experiences.

Looking at individual sources before launching into searching for information might transform the traditional pedagogy and content of research instruction. Students need guidance in confronting, reading, critically considering, and connecting information sources in unfamiliar formats. Activities that take a closer look at specific types of sources and differences between them can help students better understand and successfully incorporate information. Instead of asking students to find sources and then read and evaluate them, this approach gives students experience reading and thinking about sources to make them more successful at finding them. Rather than the mechanical process of simply finding sources on a topic, more authentic research often involves understanding or finding interest in one source and expanding from there. Academics and researchers rarely begin from an unfamiliar topic or question, but instead depart from some initial source or theory to find exam-

ples, comparisons, and extensions; therefore, helping students understand how to work with a single source brings them closer to a research
process that is less artificial than casting a wide net into an overwhelming
expanse of information. Even the words we use to alert students to the
expectations of a research assignment can be foreign and bewildering.

The following activity will help students see the value in different
types of sources—secondary or primary—and give them support in seeing the differences between them. It will also help us see how our perspective on a topic may depend on the sources we consult. Instead of
asking students to find X primary sources and Y secondary sources and
doing little to ensure their success, this activity asks them to consider
how each offers different perspectives on a topic.

* * *

PRIMARY AND SECONDARY SOURCES

Some sources of information give us a firsthand account of an event or
issue; these primary sources provide direct evidence from a time period
to understand it in terms of the experiences and understanding of the
people living during that time. Secondary sources, on the other hand,
describe, discuss, combine, or interpret information from other sources
(primary or other secondary sources). Primary and secondary sources
offer different ways of looking at the same topic.

Think about examples of each type of source and write to explore
possible uses of each. Primary sources might include archival documents,
letters, journal entries, experiment results, survey responses, or interviews. Write a summary of what you know about your topic from your
investigation of one or more primary sources. What facts, dates, or important people are included? Does the source state any opinions or theories about the topic? What else seems interesting or important about this
source to inform us about the topic? What information from this source
would you share with someone to tell them about the topic? Next, use
secondary sources (articles in journals, popular magazines and newspapers, websites, and book chapters) to answer the same questions in a
summary of the source(s).

Now think about comparing the two types of sources. How are they
different? What new information or perspectives did you find in the primary sources? What do the secondary sources add or take away from
knowledge of this topic? Is there conflicting information between the two
sources?

* * *

Numerous studies have shown how students prefer Internet search and sources, express frustration with library resources, and fail to consistently and completely apply evaluative criteria to their information sources.[8] Furthermore, students are looking for the perfect source, one that answers every aspect of their research question and gives complete and balanced evidence. Activities on individual sources or explicit comparisons can help students see how combining and synthesizing several sources provides a complete picture. These activities are designed to make information sources more familiar to students and give them a richer approach to understanding and using various sources.

Library literature often suggests giving more attention to the meaning of information and less to the tools and mechanics of search. With these activities, librarians and instructors have an alternative to focusing exclusively on search. In addition, the intent of this approach is to put the meaning-making activities first in the process. We attend to the timing of research instruction in terms of curricula, assignments, and semesters. Norgaard urges attention to "how and when to situate information literacy in the rhythms and structures of academic life."[9] Taking this charge further, we consider not just the timing of when in the semester we meet with a class for research instruction, but the planning and delivery of specific and meaningful support to students. By putting an exploration and understanding of sources first, we show students that reading is research. When carefully and critically considering information sources apart from a larger research assignment, students move away from easy answers and chunks of information toward reasoning for themselves and creating new meaning.

One of the most challenging research tasks that undergraduate students confront is combining their own reading of a primary source with other secondary sources on a related topic. The following activity addresses that confusion and uncertainty by taking an in-depth look at the relationship between the two.

* * *

POPULAR CULTURE SOURCES

Reading primary sources involves drawing your own conclusions and generalizations about a time period, event, or issue using evidence from the original time or context for that issue or event. Secondary sources on historical events or issues show you how other researchers and scholars have "read" the original context or primary sources themselves. Artifacts from popular culture of the past give us a good opportunity to explore the relationship between these two types of sources. Use the following questions to explore each type of source and better understand how you can include both in your own research.

Primary Source (television show, movie, song lyrics, advertisement, or other historical popular source from a decade earlier than now)

1. What can you learn about the time period of this source from the words or language used in the source? How do those words or language differ from what we use today?
2. What can you learn about the time period of this source from the images or visual elements used in the source? How do the visual elements of the source show that it is from a time period different from today?
3. What topics or issues are raised by the language and/or visual elements of this historic source? Possible issues may include (but are not limited to) gender roles; race relations; political or economic issues; work/career choices; leisure activities; relationships (family, romantic, friendship); status; taste/style; aging; or foreign/international relations
4. What specific language or visual elements help you compare the issue you chose from the past to today?

Secondary Source (article or book chapter about popular culture in an earlier decade)

1. Does your secondary source discuss a particular issue in historical popular culture or a particular format?
2. What specific examples of popular culture (names of television programs, movies, magazines, musical artists) does this source mention?

* * *

Considering sources before search unsettles the pedagogy of the traditional research paper, which, according to Norgaard, "has done as much as anything to make students as fearful of libraries as they are about writing courses."[10] Disrupting the traditional approach to research instruction and research paper assignments gives students support and direction for greater success, rather than simply giving them the directive to find good sources absent of any direction on what good sources look like and how they can be used. With less emphasis on format and final product, this approach of sources before search redirects the focus of research to intellectual activity rather than citations in the abstract.

LOSE THE LIST: ENRICHED EVALUATION OF SOURCES

Existing information literacy measures require students to be able to evaluate the quality of information, but this evaluation frequently involves something akin to a checklist of criteria rather than a critical reading of the information source. Lea Currie and colleagues suggest that "students are not skilled in the application of evaluative criteria, even if they know that these are important and should be attended to." [11] By giving students experience and guidance in confronting information sources before the research process, we better equip them with a critical schema, rather than present them with an artificial checklist at the beginning of the information-seeking process. Providing students the opportunity to explore information sources before they are asked to find them means that they are not just armed with a list of questions and criteria to apply to each source, but an infinite number of questions according to the information context.

Like students clinging to their vanilla-flavored sources, librarians and instructors can rely too much on the comfort and certainty of a list of criteria that make a source credible. Although students have their list of criteria for evaluating sources, and we have our own list in the form of the "Information Literacy Competency Standards for Higher Education," [12] neither provides for the complexity, potential, and richness of the research process or our role in helping students explore information sources. While the standards are necessarily succinct and process-oriented, they do provide justification for expanding the role of academic librarians beyond the selection and use of information sources. We should look beyond simple criteria and standards, however, to ways of implementing and expanding our reach and the significance of students' research endeavors.

Traditional approaches to research instruction often see librarians relying on preconceived understandings of users' needs. If students are struggling with research, we assume they are unable to find good sources. The response might be to teach more search and hand out more lists of criteria for credible sources. Instead, we can look to promote meaning making and critical thinking over efficient searching and effective use of research tools. As Nancy Dennis states, "we must shift the focus from librarians postulating what students need to know to librarians supporting students creating their own paths toward information literacy." [13]

If teaching students to evaluate information involves "formulaic value judgments about 'good' and 'bad' information," [14] it is a disservice to our students and the rich potential for librarians as partners in critical, content-based work with students. Instead, we should look to something like James Elmborg's critical information literacy: "[A] complicated set of interwoven practices . . . mobile, flexible, and malleable, residing in various places and in constant flux." [15] So we use these activities to help students build those relationships between themselves and various information sources, adding to their adeptness and flexibility in applying their growing information literacy to numerous situations.

In a 2010 study, Currie and associates found that students "used the proper terminology in describing their selection process, but clearly did not understand the definitions of the terms." [16] To remedy this disconnect, we look to student-centered learning—asking students to say something about the sources, rather than our handing out cautions and criteria. If instructors consider the learning objectives they hope their students will achieve in their research, critically evaluating sources will surely feature prominently. Instead of losing this objective in the tangle of writing the research paper, activities like these can focus students on an important but complex goal. Taking assignments apart in this way offers focus and eases frustration. Students and instructors are able to eliminate the checklist, for both research papers and source evaluation.

The following activity provides for tiered instruction and expectations in the way it introduces different types of information sources and asks students to consider them critically. Without this preparation, students may feel lost in choosing multiple sources of various types for one information need, as is often the request with a traditional research paper or project. Instead of simply telling students in their assignment description that they may not use encyclopedias, or that they need three academic journal articles, instructors can remind students that they have explored the various uses and strengths of different information sources and should consider those as they are choosing sources for a research project.

* * *

INFORMATION SOURCE JIGSAW

Find one source of a particular type: website, news/popular article, book, encyclopedia, or academic journal article. Answer the following questions about that source and then discuss them with your group. Write a reflection on how different types of sources can contribute to a research project.

1. How does this source help you understand the topic?
2. What new, unique, or surprising information is included in this source?
3. What information from this source would you use if you were presenting this topic to your class?
4. What information or perspective is missing from this source?

* * *

By explicitly asking students to analyze sources, find connections, make inferences, and draw conclusions, these activities require analytical and evaluative skills that students might otherwise be reluctant to bring to bear on their research assignments. Evaluation is not just one step in the research process, or a hurdle one has to cross, but it is implicated in each part of meaningful and authentic inquiries. Putting it before search and building students' fluency at evaluation and reflection prepares them to approach their information searches in more critical and reflective ways. We are thus encouraging a version of information literacy that "begins to extend from one centered on a particular set of skills to a view of information literacy that is situated within an information-seeking context."[17] With the support of these activities, students can begin to see how the context for information sources and their own constructions of meaning come into play when evaluating the relevance of information.

For the next activity, provide students with a recent event as an initial topic and have them work in groups to find different types of documents about it (blogs, news videos, newspapers, Tweets, magazine articles, journal articles, and books).

* * *

THE INFORMATION CYCLE

As a group, place the provided sources in the order in which they were published to document the information cycle. Consider why certain media work better for different types of information, at different stages in the cycle. Answer the following questions:

1. Who wrote this source?
2. Does the author or source provide citations for their information?
3. Why is this source important for understanding the topic?

As an extension of this activity, contact individuals that have written about a particular event (journalist, blogger, scholar, etc.) and interview them to learn about their credentials. How did they become aware of the event? How did they decide to write about it? Where did they get their information? Are they an expert in this field of study? How did they decide which medium to use to publish that information? Was there a review process of their work? From the time they collected the information and wrote about it, how long did it take for their writing to be published?

* * *

By including these activities in an information literacy program, librarians and instructors can move away from assigning students strict parameters for required source types. When students begin to understand how information sources work and how they work together, they can make more informed and authentic decisions about sources to include in their research. As Dennis suggests, "this is an improvement over the scavenger hunt (evaluation checklist), in which students scour websites for authors, sponsoring organizations, dates of updating, etc."[18] While engaged in critical thinking about source content, students can attempt more authentic evaluations of the sources by using content to consider point of view, biases, credibility, and evidence.

ENCOURAGING SYNTHESIS OF INFORMATION SOURCES

Like evaluation of sources, incorporating and synthesizing information sources into new knowledge is an important ability for students to gain. By presenting students with these opportunities to explore single sources or selected groups of sources, instructors can gently guide them away from the idea that each source must specifically and completely answer their research question. When they know more about how sources work and how they might work together, students are thereby given the tools they need to move beyond regurgitation to thoughtful synthesis. Donham and Steele point out that "students develop inaccurate mental models of the research process when they conceive of research as a process of assembly or cut-and-paste."[19]

If we are going to convince students that research papers are more than repositories for chopped up sources, we must begin, as Elmborg suggests, "engaging students as more than repositories of information."[20] It becomes necessary to encourage acts of thinking rather than simply pass along the rules of the process. Although students may be adept at search and digital interfaces, they can still confuse collecting and repeating information from sources with answering real and provocative questions with a new arrangement of evidence. Showing students how sources can address different aspects of a topic or lead to new and refined lines of inquiry corrects the expectation that every source they find will give an easily digested overview of their topic. Instead, these activities illustrate how one of several sources may provide background information, specific examples, or new and startling insights.

In the following activity, have students work in groups with three sources on one topic. Consider using three of the same type of source (three academic journal articles) or three different source types (one website, one magazine article, one YouTube video) for different approaches and outcomes for this activity. Give each group instructions and questions to find connections between the sources and determine where additional information is needed.

* * *

SYNTHESIS

Your goal with this activity is to connect the important ideas in each article to create a synthesis of all of the information for providing information on the topic. Number the sources 1, 2, and 3. Using sticky notes, write the important and interesting words or phrases from each source that you would share with your classmates if you were explaining the topic. Include any ideas, facts, or concepts that you think are essential to understanding the purpose of the source. In addition to writing the words or phrases from the source, number each note to identify its source. Once you've carefully read each source for its important and interesting information, combine the sticky notes from all three sources and group them into categories, with similar information grouped together. As you read all of the sources, and as you begin to group the information into categories, notice how you learn and understand more about the subject. In addition, different parts of the source may have more information to offer than others, and some sources will have more important or more interesting information than other sources. Give each group of sticky notes a category or name that describes all of the words or phrases on the notes you've grouped together. If you name the group and some notes don't fit, they may need to be moved to a new or different category. Looking at your groups of notes, answer the following questions before moving on the next step in the process:

1. Which categories have a lot of information? Does this group need to be separated into narrower or more specific topics? Would this category make a more interesting and focused topic for exploring and sharing than the topic you started with?
2. Are there categories with very little information? Are these important aspects, or can they be left out of a conversation about this topic? Which of the smaller categories might require additional sources to add important information?
3. What would be the best order for presenting or writing about the categories you've identified? Are there categories that are more general and others that are specific, or examples of the others? Are the categories related in some other way that suggests a good way to organize the information? This approach is how you might orga-

nize your paper or presentation if you were using these sources in a research project.

* * *

Accustomed to generic informational sites on the Internet, Wikipedia, and other tertiary sources, students feel puzzled and cheated when the sources they find in library collections do not answer their entire inquiry. The standard approach to research, with a focus on searching, gathering, and cobbling together, allows students to avoid any genuine inquiry of their own. Activities where students clearly see how a variety of sources can connect and work together will help move them beyond this simplistic view of research. Instructors concerned with issues of plagiarism can replace or enrich traditional research assignments with these more engaging and creative activities.

PUTTING IT ALL TOGETHER: SHARING EXPERTISE

The work of clarifying the connection for students between information-seeking processes and critically considering sources to make new meaning requires the involvement of both instructors and librarians. To avoid the tendency that Norgaard expresses, that "information literacy in its pedagogical expression can easily become narrowed or trivialized,"[21] these activities are left purposefully vague to allow for numerous versions and options depending on course level, discipline, connections to existing assignments and other activities, and evaluations of student needs. Success with this approach and these activities clearly involves more than simply dropping the activities into existing information literacy models or research instruction sessions. Librarians will point out that such work takes time, so this perspective requires a program of curriculum integration that takes research instruction beyond one-shot sessions.

Librarians at the University of North Carolina Charlotte are using the more general of these activities to replace traditional database searching and library orientation sessions with freshman seminar and English composition classes. The more specific and advanced activities are finding their way into integrated instruction with second- and third-year classes in academic majors, positioned in classes before sessions on search strategies and process.

* * *

COMPARING INFORMATION TYPES

The type of source you use for information makes a difference in how specific and advanced the information will be, what evidence is used, and the target audience of the source. Many information sources, including magazines, newspapers, and news websites are written for a general audience. Even someone who isn't an expert in a subject can understand and find interest in these sources. Other sources, in scholarly books and research journals, are written by researchers and experts on a topic for other people working on similar topics. The sources for this type of information are usually specific to a subject area or discipline. Compare a "popular" or general-interest source on a topic to an academic, discipline-specific source on the same topic. Looking at each source, answer the following questions:

1. Who would be most interested in the information in this source?
2. How does this source make the topic seem important to people who are reading it?
3. What kind of evidence is used to support the information in the source?
4. How would you use this source to do further research and find more information on the topic?

Considering both sources and your answers to the questions, write a reflection on how the type or level of information in a source determines how you would use it for a research project.

* * *

Bringing multiple experts to this approach allows for the activities and learning to be spread throughout an assignment, unit, or course to support student success with ongoing, tiered instruction. As we guide students through reading sources critically, this "reading as research" does not just suggest the possibility of faculty involvement but would seem to require it. In addition, working with information sources closely and directly instead of concentrating on process addresses the context deficit of some library instruction sessions and information literacy programs in general. This approach encourages librarians to extend their pedagogical and curricular involvements, but also invite departmental faculty into the library instruction sphere. The library may provide the framework for information literacy but does not isolate itself from others rightly involved in the process.

NOTES

1. David Wood, Jerome S. Bruner, and Gail Ross, "The Role of Tutoring in Problem Solving," *Journal of Child Psychology and Psychiatry and Allied Disciplines* 17, no. 2 (1976); Karen Bordonaro and Gillian Richardson, "Scaffolding and Reflection in Course-Integrated Library Instruction," *Journal of Academic Librarianship* 30, no. 5 (2004); Jean Donham and Mariah Steele, "Instructional Interventions across the Inquiry Process," *College and Undergraduate Libraries* 14, no. 4 (2007).

2. Wood, Bruner, and Ross, "The Role of Tutoring in Problem Solving," 98.

3. Bordonaro and Richardson, "Scaffolding and Reflection in Course-Integrated Library Instruction," 397.

4. Donham and Steele, "Instructional Interventions across the Inquiry Process," 11.

5. Donham and Steele, "Instructional Interventions across the Inquiry Process," 16.

6. Rolf Norgaard, Lori Arp, and Beth S. Woodard, "Writing Information Literacy in the Classroom," *Reference and User Services Quarterly* 43, no. 3 (2004): 223.

7. Donham and Steele, "Instructional Interventions across the Inquiry Process," 4.

8. Alison J. Head and Michael B. Eisenberg, "Finding Context: What Today's College Students Say about Conducting Research in the Digital Age," *Project Information Literacy Progress Report*, Project Information Literacy, 2009. Available online at http://projectinfolit.org/pdfs/PIL_ProgressReport_2_2009.pdf (accessed March 29, 2012); Vicki Tolar Burton and Scott A. Chadwick, "Investigating the Practices of Student Researchers: Patterns of Use and Criteria for Use of Internet and Library Sources," *Computers and Composition* 17, no. 3 (2000); Michelle Twait, "Undergraduate Students' Source Selection Criteria: A Qualitative Study," *Journal of Academic Librarianship* 31, no. 6 (2005); Lea Currie, Frances Devlin, Judith Emde, and Kathryn Graves, "Undergraduate Search Strategies and Evaluation Criteria: Searching for Credible Sources," *New Library World* 111, no. 3/4 (2010).

9. Norgaard, Arp, and Woodard, "Writing Information Literacy in the Classroom," 224.

10. Norgaard, Arp, and Woodard, "Writing Information Literacy in the Classroom," 222.

11. Currie, Devlin, Emde, and Graves, "Undergraduate Search Strategies and Evaluation Criteria," 122.

12. Association of College and Research Libraries, "Information Literacy Competency Standards for Higher Education" (Chicago: Association of College and Research Libraries, 2000). Available online at www.ala.org/ala/acrl/acrlstandards/informationliteracy-competency.htm (accessed March 25, 2012).

13. Nancy Dennis, "Using Inquiry Methods to Foster Information Literacy Partnerships," *Reference Services Review* 29, no. 2 (2001), 127.

14. James Elmborg, "Critical Information Literacy: Definitions and Challenges," in *Transforming Information Literacy Programs: Intersecting Frontiers of Self, Library Culture, and Campus Community*, edited by Carroll Wetzel Wilkinson and Courtney Bruch (Chicago: Association of College and Research Libraries, 2012), 93.

15. Elmborg, "Critical Information Literacy," 77.

16. Currie, Devlin, Emde, and Graves, "Undergraduate Search Strategies and Evaluation Criteria," 123.

17. Melissa Gross and Don Latham, "Experiences with and Perceptions of Information: A Phenomenographic Study of First-Year College Students," *Library Quarterly* 81, no. 2 (2011): 162.

18. Dennis, "Using Inquiry Methods to Foster Information Literacy Partnerships," 129.

19. Donham and Steele, "Instructional Interventions across the Inquiry Process," 16.

20. Elmborg, "Critical Information Literacy," 93.

21. Norgaard, Arp, and Woodard, "Writing Information Literacy in the Classroom," 224.

NINE

RAIDS for Research

Sara D. Miller, Nancy C. DeJoy, Benjamin M. Ober-dock

Many undergraduate students enter higher education with a clear idea of what they want to study and why. Others enter with the goal of learning what their strengths and passions are and how they might channel them in ways that will help them create the lives they hope for. There are, of course, all kinds of positions in between. Required first-year writing courses are one place where students can begin to explore the literacy expectations of specific fields of study. If introduced to the idea of disciplinary literacy early in their educational process, undergraduate students can begin to see the ways that "[e]mpowerment is underpinned by information literacy."[1] As Michelle Holschuh Simmons notes,

> Frequently, the domain-specific rhetorical processes are seen by the faculty members who work within the domain as the 'normal' or 'natural' or 'correct' way of writing, reading, or researching, and they expect their undergraduate students to be able to learn and adopt these ways of communicating without explicit instruction.[2]

A disciplinary literacy assignment that allows students to select their own areas of interest creates discussions about the differences between and among what is considered "normal" as a matter of course. In addition, the assignment creates an organic need for discussions about databases, scholarly sources, trade publications, and so forth, that emphasize disciplinary-based forms of information literacy. In this chapter, I illustrate the ways that a disciplinary literacy assignment engages information literacy to enhance students' knowledge about majors and related career interests.

My work agrees with the basic idea set forth by the Institute for Learning at University of Pittsburgh, "that disciplinary knowledge always co-exists with habits of thinking—and therefore literacy skills—particular to each discipline."[3] It should be further understood, however, that some of these habits of thinking—especially curiosity and openness to multimodal research—cross disciplines and enhance information literacy in more general ways.[4] In addition, reading to participate in a discipline—rather than to consume and report on what is already known—is a shift all students need to make as they progress through their undergraduate education and prepare to enter professions. Because first-year writing classes are most commonly made up of students from across the disciplines, these courses present a unique situation in which to invite explorations of disciplinary literacies. As we develop strategies for responding to the recent trends toward the five- and six-year degree trajectories and multiple changes of majors that add to time toward degree, finding ways to integrate information literacy projects that focus on disciplinary literacies early in undergraduate curricula offers a productive way to think about helping students make successful transitions to the expectations for literate behaviors in higher education and beyond.

To make this pedagogy work, however, teachers need to help students create new relationships with texts, especially those texts usually thought of as citation sources for traditional research papers. As Bruce Ballenger notes, students are often introduced to information literacy through assignments that require them to merely find sources to agree or disagree with, especially as they build an argument to prove a predetermined conclusion/thesis statement that precedes the inquiry process.[5] Reading to build new knowledge, reframe what's known for a new context, or identify and/or practice the discourse patterns of a field are goals that can challenge basic assumptions about research for students and teachers alike. Similarly, information literacy is more than the ability to access and evaluate information based on preset criteria. Disciplinary literacy is more productively understood as the ability to participate in forums of construction and/or distribution of information. The move away from research reports and toward forms of information literacy that support the construction of new knowledge challenges teachers to think differently about their students' abilities and challenges students to engage forms of literacy that they usually do not associate with the demands of school writing.

Placed in the middle of the semester as the researched essay, the disciplinary literacy project is an opportunity for students to use a variety of research methods to 1) ask questions, 2) search for and obtain information from a number of sources, 3) analyze the relationships between and among the information in those sources, 4) draw conclusions about what the diversity of information might mean, and 5) reflect on the ways that information literacy helps us create informed contexts for our decisions.

Whether first-year students are sure or unsure of what discipline they are interested in, they have little experience understanding the literacy skills connected to specific disciplines.

The disciplinary literacy assignment creates multiple opportunities for a variety of inquiry processes that emphasize reading, writing, and researching as disciplinary practices: conducting interviews; searching the Web and online databases; accessing scholarly, popular, and trade publications; and so forth. Because they are inquiring about literacy skills related to different disciplines, students come to see the skills, and the practice of those skills, as important in multiple disciplinary research contexts. In fact, the assignment is designed to position students as researchers who can learn from one another's inquiry processes. They often help one another find interview subjects through their family or other community connections. As they gather what might seem like conflicting information from different kinds of sources, they help one another figure out why these conflicts exist—and what these differences mean about information literacy more generally.

Taken as a whole, then, the assignment centers information literacy as a subject for conversation, illustrating the ways that information literacy requires participation in conversations about diversity, authority, inclusion, and exclusion: the decisions that constitute our view of the disciplines. The approach allows us to move away from checklists and skills that are perceived as connected too strongly with one project or too focused on consumption and analysis and toward practices of participating in the construction of knowledge using strategies that clearly transfer across situations.

FACILITATING NEW LITERACY IDENTITY THROUGH THE INQUIRY CYCLE

An inquiry approach[6] challenges the linear progression of behaviors inherent to creating a traditional research report, which begins by formulating a thesis statement or research question and a search strategy, followed by searching for information that meets the criteria and/or supports an idea or argument, and culminating in composing the report. Linear information-seeking processes[7] mirror the traditional compositional method of presenting a thesis and supporting it with arguments. A technical, linear approach to information seeking has been shown to reinforce use of sources for the purpose of fact-finding in favor of interaction, analysis, or active participation.[8] A linear approach to information seeking is particularly ineffective for the outcomes of the disciplinary literacies assignment,[9] which asks students to *write about writing, reading, and researching* within a discipline, a conceptual leap that is often difficult for students who may be used to approaching sources for the purpose of gleaning facts or arguments rather than examining the strategies used to create the information. While defined linear steps may make the research process easier for structuring of assessments and teaching, these steps tend to impose an artificial progression on a process that, in reality, can be messy and organic, potentially stifling a sense of exploration along the way.

Research indicates that students presented with a research assignment encounter the most difficulty in the areas of "getting started" and "defining and narrowing a topic."[10] Incorporating searching and analysis of sources as texts stimulates asking questions to move toward a research focus. In this way, sources stimulate curiosity rather than a mad search for facts and arguments. For example, we begin information literacy sessions by having students briefly analyze an article to create questions about both the subject matter and the article itself, as well as identify keywords and concepts. Beginning a project by asking questions about how sources create the information they present rather than just what information is presented introduces students to the process of knowledge creation and aids in the shift from information consumer to active participant. Once students are positioned as active participants, they can then assist in the identification and creation of analytical criteria to apply to further sources of information.[11]

For librarians who work with first-year writing classes, this approach is especially valuable because it creates shared notions that inform pedagogy, place value and focus on inquiry, and allow for alignment of information literacy and writing outcomes. As librarians move from traditional "source showcase" library instruction sessions to interactive, inquiry-based approaches, they can guide students to participate more deeply in the inquiry cycle in relation to information sources.

INQUIRY AND SOURCE EVALUATION

In traditional bibliographic or library instruction, students are taught to evaluate information and sources in an isolated or silo fashion. Before they evaluate a source, they may be taught or given a checklist of certain criteria to look for to determine if a source is good enough to use. This list may include the following characteristics: reliability, validity, accuracy, authority, timeliness, and bias. When students find a source, they go down their checklist to see if the source satisfies all, or at least most of, the criteria they have been given. If the source satisfies enough of their criteria, it is good and can be included on their list of sources. The content of the source and the thought of looking at it in relation to other sources seldom enter into the conversation. Sources are simply treated as isolated entities to be evaluated and proven worthy or unworthy of inclusion in the student's bibliography or works cited page, and not as part of a

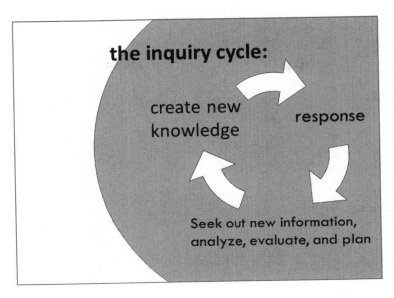

Figure 9.1.   The Inquiry Cycle. Sara D. Miller and Nancy C. DeJoy, "Assessing Collaboration: The Effect of Pedagogical Alignment and Shared Learning Outcomes for Information Literacy Instruction in First-Year Writing Classes," paper presented at LILAC Annual Conference, Limerick, Ireland, March 29, 2010.

process of joining a larger scholarly conversation about a topic. The worthiness or unworthiness of sources is not tied to the project or the pedagogical goal of helping first-year students understand the importance of participation and contribution as disciplinary values.

Most importantly, perhaps, the notion that credibility can be determined by noting the publisher, author, author credentials, and so forth, is in direct conflict with the notions of credibility and source selection required by the assignment, in which multiple sources and modes of information must be understood in relation to one another for the researcher to construct knowledge. In this framework, the content of the sources, rather than just the identifying features of the source itself, tends to be central to decisions about credibility. Within the discipline of composition studies, credibility requires analysis of the content of the source, which might identify gaps or biases in text written by authors endowed with credibility/authority in some contexts. A bad source might give useful information, pose useful dilemmas, or prompt further research in ways that searching for good sources would not.

To create more consistency throughout the value systems connected with information literacy instruction as it is embedded in first-year writing classes, library instruction in those classes was shifted from focusing on the isolated evaluation of a source to inquiry-based instruction sessions. When students find a source they think will help with their research topic or inquiry, they analyze it as an artifact, asking questions about how the information was created and made public; through this questioning, students determine what factors to consider as important to use when analyzing a source within the context of a project. Approaching and treating information sources as artifacts and assessing sources in the context of a project's purpose allows students to come up with their own list of project-related factors to consider when evaluating sources, illustrating how creating criteria is part of the inquiry cycle. For example, students analyze the invention activities necessary to the creation of the artifact and evaluate those as more or less indicative of the disciplinary practices they see at work in other sources.

Analyzing sources in relation to what counts as useful within the context of a particular purpose allows students to determine what use any given source may have, why it was written, what the author had to know to write it, and how the source may be important. Ultimately, it helps them understand and use the source in a much deeper way than superficial examination using a list of prescribed evaluative criteria could ever allow. Doing so shifts the students' focus from asking "Is the source or information good?" to "Is it relevant?" [12]

RAIDS

In our information literacy sessions, we attempt to make disciplinary writing conventions transparent, drawing explicit attention to those conventions by looking at the source as a piece of writing. Instead of using typical criteria lists to evaluate information sources, we use concepts from the course to make the connections even more obvious, thereby "teaching students to see how the genre of discourse is related to the communicative need." [13] A typical information literacy session discussion question after examining such aspects of an information source as authorship, style, or audience is, "What does this source say about communication in your discipline?"

Revising information literacy instruction to align with the inquiry-based pedagogy of the course allows us to shift toward understanding sources as containing information not only about content, but also about the activities, assumptions, organizational structures, language, and so forth, that constitute that content. To direct this kind of inquiry, we use a heuristic for reading that positions students as writers who are reading, which is how the assignment itself—and all research assignments—position students. Questions about Revision, Arrangement, Invention, Delivery, and Style (RAIDS) serve two major pedagogical goals: They position inquiry as the primary activity at the heart of writing, and they reconnect reading and writing, inviting students to see the texts they read as pos-

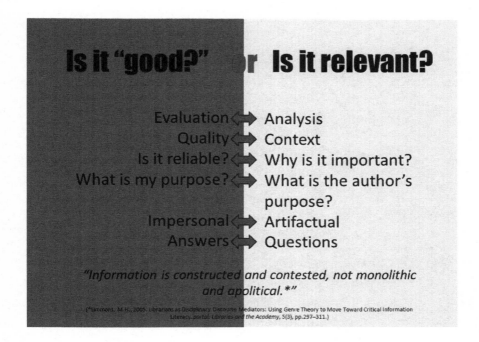

Figure 9.2. Evaluative Criteria

sible sources for learning about writing across modes and situations. Shared across library and writing classroom teaching and learning situations, this pedagogy challenges the initiate-respond-evaluate pattern that many students come to expect in their high school language arts classrooms focused primarily on responding to literary texts.[14] As A. Petrosky, S. McConachie, and V. Mihalakis note, "one-way discussion predicated on teacher questions, students' responses, and teacher evaluation is often interspersed with lectures and individual seatwork" in classes preceding higher education.[15]

Similarly, information literacy standards, including the Association of College and Research Libraries' (ACRL) "Information Literacy Competency Standards for Higher Education,"[16] tend to emphasize discrete skills and concepts that fit easily into the traditional stages of a research report: thesis statement, search strategy, find supporting sources, compose. Situating information literacy standards within RAIDS provides two important opportunities: the creation of a shared framework for analyzing information sources as written artifacts and the chance to transfer the generative and analytic skills they are using in class to sources of information they will encounter or search for in other contexts. This approach also provides opportunity for addressing the issues that Simmons indicates as follows:

> (to) help our students see—that knowledge is constructed and contested. Therefore, we need to communicate to students—both explicitly through explanation and implicitly through modeling—that research is not about finding information or facts, as most of the ACRL standards suggest, but instead that research is about constructing meaning through active engagement with the ideas and asking questions surrounding the information itself.[17]

In the following section, I present RAIDS as it appears in the student handbook required in first-year writing classes, adding selected information literacy standards and concepts important to source-based assignments. I hope to present all three sets of concept, writing, reading, and information literacy, together in the next version of the handbook. I also include suggestions for questions to stimulate discussion about the information literacy concepts when responding to a text or other information source. Integrating the standards into actual reading and writing activities that support effective research practices creates a more holistic framework for application of standards that otherwise seem decontextualized. I invite students to think about how the information literacy of source authors is engaged in the artifacts they use to create their projects. In this way students broaden their repertoires for writing as they analyze the artifacts and evaluate the effectiveness of the sources' uses of information.

For example, if an author from political science uses popular sources to show the difference between how those sources address a political issue as compared to more scholarly sources, students gage the effectiveness of the comparison; however, they also see a comparative activity at work and can engage that strategy as an invention activity as they build their own projects. ACRL standards, then, are applied to analyze sources, as well as guide information literacy instruction and assessment of students' information literacy skills.

RAIDS: REVISION, ARRANGEMENT, INVENTION, DELIVERY, AND STYLE

Note: Order is changed from the acrostic.

Invention

Writing

What am I/are we inventing? What ideas, practices, changes, and so forth define our purpose? What is invention? What activities will support the inquiry and writing processes necessary to meet that purpose?

Reading

What's being invented? What ideas, practices, changes, and so forth is the author trying to manifest? What is invention? What activities did the author have to engage in to create the text?

Information Literacy Concept Questions Related to Invention

Note: ACRL Standards appear in italics after the questions to which they are related. ACRL standards relate to either student processes or source author processes.

What makes a writer qualified? How might this concept change across genres or types of information? *Identifies a variety of types and formats of potential sources of information (1.2), retrieves information online or in person using a variety of methods (2.3), articulates and applies initial criteria for evaluating both the information and its sources (3.2), constructs and implements effectively designed search strategies (2.2).*

What kinds of citations are used? How do other sources affect the author's invention process? Can you identify any sources of influence that are not named in a bibliography? (i.e., personal experience, etc.) *Applies new and prior information to the planning and creation of a particular product or performance (4.1), validates understanding and interpretation of the information through discourse with other individuals, subject-area experts, and/ or practitioners (3.6), defines and articulates the need for information (1.1).*

What factors influenced the author to write this material? *Validates understanding and interpretation of the information through discourse with other individuals, subject-area experts, and/or practitioners (3.6), defines and articulates the need for information (1.1), summarizes the main ideas to be extracted from the information gathered (3.1).*

Are there any factors that indicate a possible bias on the author's part? *Articulates and applies initial criteria for evaluating both the information and its sources (3.2).*

Arrangement

Writing

What's being arranged? What am I/are we putting in relationship with what? What is arrangement? How can we create these relationships in ways that will be effective for us and for our audience?

Reading

What's being arranged? What's being put in relationship with what? What is arrangement? How are things being put in relationship with one another?

Information Literacy Concept Questions Related to Arrangement

Note: ACRL Standards appear in italics after the questions to which they are related. ACRL standards relate to either student processes or source author processes.
How is the presentation of information different across genres? What does this indicate about the relationship of the sources to one another? *Compares new knowledge with prior knowledge to determine the value added, contradictions, or other unique characteristics of the information (3.4).*
What is the relationship between you as a researcher and the resources that you are finding and using? *Constructs and implements effectively designed search strategies (2.2), determines whether the new knowledge has an impact on the individual's value system and takes steps to reconcile differences (3.5).*
What is the relationship between your discipline and the way that information is presented, organized, stored, or discovered? *Extracts, records, and manages the information and its sources (2.5).*
How does what you want to find out relate to your options for finding information? *Identifies a variety of types and formats of potential sources for information (1.2), refines the search strategy if necessary (2.4), determines whether the initial query should be revised (3.7).*
What is the relationship between the library session, your assignment, and the rest of the course (i.e., scaffolding, design, relevance, etc.)?

Revision

Writing

What's being revised (may share some features with what's being invented)? What changes does the text seem to be directed toward? What changes—if any—resulting from the process of creating the text should be apparent in the text? Examples: A change of thought? A new practice?

A specific action the reader should take that would not have been taken before reading the text?

What is revision? What things can the writer/writers do to help the text meet its revisionary purpose(s)? For example, inclusion of new statistics or stories? Presentation of benefits that readers will find hard to resist?

Reading

What's being revised (may share some features with what's being invented)? What changes does the text seem to be directed toward? Examples: A change of thought? A new practice? A specific action the reader should take that would not have been taken before reading the text?

What is revision? What things does the text do that are most clearly engaged to make the revision happen? For example, inclusion of new statistics or stories? Presentation of benefits that readers will find hard to resist?

Information Literacy Concept Questions Related to Revision

Note: ACRL Standards appear in italics after the questions to which they are related. ACRL standards relate to either student processes or source author processes.

What is the author trying to do? *Synthesizes main ideas to construct new concepts (3.3).*

How might the author's purpose be affecting the view of the issue? *Determines whether the new knowledge has an impact on the individual's value system and takes steps to reconcile differences (3.5).*

Looking across several types of sources, what is the range of discourse on this topic that you might find within a discipline? *Compares new knowledge with prior knowledge to determine the value added, contradictions, or other unique characteristics of the information (3.4), reevaluates the nature and extent of the information needed (1.4).*

Who is communicating to whom? Why is this communication important to your discipline? *Revises the development process for the product or performance (4.2).*

How does this information compare to other information about this issue that was written at an earlier or later date? *Compares new knowledge with prior knowledge to determine the value added, contradictions, or other unique characteristics of the information (3.4).*

How does this material affect your initial question or search strategy? Would you change it? What would you do next in your information search? *Determines whether the initial query should be revised (3.7), refines the search strategy as necessary (2.4).*

Style

Writing

Which style is most appropriate in this composition situation? High? Middle? Low? A style only insiders would understand or one geared toward a general audience? The use of vocabulary that not everyone would understand and/or agree about the meaning of? Should the audience be directly addressed, or should the style be more detached? What are the effects of the style likely to be on the audience's interpretation of the message?

Reading

Which style is used? High? Middle? Low? A style only insiders would understand or one geared toward a general audience? The use of vocabulary that not everyone would understand and/or agree about the meaning of? Is the audience directly addressed, or is the style more detached? What are the effects of the style on your interpretation of the message?

Information Literacy Concept Questions Related to Style

Note: ACRL Standards appear in italics after the questions to which they are related. ACRL standards relate to either student processes or source author processes.

What does the language used tell you about the audience for this source? *Articulates and applies initial criteria for evaluating both the information and its sources (3.2), communicates the product or performance effectively to others (4.2).*

Why might a certain type of information source (i.e., popular, scholarly, or trade article) be useful in your writing and research context? *Identifies a variety of types and formats of potential sources for information (1.2).*

What types of communication might you have to produce in your discipline and for whom? *Communicates the product or performance effectively to others (4.2).*

What does the style of a text tell you about writing expectations and conventions for your discipline? *Articulates and applies initial criteria for evaluating both the information and its sources (3.2), acknowledges the use of information sources in communicating the product or performance (5.3).*

Delivery

Writing

What mode of delivery will be most effective? How will this mode of delivery affect the message and your audience's interpretation of the message?

Reading

What mode of delivery is used? How does this mode of delivery affect the message and your interpretation of the message?

Information Literacy Concept Questions Related to Delivery

Note: ACRL Standards appear in italics after the questions to which they are related. ACRL standards relate to either student processes or source author processes.

Where is this information published? *Acknowledges the use of information sources in communicating the product or performance (5.3), identifies a variety of types and formats of potential sources for information (1.2).*

Where would people look to find this particular type of information? *Selects the most appropriate investigative methods or information retrieval systems for accessing the needed information (2.1).*

What type of publication might you write for if you wanted to communicate an issue in your field to the general public? To others in your field? *Communicates the product or performance effectively to others (4.3).*

Observations

In identifying the relevant ACRL standards and placing them within the RAIDS heuristic, some factors stand out. Style, which is heavily emphasized in our information literacy sessions as a key concept to help students both view information sources as pieces of writing and begin to evaluate them in context, has the least explicit correspondence to the standards. In contrast, the concepts of invention and revision had the largest number of standards with which they could be easily associated. This observation highlights an interesting area for further consideration about the relationship between RAIDS, the ACRL standards, and information literacy more generally.

INTEGRATED DISCIPLINARY AND INFORMATION LITERACIES

Creating a space to integrate disciplinary literacy and information literacy instruction in first-year writing facilitates faculty/instructional librarian collaborations around an issue that is key to student interest and success during the transition to identifying and meeting the expectations for writing, reading, and researching in higher education. The shift to inquiry-based teaching and learning can be challenging because of the ways it refigures our understanding of the relationships between and among multiple sets of standards and assessment criteria, but integrated versions of our standards and performance scales helps us understand our educational contexts in richer, more generative ways.

As we have introduced colleagues to this integrated approach, we have been aware of the particular difficulties caused when questions generally assumed to have one referent—e.g., student performance—are engaged for other purposes. Modeling the practices addressed by ACRL standards within a disciplinary context to relate to the major concepts that we use in writing classes has allowed us to integrate information literacy into the course conceptually in ways that enhance the relationships that lead to good research products: writing, reading, and the use of a variety of sources. Doing so in relation to the issues surrounding disciplinary literacy allows our students to explore the kinds of work they will do as emerging experts in the fields of study that they are interested in.

As a result, information literacy is repositioned not merely as a set of skills, but as a set of practices that can enhance lifelong learning in two specific ways: as practices that help us make informed choices, and approaches to developing the analytic and generative skills necessary to keep up with the trends that define effective practices across our educational and professional lives. Creating a pedagogy that demonstrates the ways that research can simultaneously give us content-based information and insights into how to create texts that enter into conversations in effective ways deepens the opportunities we have to help our students become participating members of the communities and organizations they will belong to throughout their lives.

APPENDIX A: FIRST-YEAR WRITING MICHIGAN STATE UNIVERSITY DISCIPLINARY LITERACY BASE ASSIGNMENT

Note: DeJoy requirements appear in italics.

Background: Earlier assignments for this course gave you opportunities to identify themes and terms for analysis so that you could begin to understand and practice meeting the expectations for writing in higher education. Paper three allows you to continue engaging effective invention, arrangement, revision, style, and delivery practices. It also introduces you to the ways that research and participating in important academic discussions prepare you to use literacy in successful ways in the various types of writing situations you will find yourself in in higher education and, perhaps, beyond.

Requirements: Different academic disciplines have different ways of presenting and analyzing information, building knowledge, and presenting knowledge in written form. This paper gives you the opportunity to begin building your own understanding of how writing, reading, and researching operate within a discipline of interest to you. You may choose any discipline you wish to examine for this project. Whichever you choose, you must engage in at least the following invention activities:

1. Analyze at least one scholarly article from that discipline.
2. Analyze at least one article from a trade publication related to that discipline.
3. Conduct an interview with a person who teaches major courses and/or does research in that discipline.
4. Conduct an interview with a person who practices in a field related to that discipline.
5. *Enroll on the career services website (a consultant from career services will attend our class to demonstrate this system).*
6. *Analyze an introductory piece about economic and quality of life issues related to the literacy work done in that discipline or career field.*

Your research will include additional reading and interviewing as determined by your individual projects. Papers must be at least seven to nine pages in length, in twelve-point font, with one-inch margins (*or the equivalent*). Your visual should communicate a specific, important piece of information; graphs and charts are commonly used for this purpose.

Writing Context: Many students come to higher education with only a vague idea of what it means to become a participating member of an academic discipline. Your purpose in this essay is to give students who are new to the academic discipline/field you have chosen an introduction to the expectations for writing, reading, and researching in that discipline. Your paper should ultimately help your audience understand how literacies are used to create and communicate knowledge in the discipline/field you choose to explore.

This assignment gives you the opportunity to continue practicing successfully meeting the learning goals connected with previous assignments. It also helps you begin to integrate the skills related to the following learning outcomes. As always, the undergraduate learning outcomes that relate to our first-year writing program goals appear in parentheses.

Writing

Demonstrate an understanding of writing as an epistemic and recursive process; effectively apply a variety of knowledge-making strategies in writing (integrated reasoning)

Reading

> Demonstrate an understanding of reading as an epistemic and recursive meaning-making processes (integrated reasoning, cultural understanding)
> Understand that various academic disciplines and fields employ varied genre, voice, syntactical choices, uses of evidence, and citation styles that call for a variety of reading strategies (analytical thinking, integrated reasoning, communication)

Inquiry/Research

> Demonstrate the ability to locate, critically evaluate, and employ a variety of sources for a range of purposes (analytical thinking, integrated reasoning)

APPENDIX B: DESCRIPTION OF SAMPLE INFORMATION LITERACY SESSION ADDRESSING DISCIPLINARY LITERACY

Note: This session is modeled after the inquiry cycle (see figure 9.2).

1. *Response:* The class begins with the display of an online article, video, or other source, usually from the website of a professional organization. Students read and respond to the article to generate aloud a list of related questions and keywords as a group. Sample questions asked of the students are "What was the article about?" "What was the author's purpose?" "What disciplines or fields are represented?" "Why would this article be important in the discipline of _____?"

2. *Seek out new information, analyze, evaluate, and plan:* Students are put into small groups and use the responses generated by the class to search for different genres of sources that reflect the content or discipline of the original source. Each group is tasked to find either a scholarly article, background information, an opinion, a book, or website. Students are encouraged to search as they normally would (most beginning with Google or a search engine). Groups then decide on the one source within their group that they like the best.

3. *Create new knowledge:* One spokesperson from each group demonstrates to the class how the source was located, and the librarian initiates a discussion about the nature of the material, drawing from the sample questions addressed in the RAIDS section of this chapter. As the students bring analytical criteria into their discussion, the librarian identifies and creates a list of these criteria (e.g., authority, bias, currency) on a separate display surface. As all five groups demonstrate and discuss their sources, the librarian guides discussion as needed to bring attention to other criteria for a complete list. After each group has discussed their respective source, the librarian briefly demonstrates a library resource that is ideal

for locating that type of information as an alternative to (or further demonstration of) the source that the students first used. Librarian demonstration is limited to allow maximum time for discussion and student interaction with sources and one another.

A thorough online course guide, structured to mirror the format of the class, with details of library resources, online modules, research guides, librarian contact information, and other mechanics, is prepared for the students and presented at the end of class to facilitate future research and classroom activities. We rely on this guide heavily for providing more traditional "show-and-tell" textual and list-based content so that that it frees up more class time for inquiry-based exercises. It also provides a more structured guide for students who work well on their own.

4. *Response:* At the end of class, students should write a brief minute paper answering the questions, "What was the most important thing you learned today" and "What would you still like to know more about?"

NOTES

1. Mark Hepworth and Geoff Walton, *Teaching Information Literacy for Inquiry-Based Learning* (Oxford, UK: Chandos, 2009), 3.

2. Michelle Holschuh Simmons, "Librarians as Disciplinary Discourse Mediators: Using Genre Theory to Move toward Critical Information Literacy," *Portal: Libraries and the Academy* 5, no. 3 (2005): 298.

3. S. McConachie and A. Petrosky, eds., *Content Matters: Improving Student Learning through Disciplinary Literacy* (New York: Jossey-Bass, 2010).

4. Hepworth and Walton, *Teaching Information Literacy for Inquiry-Based Learning;* Seth Godin, *Tribes* (London: Penguin, 2008); Bruce Ballenger, *The Curious Researcher: A Guide to Writing Research Papers,* 6th ed. (New York: Longman, 2009).

5. Bruce Ballenger, *Beyond Note Cards: Rethinking the Freshman Research Paper* (Portsmouth, NH: Boynton/Cook, 1999).

6. Ballenger, *Beyond Note Cards.*

7. For an excellent comparison of common information-seeking process models, see the chart in Mandy Lupton, *The Learning Connection: Information Literacy and the Student Experience* (Adelaide, Australia: Auslib Press, 2004), 23.

8. Louise Limberg, "Is There a Relationship between Information Seeking and Learning Outcomes?" in *Information Literacy around the World: Advances in Programs and Research,* edited by Christine Bruce and P. Candy, 193–218 (Riverina, Australia: Centre for Information Studies, Charles Sturt University, 2000).

9. See appendix A at the end of this chapter for the full text of the disciplinary literacies assignment.

10. Alison J. Head and Michael B. Eisenberg, "Truth Be Told: How College Students Evaluate and Use Information in the Digital Age," *Project Information Literacy Progress Report,* Project Information Literacy, 2010, 3. Available online at http://projectinfolit.org/pdfs/PIL_Fall2010_Survey_FullReport1.pdf (accessed March 25, 2012).

11. See appendix B at the end of this chapter for a description of a sample information literacy session addressing disciplinary literacies.

12. Nancy C. Dejoy, Sara D. Miller, and Benjamin M. Oberdick, "Disciplinary Literacy: A Context for Learning Critical Information Literacy," paper presented at the LILAC Annual Conference, Glasgow, Scotland, UK, April 11, 2012.

13. Simmons, "Librarians as Disciplinary Discourse Mediators," 302.

14. A. Applebee, *Literature in the Secondary School: Studies of Curriculum and Instruction in the United States* (Urbana, IL: National Council of Teachers of English, 1993).

15. A. Petrosky, S. McConachie, and V. Mihalakis, "Disciplinary Literacy in English Instruction," in *Content Matters: Improving Student Learning through Disciplinary Literacy,* edited by S. McConachie and A. Petrosky (New York: Jossey-Bass, 2010).

16. Association of College and Research Libraries, "Information Literacy Competency Standards for Higher Education" (Chicago: Association of College Research Libraries, 2000). Available online at www.ala.org/ala/mgrps/divs/acrl/standards/informationliteracycompetency.htm (accessed May 25, 2012).

17. Simmons, "Librarians as Disciplinary Discourse Mediators," 308.

TEN

College Students as Wikipedia Editors: New Pathways to Information Literacy

Davida Scharf

How can information literacy be effectively taught? In addressing this question as a librarian at the New Jersey Institute of Technology (NJIT), I engaged several professors of technical writing to turn college students into Wikipedia authors with surprisingly positive results. Most librarians agree that Wikipedia can be a good place to gain background for a research project, although librarians usually suggest that it should not be cited in a college term paper. We use encyclopedias and other reference tools to open the door to knowledge. Even as a doctoral student, I have used my old *Britannica* to refresh or learn about concepts or facts relevant to the work at hand. Some faculty and librarians deplore the use of Wikipedia, but as Chris Harris points out in an editorial in *School Library Journal* entitled "Can We Make Peace with Wikipedia?," the *Oxford English Dictionary* was the original collaborative reference work, and librarians worship it.[1] This thought led to an exploration of Wikipedia that provided the basis for an assignment for a third-year undergraduate technical communication course. The assignment positively affected student motivation and resulted in a successful learning experience, one that integrated research, writing, critical thinking, and presentation skills. It suggested a new approach to the incorporation of Web 2.0 technology into information literacy instruction. This chapter describes our curriculum, instruction, and assessment methodology and suggests benefits and avenues for future research.

LITERATURE REVIEW

Student engagement is a recurrent theme in research on academic success in college.[2] Educators have long recognized the importance of addressing the affective dimensions of learning and identified motivation to learn as one important factor in student engagement.[3] Educators have discussed the broad role of libraries in student engagement[4] and the related role of self-efficacy,[5] and some mention engagement as a technique to enhance instruction.[6] In our field, instructional librarians know well Constance A. Mellon[7] and Carol Kuhlthau's[8] work on the concept of library anxiety as an affective dimension of the research process. Kuhlthau's work on guided inquiry[9] suggests evidence of student learning during the search process, but this knowledge has not been embodied in the performance indicators that are part of the Association of College and Research Libraries' "Information Literacy Competency Standards for Higher Education."[10] Teresa Yvonne Neely found significant correlations between such sociological and psychological factors as exposure, experience, and attitude with information literacy skills, as measured through students' self-reporting.[11] Diane Nahl[12] and Lesley J. Farmer[13] studied the relationship between information and emotion, considering, in particular, the role of self-efficacy, a person's belief in his or her own ability to complete a task or achieve a goal. While these studies have added to our knowledge of some of the noncognitive aspects of learning, more detailed examinations of the effect of instructional design on student motivation and engagement would certainly help practitioners of information literacy instruction.

Rapidly developing and disruptive digital technologies have created both cognitive and affective gaps between students and faculty—a form of generation gap. Some faculty members still place restrictions on students' use of Web-based sources. Faculty, whether or not they embrace digital technologies in the service of scholarship, may make assumptions and have frameworks for understanding scholarly communication that are quite different from that of their students.[14] These disconnections are frequently manifested in the types of research assignments they give students and the weak engagement they engender. Both faculty and students may also express a failure to connect in emotional terms as they lament, in their own ways, the lack of engagement, each blaming the other. In his valuation of student engagement and satisfaction, McGuinness has studied reflective journals as examples of authentic student work that seem to bridge this gap.[15]

Study and practice in the use of various digital technologies as tools for increasing student engagement in information literacy learning have also been relatively limited. Clickers, a technology that enables real-time polling in traditional classroom settings, are designed only for face-to-face engagement. In "Using iClickers in Library Instruction to Improve

Student Engagement," Bobby Hollandsworth and Ed Rock explain how they used Clickers to create interactivity in source identification and search strategy formation.[16] The practice of using library scavenger hunts as instructional devices in college can be traced as far back as 1957.[17] Such games, even as they were adapted for the current technological environment, have had some degree of success in meeting learning goals and reducing library anxiety, yet librarians' acceptance has been limited.[18] A few librarians attempted to create instructional video games but struggled with resource limitations and other obstacles, including the extremely high bar for engagement set by the commercial video game industry. An information literacy game development initiative at NJIT suffered from these problems.[19] Maura A. Smale's discussion covers the potential benefits of and obstacles presented by the use of gaming for information literacy instruction.[20]

Meanwhile, librarians' understanding of the research habits of the Net Generation is growing. It has been a research focus for almost a decade, as evidenced by such major projects as those undertaken by the Pew Research Center,[21] the University of Rochester Library,[22] Project Information Literacy,[23] and many others; however, librarians are only beginning to translate this deepening knowledge into practice. Few studies thus far have documented the application of this growing body of knowledge into assignments specifically designed to be engaging. One early study of Gen Y students used a traditional library assignment focused on search mechanics, but it was presented in ways designed to reduce boredom, and it did, although the authors could not isolate which of the many changes to the course made the difference.[24]

Video-based tutorials and screencasts have been the subject of much development activity among instructional librarians, as evidenced by the plethora of shared learning objects available through such sites as PRIMO, Merlot, LionTV, and YouTube. Engagement has only rarely been considered in discussions of their effectiveness.[25] These seem aimed at the MTV rather than the Net Generation and are, alas, still passive tools not requiring the type of engagement and interactivity associated with practicing research skills. One application designed as a test with Net Gen students in mind is iSkills™, a test developed by the Educational Testing Service (ETS).[26] It is a unique computer-based adaptive test that was based upon the information, communication, technology (ICT) literacy construct. ICT competencies include cognitive skills, traditional literacy, and technology skills as critical components of the construct. They address the ability to define, access, manage, integrate, evaluate, create, and communicate, concepts familiar to instructional librarians.[27] Test takers must respond to complex scenarios that require what seem like constructed responses, but they are actually restricted to a limited set of choices. According to Irvin R. Katz, senior researcher at ETS, iSkills™ test takers did not perform as well as hoped. Even so, more than 60 percent said that they enjoyed taking the test.[28] Given this unexpected outcome, iSkills™ shows promise not only as a test, but as an instructional device, since enjoyment might also increase motivation and engagement. Perhaps the use of iSkills™ will spread, but, for now, research papers, annotated bibliographies, and other traditional types of research assignments are still the prevalent assignment models.

Motivation may be understood as the drive for satisfaction of human needs, with self-actualization at the top of Abraham Maslow's hierarchy.[29] Educational activities that support independent and active learning fit well in the higher levels of his model. Motivation may also be understood as responsive to intrinsic and extrinsic rewards, as Frederick Hertzberg found in relation to job satisfaction.[30] Such extrinsic rewards as salary, or in this case, grades, are important, but not sufficient, for satisfaction and engagement. Thus, assignments that spark genuine interest generally provide stronger incentives than grades or punishments. These theories of motivation helped us understand how using Wikipedia might improve student engagement.

Wikis have been around for more than a decade[31] and have been embraced by many educators as a new media tool for writing instruction. As a collaboration vehicle for the digital era, they have already garnered a substantial literature on their use in teaching rhetoric.[32] The collaborative aspect of Wikipedia was initially used to pilot the development of a wiki publishing environment for student work.[33] Researchers have also noted the positive effects on students when the role of audience shifts from instructor to the Wikipedia community, in which case the instructor becomes coach rather than judge.[34] Good coverage with examples of using Wikipedia as a teaching tool in higher education can be found within Wikipedia itself.[35] Piotr Konieczny, both a scholar and a Wikipedian, also summarizes many of the techniques and benefits[36] ; however, in a survey of librarians' use of Web 2.0 in the information literacy classroom, Lili Luo found only sporadic case studies. She quotes just one Wikipedia-using librarian who asked students to change an article to "demonstrate the active participation of the Web nowadays."[37] Wikipedia has been commonly used in instructional lessons on evaluating sources, but so far the library literature includes little evidence that students have been asked to contribute to Wikipedia as part of information literacy instruction.

The composition[38] and library literature[39] have promoted authentic assignments as student-centered learning tools recommended for their ability to promote engagement. Other postsecondary educators have used Wikipedia to enhance content knowledge as described in a Wikimedia brochure of case studies and on Wikipedia itself.[40] Many examples are available through the school and university WikiProject on Wikipedia.[41] The high visibility it can provide on the Web has been attractive to many scholars and others with a passion for a particular subject. Instructional librarians' use of Wikipedia has been largely limited to a discussion of the quality and utility of Wikipedia as an initial reference source.[42] Vivien Elizabeth Zazzau explores the use of Wiki software for library instruction as a tool for teaching critical thinking through team-based learning.[43] Although she did not use Wikipedia, her survey of two classes revealed that none of the forty-four respondents realized that they could edit Wikipedia. They did not conceive of it as a social networking tool.

These gaps in research and understanding are significant because information literacy has been identified as an important skill for twenty-first-century learners and workers. Seeking better ways to engage and teach information competencies, academic librarians and faculty are compelled to ask how information literacy instruction can utilize educational strategies that improve student engagement. How can we bridge the gaps between the assumptions about information made by faculty and those made by students? An assignment that effectively engages students in learning to improve their research and critical thinking skills is gratifying for individual teachers and learners alike—indeed to all who are held accountable for program and institutional effectiveness. Can assignments be created that speak to both interests and information behaviors of digital natives while fulfilling faculty objectives for information literacy? At NJIT, beginning in 2007, we sought to answer in the affirmative, using Wikipedia as a teaching tool.

OBJECTIVE

The objective was to develop and pilot an information literacy curriculum for undergraduate students that would address both affective and cognitive dimensions of information literacy instruction. We hypothesized that a nontraditional writing assignment would better motivate students and integrate course objectives in both writing and information literacy. The project began with our exploration of Wikipedia from the point of view of an editor and teacher, rather than a reader. Just as teachers sometimes use comic books to engage young readers, Wikipedia, with its low entry barriers, could be used to engage college students in research. We asked ourselves if students in a technical communication course could learn about audience, authority, and objectivity, along with information ethics and proper citation, by writing for Wikipedia; we decided to try it.

WIKIPEDIA PRIMER

Wikipedia, a Wikimedia Foundation project, is an open-access encyclopedia using an open source platform. It aims to encourage the growth, development, and distribution of the world's knowledge to the public, free of charge, using networks of volunteers.[44] Anyone with Internet access can edit Wikipedia, and, although it is not necessary to register to edit an article, setting up a log-in confers some privileges and enables anyone to view changes by an individual editor. More than 100,000 volunteers worldwide do the work of administration, editing articles and writing software.[45] This means that volunteer editors manage all activities, including communication, discussion, edits, dispute resolution, and even automated article review using bots. Still, a small percentage of users is responsible for the majority of work.[46] The typical active volunteer, called a Wikipedian, is a male student in his twenties from the developed world. An even smaller percentage of these editors gain administrative privileges that enable them to block other users who violate Wikipedia principles, as well as delete, restore, and protect pages. Other admins bestow these privileges to those who are active editors and who have gained the trust of the community. Communities of interest come together in WikiProjects, where broad topics or related groups of topics are coordinated, organized, and managed through voluntary collaboration.

The overall editorial guidelines for Wikipedia, also developed by the volunteers, are defined in the Five Pillars[47] and developed in other Wikipedia articles. Wikimedia provides no official instruction manual; guidelines and practices are evolving and must be discovered through exploration and engagement. Every article on Wikipedia has some similar basic structure; each begins with an introductory section that defines the term or provides an overview of the content to be covered. The sections that follow can vary greatly in size and number depending on the subject of the article. Any term in the text can be linked within Wikipedia to a corresponding article, resulting in extensive internal cross-referencing. Such headings as "Background," "History," and other content-specific terms break up the content. There are also some common headings used in many articles, including "References," "External Links," and "See Also." These three sections are a major reason why Wikipedia serves as the initial and sometimes only stop for many researchers in college. "References" are the sources used to support content in the article. The "External Link" is used for those things referred to in the article or directly related to the article content but not cited. The "See Also" section is for material an editor felt a reader might be interested in reviewing. Wikipedians are free to make other types of connections and headings as they see fit; however, these three are seen throughout Wikipedia, and their usage is key to the case study that follows.

The absence of an editorial board typically engenders questions about accuracy. Stephen Colbert famously mocked this aspect of Wikipedia in a satire we share with our students.[48] While Wikipedia may benefit from the wisdom of crowds,[49] it is indeed the result of a complex set of conditions and interactions.[50] For the most thorough analysis to date of the scholarship associated with Wikipedia, see Nicolas Jullien's review of the subject.[51] As librarians well know, the popularity and utility of Wikipedia is undisputable. That people often favor easy-to-access sources of information over quality did not diminish our enthusiasm for using it as a teaching tool, as its popularity made it all the more likely to be a successful tool for student engagement.

Wikipedia allows users to see the history of edits and comments made about any article. Through the "View History" or "Talk" tabs on each article, anyone can see the entire history of edits and review or engage in comparisons and discussion of the changes, as well as undo changes that were made. For instructional purposes, this ability to see all the work done in context is a valuable tool for the teacher. An edit can be challenged, changed, or reversed at any time, forcing students to be active participants in a real-world experience in which the edits have real consequences and are instantly posted globally.

WIKIPEDIA ASSIGNMENT EVOLUTION

At NJIT, humanities professors and their liaison librarian were already collaborating at an institution where the librarian–faculty environment is collegial, and where at least one master teacher and longtime humanities professor has proclaimed the "end of the essay."[52] In this context, the librarian suggested that a nontraditional writing assignment might better motivate students, while also integrating course objectives in both writing and information literacy. Upon completion of the course, students are expected to produce an effective professional communication package that accomplishes a predetermined goal for a given situation and target using specialized forms of writing and mediums. One reason for the selection of this course for the Wikipedia assignment was that the demographic profile of these students was quite similar to that of the typical Wikipedian. We thought this might mean that our students would find Wikipedia editing tasks engaging. It was also selected for this pilot because the course goals encompass writing and research. In addition, previous assessment of student portfolios in this course had pointed to weaknesses in the students' ability to cite their sources.[53]

Initially, one professor agreed to test the new assignment in two sections, an online class and a face-to-face section, and report the findings. To these first classes of students at NJIT to become Wikipedians, the assignment was stated simply as the following: "Contribute to the dynamic online world database by becoming a Wikipedia editor. Create a new article or modify an existing one." The first glimmer of success came early on, when a few students began tackling the Wikipedia assignment on their own, ahead of schedule. These Net Gen students attending a science and technology university had few problems with the technical aspects of searching, creating, and editing Wikipedia articles. They were highly motivated by our recommendation that they select a topic about which they felt they already had knowledge or expertise. The students became intensive and active information seekers. Our assignment mimicked real life, where authors are frequently experts on their subjects, rather than the frequently manufactured-for-the-assignment topics that put students in a dulled expository writing mode. Without being directed, some students used their independent learning skills to discover how Wikipedia worked and what they were being asked to do.

The second term, a different professor agreed to test the Wikipedia assignment in two sections, one online class and one face-to-face section, and report the findings in a wrap-up session for all technical writing instructors after the end of the semester. During this semester, students were not only asked to propose an article for improvement, but to make a case for why it would be a substantial improvement to Wikipedia. Students could improve the article by adding material or editing it and documenting with reliable sources. They were asked to consider the audience and context in making internal and external links to relevant material, or by adding or changing the categories under which the article was listed. They were encouraged to engage in discussion with the Wikipedia community involved in their chosen topic and use it to strengthen their case and improvements. The professor stipulated that if student edits were largely removed by other Wikipedians prior to the end of the semester, the student grade could be negatively affected.

At the official start of the assignment, the librarian delivered a presentation designed to address some of the weaknesses uncovered in the previous semester. She also introduced Wikipedia basics, guidelines for editors, and suggestions for selecting a topic. Although most students already had experience in using the library, she reviewed library and Web research tools, source evaluation, and citation. These communications also took the form of videos and PowerPoint presentations for use in the online section. Work on the assignment took place during a three-week period and constituted 5 percent of the course grade. After the in-class presentation and some initial research, students were encouraged to sign on as editors, explore the site, and find topics of interest they could add, correct, or enhance. They were asked to prepare a five-minute presentation on their chosen Wikipedia topics that was critiqued in class, with the librarian participating. Students were encouraged to consult with the librarian as needed throughout the project, and many did seek her out. Student interest was high, and seeing one another present the topics led to more discussion, cooperation, and engagement.

Based upon the end of semester review of student work, we revised the assignment to make it easier for students to understand and access support materials. We also identified important factors for success. Students needed to start early, and we had to break the task into smaller pieces to allow time for feedback from the librarian and professor. We planned interventions and set up the tasks in a way that would force students to overcome a series of smaller obstacles because some found it extremely difficult to accomplish the entire task on their own. Some milestones identified were as follows:

1. Register for a Wikipedia editor ID.
2. Select a topic.
3. Find, cite, and evaluate one potential source to support your work.
4. Receive feedback from peers and teachers.
5. Proceed with the editing.

Another aspect needed to improve the task was related to the transparency of the assessment. It was important for the students to have a clear picture of what was being asked and how it would be judged. We used a scaffolded sequencing of tasks for the revised assignment. We asked students to do the following:

1. Identify the project goals clearly and precisely.
2. Identify the context, audience, and targets.
3. Select the appropriate scope of work.
4. Find and evaluate sources of information for quality and appropriateness.
5. Use information appropriately to understand, support, or clarify.
6. Use clear language and communication techniques.
7. Adopt appropriate tone and adjust tone when needed.
8. Critique their own work and that of others to develop good judgment in making decisions.

With this in mind, we used a rubric to judge final work and make students aware of what was expected and how it would be graded.

The librarian and instructor evaluated the students' work using two rubrics. The first formative assessment was developed quickly to evaluate and respond to student proposals. These were different for the online and face-to-face classes, where presentations were made to the classroom audience. The professor graded the final work, but another rubric was used as a summative assessment of the assignment and provided insights to the instructional team that were incorporated the following semester. The criteria used for student performance evaluation were primarily those established by Wikipedia and good academic practice.

The assignment evolved and expanded during the span of several semesters, with the librarian and three different instructors teaching this advanced course in technical communications, which is required by most engineering majors and aimed at upper-level undergraduates. By assessing the task effectiveness each semester and making incremental improvements to optimize outcomes, the task developed from the initial test phases into an integral part of several sections of the course.

Throughout the iterations of the Wikipedia assignment described here, we identified some common student errors. Beyond technical issues with editing, we encountered several obstacles as students worked to complete the task. "What Wikipedia Is Not"[54] addresses issues of style, content, and community norms. Students who did not read these guidelines were forced to discover them when choices they made regarding their own entries did not follow the Wikipedia protocols. For example, at first, many students elected to describe a company or product, usually connected with their place of employment. Almost immediately, the invisible hand of a Wikipedian with experience and authority often deleted such articles. Students tinkered with the entries, eventually coming to understand the restrictions against commercial sites by trial and error. Bots automatically tagged articles lacking references, with the notice that, "This article does not cite any references or sources." Students began paying even closer attention to this assignment. Their entries were not only for their professor's eyes or classmates' peer review, but for them it seemed the entire world was watching. This pressure of possible deletion was a key factor that cannot be easily simulated by a single professor, linking to a page that discusses the issue, or telling the student the problem may arise. By introducing a low-stakes task earlier in the semester, students in subsequent classes learned about the community interface sooner and saw the need to do a better job of editing and communicating.

In choosing topics, many students made poor selections or started too late. Poor topics were often ones that reflected personal interests for which published documentation was difficult to find or nonexistent. For example, some students wanted to write about their high school sports team, college club, or hobby. Students who chose topics like a favorite video game, product, or celebrity often found that the only supporting documentation that could be found was on another website, often a commercial or promotional one. This resulted in students copying material from one website into Wikipedia and citing only that one, often biased, source. Another choice that proved to be problematic involved topics that were controversial. Some students could not see past their passion for their chosen topic and were unable to keep their articles neutral and balanced. A related issue occurred when they saw it as an easy assignment and did not take the time to evaluate the quality of their sources or use proper citation format. They confused references and external links, and many did not adequately explore related articles to understand fully and make the hyperlinks between their article and others already in Wikipedia. In summary, students did not give much thought to the importance of their choice of topic, did not know how to evaluate their sources for quality, ignored issues of scope and audience, and generally did not adhere to the Wikipedia guidelines. Despite these issues, most students reported that the assignment was interesting, valuable, and engaging, regardless of their final grade.

Even when the students started early, topic selection was challenging for many of them. They often had difficulty finding an interesting subject appropriate to the task, and for which they could locate acceptable sources. Many students did a great deal of searching and sought help from classmates, the instructor, and the librarian before settling on a topic. Experience taught us that articles that were already well developed proved to be overwhelming in terms of the time needed to make a significant contribution, so we directed students to articles already identified as needing improvement. Many WikiProjects exist for broad subject areas, and project members have created lists of articles rated for quality and importance from which students can pick topics of interest where they can make a contribution. Articles that are designated as starter articles or that have low quality ratings are ripe for improvement. If these also have importance ratings that are high, this too can be a strong indication that the contribution made by our student will be significant. Next the student must consult the library and Web resources on the topic to see if reliable documentation is available on the subject. This also brings students back with questions. In addition, experience taught us to suggest a "reverse engineering" strategy, wherein a student locates some reliable sources on a topic of interest and, after looking through them, tries to locate a place in Wikipedia where some information from the source could logically be added.

Armed with an improved understanding of the difficulties students encountered, we found it easier to assist them, and student work was of higher quality in subsequent semesters. Moreover, since Wikipedia is always changing, we did not need to adjust the assignment each term to avoid plagiarism or overcome staleness. Although some students had trouble with the freedom this task provided, most liked the fact that they could make their own choices and pursue goals that met personal needs and interests. Many students went beyond the minimums listed in the assignment to edit more pages, and some even continued to be active editors after the semester was over.

WHAT DID THEY LEARN?

Besides enjoying the novelty of the assignment, students learned several important lessons along the way. Most simply, they practiced finding and citing reliable sources. They learned the difference between fact and opinion, and that each fact should be verifiable, preferably in more than one source. They learned that an encyclopedia is supposed to represent generally accepted knowledge and, as such, must rely on quality and multiple sources of authority. In addition, they learned how to write in a neutral academic style and create definitions that were meaningful. Indeed, they learned just how difficult it can be to find sources, and sources that agreed, even on simple facts. Writing on a topic for an encyclopedia bears resemblance to academic writing in several ways. It requires documentation, accuracy, and currency, but without the argument. If students can master this small proxy for a literature review through this assignment, it may help them master a fundamental skill required for further scholarship.

Students also learned about the scope and quality of Wikipedia. From their course evaluations, we learned that their enriched understanding would probably make many of them more diligent in their use of Wikipedia, and more critical of all sources. They also learned about social norms and conventions. As Wikipedia editors, they engaged with their community of interest when they were forced into conversation with Wikipedians who commented or edited their work. This, too, mimics the world of scholarship, where peers in a community of interest comment publicly in a collegial way.

CONCLUSION

The Wikipedia writing assignment employs active learning and fosters student engagement. Learning is largely the result of students discovering the parameters and protocols of a community of authors on their own. The assignment motivates students at first because it seems "cool," and later because they realize their entry, if well done, might remain on the Web for all to see. It heightens their awareness of the difference between fact and opinion. The purpose and point of citations become clear. It changes their perceptions of the purpose of writing from a static, class-assigned exercise to a dynamic, source rich writing activity that uses a topic about which they care deeply, and on which they can publicly contribute to an authoritative article.

Our Wikipedia assignment here at NJIT is ongoing and has already been adapted to courses in addition to technical writing. The assignment achieved our purpose, as it was not only highly engaging, but it imparted a range of information literacy skills applied in an authentic setting. Wikis and Wikipedia are changing and evolving, so the conditions could change. Nevertheless, the current opportunity created by Wikipedia for engaging students in active learning of integrated research and writing skills should not be missed.

NOTES

1. Chris Harris, "Can We Make Peace with Wikipedia?" *School Library Journal* 53, no. 6 (2007): 26.

2. Ernest T. Pascarella and Patrick T. Terenzini, *How College Affects Students: A Third Decade of Research* (San Francisco, CA: Jossey-Bass, 2005); Alexander W. Astin, "Student Involvement: A Developmental Theory for Higher Education," *Journal of College Student Personnel* 25, no. 4 (1984): 297–308; George D. Kuh and Robert M. Gonyea, "The Role of the Academic Library in Promoting Student Engagement in Learning," *College and Research Libraries* 64, no. 4 (2003): 256–82; Vincent Tinto, "Classrooms as Communities: Exploring the Educational Character of Student Persistence," *Journal of Higher Education* 68, no. 6 (1997): 599–623; Ernest L. Boyer, *College: The Undergraduate Experience in America* (New York: Harper & Row, 1987).

3. Ralph W. Tyler, *Basic Principles of Curriculum and Instruction* (Chicago: University of Chicago Press, 1949); Benjamin S. Bloom, *Taxonomy of Educational Objectives: Handbook I, Cognitive Domain* (New York: David McKay, 1956); David R. Krathwohl, Benjamin S. Bloom, and Bertram B. Masia, *Taxonomy of Educational Objectives: The Classification of Educational Goals: Handbook 2, Affective Domain* (New York: David McKay, 1964).

4. George D. Kuh and Robert M. Gonyea, "The Role of the Academic Library in Promoting Student Engagement in Learning," *College and Research Libraries* 64, no. 4 (2003): 256–82; Bonnie Gratch-Lindauer, "Information Literacy-Related Student Behaviors: Results from the NSSE Items," *College and Research Libraries News* 68, no. 7 (2007): 432–41; Amy E. Mark and Polly D. Boruff-Jones, "Information Literacy and Student Engagement: What the National Survey of Student Engagement Reveals about Your Campus," *College and Research Libraries* 64, no. 6 (2003): 480–93.

5. Penny M. Beile and David N. Boote, "Does the Medium Matter? A Comparison of a Web-Based Tutorial with Face-to-Face Library Instruction on Education Students' Self-Efficacy Levels and Learning Outcomes," *Research Strategies* 20, no. 1/2 (2004): 57–68; Qun G. Jiao and Anthony J. Onwuegbuzie, "Information Search Performance and Research Achievement: An Empirical Test of the Anxiety-Expectation Mediation Model of Library Anxiety," *Journal of the American Society for Information Science and Technology* 55, no. 1 (2004): 41–54; S. Serap Kurbanoglu, Buket Akkoyunlu, and Aysun Umay, "Developing the Information Literacy Self-Efficacy Scale," *Journal of Documentation* 62, no. 6 (2006): 730–43; Maria Pinto, "Design of the IL-HUMASS Survey on Information Literacy in Higher Education: A Self-Assessment Approach," *Journal of Information Science* 20, no. 10 (2009): 1–18; Wen-Hua Ren, "Library Instruction and College Student Self-Efficacy in Electronic Information Searching," *Journal of Academic Librarianship* 26, no. 5 (2000): 323–28; Adeyinka Tella, Adedeji Tella, C. O. Ayeni, and R. O. Ogie, "Self-Efficacy and Use of Electronic Information as Predictors of Academic Performance," *E-JASL: The Electronic Journal of Academic and Special Librarianship* 8, no. 2 (2007).

6. Trudi Jacobson and Lijuan Xu, "Motivating Students in Credit-Based Information Literacy Courses: Theories and Practice," *Portal: Libraries and the Academy* 2, no. 3 (2002): 423–41; Stephanie M. Mathson and Michael G. Lorenzen, "We Won't Be Fooled Again: Teaching Critical Thinking via Evaluation of Hoax and Historical Revisionist Websites in a Library Credit Course," *College and Undergraduate Libraries* 15, no. 1/2 (2008): 211–30; Susan B. Kanter, "Embodying Research: A Study of Student Engagement in Research Writing" (Ph.D. diss., Indiana University of Pennsylvania, 2006).

7. Constance A. Mellon, "Library Anxiety: A Grounded Theory and Its Development," *College and Research Libraries* 47, no. 2 (1986): 160–65.

8. Carol Kuhlthau, "Developing a Model of the Library Search Process: Cognitive and Affective Aspects," *Reference Quarterly* 28, no. 2 (1988): 232–42.

9. Kuhlthau, Carol, Ann K. Caspari, and Leslie K. Maniotes, *Guided Inquiry: Learning in the 21st Century* (Westport, CT: Libraries Unlimited, 2007).

10. Association for College and Research Libraries, "Information Literacy Competency Standards for Higher Education" (Chicago: Association of College and Research Libraries, 2000). Available online at www.ala.org/ala/acrl/acrlstandards/informationliteracy-competency.htm (accessed March 28, 2013).

11. Teresa Yvonne Neely, "Aspects of Information Literacy: A Sociological and Psychological Study" (Ph.D. diss., University of Pittsburgh, 2000).

12. Diane Nahl, "Affective Monitoring of Internet Learners: Perceived Self-Efficacy and Success," *Proceedings of the Annual Meeting-American Society for Information Science,* 33 (1996): 100–109; Diane Nahl and Dania Bilal, *Information and Emotion: The Emergent Affective Paradigm in Information Behavior Research and Theory* (Medford, NJ: Information Today, 2007).

13. Lesley J. Farmer, "Developmental and Social-Emotional Behavior and Information Literacy," in *Information and Emotion: The Emergent Affective Paradigm in Information Behavior Research and Theory,* edited by Diane Nahl and Dania Bilal, 99–119 (Medford, NJ: Information Today, 2007).

14. Gloria J. Leckie, "Desperately Seeking Citations: Uncovering Faculty Assumptions about the Undergraduate Research Process," *Journal of Academic Librarianship* 22, no. 3 (1996): 201–8.

15. McGuinness, Claire, and Michelle Brien. "Using Reflective Journals to Assess the Research Process." *Reference Services Review* 35, no. 1 (2007): 21-40.

16. Bobby Hollandsworth and Ed Rock, "Using iClickers in Library Instruction to Improve Student Engagement," in *Proceedings of the Charleston Library Conference,* 259–64 (West Lafayette, IN: Purdue University Purdue e-Pubs., 2009).

17. National Council of Teachers of English, "Cooperation of the Composition/Communication Teacher and Library Personnel." *College Composition and Communication* 8, no. 3 (1957): 194–95.

18. Cheryl McCain, "Scavenger Hunt Assignments in Academic Libraries," *College and Undergraduate Libraries* 14, no. 1 (2007): 19–31.

19. Maura A. Smale, "Learning through Quests and Contests: Games in Information Literacy Instruction," *Journal of Library Innovation* 2, no. 2 (2011): 36–55; Davida Scharf and Heather Huey, "Zeek2Find: A Constructivist Approach to Information Literacy Training Using a Computer Game," paper presented at *Moving Targets: Understanding Our Changing Landscapes,* Thirty-Third National LOEX Library Instruction Conference, Nashville, TN, 2006.

20. Smale, "Learning through Quests and Contests," 36–55.

21. Pew Research Center, "Pew Internet and American Life Project," *Pewinternet.org,* 2013. Available online at www.pewinternet.org/ (accessed March 28, 2013).

22. Susan Gibbons, *The Academic Library and the Net Gen Student: Making the Connections* (Chicago: American Library Association, 2007).

23. Project Information Literacy, "Project Information Literacy: A Large-Scale Study about Early Adults and Their Research Habits," *Projectinfolit.org,* April 1, 2013. Available online at http://projectinfolit.org/ (accessed March 28, 2013).

24. Kate Manuel, "Teaching Information Literacy to Generation Y," *Journal of Library Administration* 36, no. 1/2 (2002): 195–217.

25. Melissa Gross and Don Latham, "Undergraduate Perceptions of Information Literacy: Defining, Attaining, and Self-Assessing Skills," *College and Research Libraries* 70, no. 4 (2009): 336–50.

26. Educational Testing Service, "The iSkills™ Assessment from ETS," *ETS.org,* 2013. Available online at www.ets.org/iskills/about (accessed March 28, 2013).

27. Irvin R. Katz, "Testing Information Literacy in Digital Environments: ETS's iSkills Assessment," *Information Technology and Libraries* 26, no. 3 (2007): 3–12.

28. Katz, "Testing Information Literacy in Digital Environments," 3.

29. Abraham H. Maslow, "A Theory of Human Motivation," *Psychological Review* 50, no. 4 (1943): 370.

30. Frederick Herzberg, *The Motivation to Work* (New York: Wiley, 1959).

31. Bo Leuf and Ward Cunningham, *The Wiki Way: Quick Collaboration on the Web* (Boston: Addison-Wesley, 2001).

32. Robert E. Cummings, *Lazy Virtues: Teaching Writing in the Age of Wikipedia* (Nashville, TN: Vanderbilt University Press, 2009); M. Kuteeva, "Wikis and Academic Writ-

ing: Changing the Writer–Reader Relationship," *English for Specific Purposes* 30, no. 1 (2011): 44–57.

33. Andrea Forte and Amy Bruckman, "From Wikipedia to the Classroom: Exploring Online Publication and Learning," paper presented at the Seventh International Conference on Learning Sciences, Bloomington, IN, June 27, 2006–July 1, 2006, 82–188.

34. Forte and Bruckman, "From Wikipedia to the Classroom," 185.

35. Wikimedia Foundation, "Wikipedia as a Teaching Tool (Bookshelf)," *Wikimedia.org*, November 19, 2012. Available online at http://outreach.wikimedia.org/wiki/Wikipedia_as_a_Teaching_Tool_(Bookshelf) (accessed March 28, 2013).

36. Piotr Konieczny, "Wikis and Wikipedia as a Teaching Tool: Five Years Later," *First Monday* 17, no. 9 (2012); Piotr Konieczny, "Wikis and Wikipedia as a Teaching Tool," *International Journal of Instructional Technology and Distance Learning* 4, no. 1 (2007).

37. Lili Luo, "Web 2.0 Integration in Information Literacy Instruction: An Overview," *Journal of Academic Librarianship* 36, no. 1 (2010): 36.

38. Ken Macrorie, *The I-Search Paper: Revised Edition of "Searching Writing"* (Portsmouth, NH. Heinemann Educational Books, 1988).

39. Kuhlthau, Caspari, and Maniotes, *Guided Inquiry*.

40. Outreach Wiki and Wikimedia Foundation, "Education/Case Studies," *Wikimedia.org*, November 9, 2012. Available online at http://outreach.wikimedia.org/wiki/Education/Case_Studies (accessed March 28, 2013).

41. Wikipedia, "School and University Projects," *Wikipedia.org*, March 23, 2013. Available online at http://en.wikipedia.org/wiki/Wikipedia:School_and_university_projects (accessed March 28, 2013).

42. H. Thornton-Verma, "Reaching the Wikipedia Generation: Reference Roundtable Tackles Trends and Thorny Issues," *Library Journal* (April 18, 2012). Available online at http://lj.libraryjournal.com/2012/04/publishing/reaching-the-wikipedia-generation-lj-recently-gathered-publishers-aggregators-and-librarians-to-discuss-trends-and-thorny-issues-in-reference/ (accessed March 28, 2013).

43. Vivien Elizabeth Zazzau, "Exploring Wikis in a Library Credit Course," *Communications in Information Literacy* 3, no. 1 (2009): 58–64.

44. Wikimedia Foundation, "Strategic Plan: A Collaborative Vision for the Movement through 2015," *Wikimedia.org*, November 10, 2012. Available online at http://strategy.wikimedia.org/wiki/Wikimedia_Movement_Strategic_Plan_Summary (accessed March 28, 2013).

45. Wikimedia Foundation, "List of Wikipedias," *Wikimedia.org*, March 21, 2013. Available online at http://meta.wikimedia.org/wiki/List_of_Wikipedias (acessed March 28, 2013).

46. Wikipedia, "Wikipedians," *Wikipedia.org*, March 31, 2013. Available online at http://en.wikipedia.org/wiki/Wikipedia:Wikipedians (accessed April 1, 2013).

47. Wikipedia, "Wikipedia: Five Pillars," *Wikipedia.org*, March 27, 2013. Available online at http://en.wikipedia.org/wiki/Wikipedia:Five_pillars (accessed March 28, 2013).

48. Stephen Colbert, "The Word Wikiality," *Colbertnation.com*, July 31, 2006. Available online at www.colbertnation.com/the-colbert-report-videos/72347/july-31-2006/the-word---wikiality (accessed June 27, 2012).

49. James Surowiecki, *The Wisdom of Crowds* (New York: Anchor Books, 2005).

50. Aniket Kittur, Ed Chi, Bryan A. Pendleton, Bongwon Suh, and Todd Mytkowicz, "Power of the Few vs. Wisdom of the Crowd: Wikipedia and the Rise of the Bourgeoisie," paper presented at the Twenty-Fifth Annual ACM Conference on Human Factors in Computing Systems, San Jose, CA, April 28, 2007–May 3, 2007, 1–9.

51. Nicolas Jullien, "What We Know about Wikipedia: A Review of the Literature Analyzing the Project(s)," in *Social Science Research Network*, May 7, 2012. Available online at https://docs.google.com/viewer?a=v&q=cache:MJ_X86FYtFcJ:https://portail.telecom-bretagne.eu/publi/public/

fic_download.jsp?id%3D11500+Jullien+and+%E2%80%9CWhat+We+Know+about+Wi kipedia (accessed March 28, 2013).

52. Norbert Elliot, *The End of the Essay: Writing in a Mediated Environment*, audio podcast in seven parts, 2007.

53. Carol Siri Johnson, "The Analytic Assessment of Online Portfolios in Technical Communication: A Model," *Journal of Engineering Education* 95, no. 4 (2006): 279–87.

54. Wikipedia, "What Wikipedia Is Not," *Wikipedia.org*, March 31, 2013. Available online at http://en.wikipedia.org/wiki/Wikipedia:What_Wikipedia_is_not (accessed April 1, 2013).

ELEVEN

Training the Trainer: Librarians as Faculty Coaches and Workshop Designers

Beth Bloom

For the past several years, librarians have examined the effect one-shot librarian instruction has had on student retention of the research process, the ability to think critically about how, where, and when to find information appropriate for assigned research tasks. Studies have shown that without reinforcement and repetition, student skills in these areas erode, and students revert to habits developed during their formative years in grade, middle, and high school.[1]

Most often, incoming college students use such popular search engines as Google, Ask, and Wikipedia, sources they understand to contain the most accurate and up-to-date information.[2] They tend to initiate such online research before thinking about an approach to their research, which would include understanding the scope and implications of their topic, narrowing their research question, and examining the best ways to utilize the features of their chosen database.[3] Research has also indicated that students do not initiate their online research in library databases.[4] Many of those who have tried to use the library databases are befuddled by the common complexities of library home pages, often being confused by the routine silo approach to library information storage, or perhaps the students do not have a clear understanding of the difference between information genres and/or structures.[5]

However, pressed for time during the semester, teaching faculty typically hesitate to ask for librarian intervention in their classrooms once they have assigned a research topic. According to Evan I. Farber, teaching

171

faculty often have established reasons for not requesting library instruction.[6] They might feel uncomfortable about sharing classes with other faculty, or that although library instruction is important they have other priorities set for their classes, or that there is not enough time to set aside for a library orientation. In our experience, this disconnect between opportunity and avoidance occurs because many teaching faculty assume that their students know how to do academic online research, an assumption that is based on students' involvement with peer-to-peer networking and their unrelenting reliance on the Internet as they go about their daily lives. They might assume that their students will visit the library individually for help or that faculty classroom guidance is enough, or the teachers themselves might be unaware of the latest advances in academic research tools and databases.

Perhaps the most important disconnect lies in the teaching faculty's underestimation of the role librarians can play in student academic success. Librarians are aware of the need to continually support academic information-literacy skill building. The one-shot, fifty-minute library instruction session is only as good as the curriculum's ability to augment and support that session. Librarians must be included in the process of developing students' information literacy skills, either through a required for-credit course, by scaffolding (a series of librarian interventions where increasingly advanced research skills are built upon one another), or by partnering librarians with faculty on a per-course basis. This chapter presents a viable alternative to the various models of collaboration between faculty and librarians—one in which the librarians train the trainer, helping teaching faculty implement information literacy in their classes.

Seton Hall University (SHU), a midsized diocesan Catholic liberal arts doctoral institution, lies fourteen miles west of New York City. Boasting a faculty and student body of multiple ethnic, socioeconomic, and religious backgrounds, it prides itself on its inclusiveness, excellent freshman studies and honors programs, prize-winning School of Business, School of Diplomacy, and various other graduate programs. SHU's moniker is "the Catholic University of New Jersey," and it attempts to derive its student body from the sizable New Jersey Catholic population; however, it lies in an area populated by such universities as Rutgers, Montclair, and William Paterson. To become competitive in the greater New York/New Jersey environment, SHU faculty and administrators developed the most important academic initiative at SHU in recent years with the creation of a new Core Curriculum to address the issues of general education and the essential competencies that students must acquire to prepare them for lifelong learning. This core would evolve away from the two-column restaurant-menu course selection process into one that offers a common intellectual experience for all Seton Hall students.

Following the university administration's charge to the Faculty Senate, it held a special election to form a Committee to Develop a New Core Curriculum (CCC). Because SHU librarians were faculty and therefore served in the Faculty Senate, they campaigned to ensure that they would play a key role in developing the Core. The Faculty Senate consequently elected two library faculty members to serve on the CCC.

DESIGNING THE CORE

After much internal discussion and input from constituencies around campus, the CCC agreed that the core should consist of a combination of the following three elements (see table 11.1 for two of these components):

1. A series of new *Signature* courses that all SHU undergraduates would be required to take;
2. The infusion of five essential *proficiencies* into existing and/or new courses; and
3. The infusion of six essential *literacies* into existing and/or new courses.[7]

The CCC determined that the Signature courses should be designed to accentuate the Catholic Intellectual Tradition and mission, as well as address transformative issues that face all human beings, particularly freshmen and sophomores. The courses would achieve this goal by requiring community service, attendance at a series of films that addressed the human condition, and, most important, the incorporation of works selected from the canon of great philosophical writings into class readings and discussion.

The proficiencies developed as a substrate for student excellence. The Core design specified that a certain percentage of courses in any regular departmental curriculum have a particular proficiency designation. Before a course could be so designated, its syllabus would have to address and focus on one or several of the proficiencies.[8] Students in these courses would be specifically assessed on their understanding of and performance in the listed proficiency. An oversight committee consisting of practitioners of each proficiency would determine if a given course satisfied articulated proficiency guidelines before officially designating it as such.

THE LIBRARIANS AND THE CORE

Establishing their role in defining the proficiencies presented a particular challenge for the librarians on the CCC. Their objective was to convince their fellow faculty that information literacy is a skill essential to learning; therefore, it would be crucial for the new Core. On multiple occasions,

Table 11.1.   Essential Components of the New Core Curriculum

Core Proficiencies	Required Courses
information fluency	Journey of Transformation (Signature I), taken in the freshman year (developed by committee)
reading/writing	Christianity and Culture in Dialogue (Signature II), taken in the sophomore year (developed by committee)
oral communication	Odyssey of the Mind, Heart, and Spirit (Signature III), taken in the junior year (developed by department)
numeracy	A capstone course, taken in the senior year (developed by departments)
critical thinking	

librarians introduced information literacy into discussions with teaching faculty about effective pedagogies, but it was difficult to maintain the focus of such conversations. To solidify their claims, the librarians used documents that the Association of College and Research Libraries (ACRL) prepared especially for teaching faculty. Nevertheless, CCC members tended to become easily distracted whenever the librarians broached the issue of information literacy. This was not entirely surprising, based on the common assumption that students already know how to do online research, or the fact that those faculty who do see a need for information literacy instruction believe that they are doing so by assigning a research paper.

Thus, the librarians revisited the strategies they used to convince participating faculty that students need information literacy instruction. They began to challenge CCC members to attest to the quality of student research, asking them if the following student behaviors seemed familiar: 1) they say there is "nothing out there on my topic," 2) they try to do a paper on an impossibly broad topic, 3) they often look for an article or book exactly on their topic, 4) they confuse information formats, or 5) they Google their paper topics and use inappropriate websites. The reality of these scenarios challenged the faculty on the committee to direct their discussions more toward information literacy.

Concurrently, a visit from the Middle States Commission on Higher Education (MSCHE) loomed large. MSCHE had recently articulated new requirements for information literacy training on college campuses.[9] Faced with the impending evaluation visit from the association, the SHU administration mandated a campus-wide information literacy initiative. Library faculty took advantage of their expertise in the field to establish their position as the main players in this initiative. They partnered with freshman studies and the freshman English program to have multiple contacts with all incoming students. They worked with the Faculty Senate Library Committee to educate faculty on the true nature of information literacy, that is, to address the commonly misunderstood distinction between information literacy and information technology. [10]

This availed the librarians on the committee the opportunity to solidify the conversation toward goals, [11] asking their teaching colleagues about the qualities they would like to see exhibited in their students' research and the skills they would like their students to carry into the world beyond academe. The members of the committee agreed that the students should display a research or *information literacy proficiency*. They also agreed that their students generally lacked understanding of this proficiency. If the librarians' expertise addressed these issues, then it would appear that the library faculty might, in fact, be essential players in achieving the goals of the new Core Curriculum. Designers of the Core, thus, recognized and articulated information literacy. They preferred the term *information fluency* (IF) and determined to refer to it as such in descriptions of the new Core Curriculum. IF, therefore, took its rightful place as part of the group of five proficiencies.

THE CORE PROFICIENCY WORKSHOPS

A select subgroup of the CCC worked out a training plan for the faculty slated to participate in the new Core. They sent out a call for faculty volunteers who would agree to participate in five subgroups that would represent each of the five proficiencies. Once the groups formed, the CCC monitored and oversaw their functioning. The following missive to the IF subgroup is an example of the initial communication from the CCC:

> Your acceptance of a role in this Core Curriculum Faculty Development workshop means that you have agreed to incorporate information literacy into at least one course you teach each semester during the academic year. Rather than an add-on, we would like you to think of ways that information literacy can be used to enhance all aspects of the curriculum and how it can help you accomplish the educational goals you have for your students. We are using a Blackboard course as our project database. We ask that you be a frequent contributor to the database, that you fulfill all assignments in a timely fashion, and that you let us know at once about scheduling conflicts.
> - Attend summer retreat and three workshops each semester
> - Participate in all workshop activities
> - Post the syllabi for IL-intensive courses being taught each semester
> - Post all IL assignments, formal and informal
> - Use Blackboard in the IL course you are teaching

The CCC required faculty participants to present preliminary syllabi and frequently revise them so that once the seminar series was over, they would have addressed the Core proficiency such that their students would be able to develop it. During that first year, to illustrate their commitment to the project, the Office of the Provost rewarded group leaders with a course reduction, in addition to $3,000 for a one-year commitment to the program, and faculty participants received $1,000.

The IF subgroup was fortunate to be able to present Dr. Carol Kuhlthau as guest speaker and consultant at its initial meeting. Kuhlthau summarized essential steps in the information-seeking process, as illustrated in her book *Seeking Meaning: A Process Approach to Library and Information Services*.[12] Within the hour, she had successfully illustrated the reasons that students have so much difficulty producing quality research assignments. She has theorized that to do successful research and writing, some confusion and uncertainty are necessary before synthesis and result formulation in the research process. She demonstrated how students often skip essential steps in the research process and most often avoid the requisite uncertainty phase in the process of gathering and synthesizing information.

Dr. Kuhlthau's presence proved to be indispensable to the IF subgroup, as well as to the librarian group leaders. Her ability to explain this common problem in a few short moments confirmed and supported in no uncertain terms the very issues upon which the librarians had focused for years. Her solid research was irrefutable. Librarians on the subcommittee benefited from this, as their claims about student behavior were substantiated. They commanded newly found respect as experts in the field of IF.

As the fall workshops progressed, the group leaders found that the discussions took on a life of their own. They continually had to scrap the meeting agendas (see table 11.2 for discussion topics). Disparate perceptions of what IF consisted of emerged as a major issue and had to be addressed. There were as many definitions of IF as there were people in the room. Discussions appeared to go nowhere and to be a waste of precious (and expensive) time. Participating faculty disagreed on how, or even if, IF instruction was necessary for their particular assignments or areas of expertise. The historians, for example, strongly suggested that IF training was a natural outgrowth of the historical method. Other faculty saw no necessity in such training, particularly if their courses focused on literary analysis. Several faculty members valued the immediate benefits of IF training in their own or students' research, but they had not really thought about its long-term benefits in instilling in students skills for lifelong learning.

The librarian group leaders on the committee knew that many faculty still believed that sending students to the library and asking librarians for research triage would satisfy the basic IF Core proficiency requirement.

They had to convince their faculty colleagues that information structures, mode, standards, and language are also essential aspects of IF, not to mention vitally important stages in the research process. Preliminarily exploration of subject, understanding the scope of the research problem, designing the research question, formulating the research plan, resource gathering, and application of search strategies and technique all help the student find relevant resources whose content will lead to synthesis and, eventually, the creation of new knowledge.

Most telling, however, was the gap between the librarians' and teaching faculty's approach toward the application of IF concepts. Librarians insisted that IF was a process and should be taught in stages, or scaffolded. The teaching faculty wanted their students to use IF concepts to produce a specific product. They were not immediately concerned about the long-term usefulness of such instruction. Discussions led to compromise, however. The librarians on the committee needed to relinquish the idea that IF was an extension of their skill, and that they were the sole experts on the subject. They had to accept the fact that, no matter how ideal it would be for students to be allowed time to internalize IF concepts and practices, those students had to produce acceptable research by semester's end. Teaching faculty, on the other hand, had to concede to the idea that, although librarians were generalists, they could learn much about the research process from them—that, despite the fact they, as faculty, might be experts in their given field of study, librarians had the facility and means to understand the research process and locate pertinent information in all disciplines.

Indeed, the discussions that had seemed to lead nowhere actually were a necessary part in establishing the mutual respect between teaching and library faculty, and in the synthesis of ideas that would eventually lead to a productive outcome. For the participants to share IF training techniques with their fellow faculty members, they had to understand the concepts themselves. [13] In an uncanny way, the IF subgroup's process of discussion, disagreement, and confusion as antecedent to mutual understanding and synthesis of ideas seemed to parallel the stages of the research process as articulated by Kuhlthau. Once all participants agreed that it was permissible to disagree on their definition of IF—once they understood that the nature of IF varied according to discipline and educational level—committee members were prepared to learn how to infuse IF into their curricula and syllabi.

As the meetings progressed, participants used the Blackboard course discussion board to share ideas and draft syllabi. Incorporating Kuhlthau's theories, several faculty members began to stage their research assignments and introduce evaluation into each stage. It was exciting to see how faculty participants began to introduce process into their research assignments. They planned to ask their students to keep a research and learning journal and enter librarians into Blackboard as participants, consultants, and coinstructors in many research courses.

The workshops that first year produced a series of training documents for faculty who might, in the future, be interested in infusing IF into their syllabi. Using Blackboard as the course management tool, they also included various ACRL information literacy documents and examples of IF best practices from other universities. Faculty workshop participants began to rework several of these documents, for example, Information Literacy Guidelines, to suit our university's needs. They also began to design grading rubrics, information on developing course-specific and discipline-specific assignments, research paper guidelines, and guidelines for developing IF-specific courses at SHU.

The second year of the workshops introduced an exciting innovation: large course redesign. Whereas the participants in the 2005–2006 academic year produced many individual course documents, participants in the 2006–2007 workshops understood that large course redesign would require detailed materials for instructors, including guidelines, sample assignments, and assessment tools. At this point in the evolution of the Core, the SHU Teaching Learning Technology Center (TLTC) funded a major portion of the workshops, with the proviso that participants would develop learning objects, supporting technologies for the new Core, and rubrics for assessment. Budgetary constraints in this second year of the workshop series mandated smaller stipends, which in turn resulted in reduced scheduling: three ninety-minute sessions at the TLTC Summer Institute (introductory, tech, and hands-on working sessions) and two regular meetings per semester (one to share plans and the other to share results) that totaled five hours (see table 11.3).

Indeed, in the second year of the workshops, the participants successfully redesigned large courses to include IF, and they included assessment rubrics and guidelines as an added benefit. Assessments included assignments, in-class activities, homework assignments, and tests/quizzes. Assessments varied by curricular area. Faculty in the humanities generally based their assessments on the final project or paper. The science faculty participant based her IF assessment on basic search strategy in the science databases for a given topic and the appropriateness of the resulting articles. Two faculty members worked on redesigning a business writing course. One availed students of several videoclips on controversial issues in the business world. He then asked students to take a side in a controversy, write a logical response, and then back up their conclusion with appropriate resources. The following are some IF standards as articulated by SHU English faculty:

Understand the structure of information within the field of literary research:

Table 11.2.   Summer 2005 Initial Subgroup Meeting Agendas

Meeting Date	Topic or Assignment
June 15	Carol Kuhlthau's presentation
	Faculty discuss frustrations with students' performance
	Bring in an assignment topic for discussion
June 17	Discuss effective research assignments
	Post topic
	Introduce to key databases
	Develop assignment based on discussions. Post in Blackboard
June 30	Sample effective syllabi
	Journaling and discussion: challenges in developing new syllabi and course assignments

1. Identify and use key literary research tools to locate relevant information.
2. Plan effective search strategies and modify search strategies as needed.
3. Recognize and make appropriate use of library services in the research process.
4. Understand that some information sources are more authoritative than others and demonstrate critical thinking in the research process.
5. Understand the mechanical and ethical issues involved in writing research essays.
6. Locate information about the literary profession itself.

The large course redesign for the Freshman English 1202 program included stages, several of which addressed IF: discussion of what constitutes research; the congruence of IF and "careful reading"; and identifying, searching for, selecting, understanding, and incorporating sources. The historian who participated in the workshop first argued that assigning a paper alone addressed IF. After participating in the workshop, he altered his syllabus to include discussion of the distinction between primary and secondary sources, study of the different kinds of secondary sources, and distinctions between different kinds of online sources. In addition, he required that the following be attached to each paper:

1. A bibliography (of course!).

Table 11.3.   Annual Timelines

Year 1

June 2005	July 2005	Fall 2005	Spring 2006
consultant's presentation	initial discussions	three meetings	three meetings
Three half-day sessions	9 hours	9 hours	

Year 2

August 2006	Fall 2006	Spring 2007
TLTC Summer Institute	two meetings (5 hours)	two meetings (5 hours)
Three 90-minute meetings		

Recent Years: Librarian-Led Online Workshops for Faculty

September/ January	November/April	December/May
initial meeting	follow-up meeting	final syllabus due and librarian evaluation

2. An indication of the paper's major primary source or sources and where you found it or them.
3. An explanation of *why* you considered it or them the major primary source/s for your work. Was it because of content, availability, accessibility of style, obvious contemporary significance?
4. An indication of the major book or books you used for the paper.
5. An explanation of *why* you considered these books, and not others, useful.
6. An indication of the major scholarly article or articles you used for the paper.
7. An explanation of why you considered these articles, and not others, useful.[14]

The official Core Curriculum rollout occurred in fall 2008. Since then, the Faculty Senate has approved all proficiency guidelines developed by group leaders. IF infusion faculty workshops have continued and are, at present, an integral part of the established Core Curriculum. Participants in IF workshops represent an ever-widening variety of departments: nursing, education, communications, and mathematics. Workshop guidelines still require at least two meetings between faculty and librarians; however, the increasing number of workshop participants has necessitated a different model in the form of asynchronous online tutorials designed and developed by the group leaders and accessible through the Blackboard course management system. The librarian group leaders created their online tutorial to include specific readings and such discussion topics as 1) defining IF, 2) researching IF at other universities, 3) creating an IF assignment, 4) sequencing IF assignments, and 5) sample IF-infused syllabi. The workshop also includes due dates for staged syllabi and self-assessment based on rubrics that the librarian group leaders designed.

Faculty workshop participants in all five proficiency subgroups must submit completed course syllabi into the Blackboard grading system. As the semester progresses, all group leaders are responsible for following participating faculty's progress in redesigning their syllabi to include instruction in the proficiency they are developing. Once the project leaders determine that all requirements for infusion are satisfied, they sign off on the syllabi, which are then added to the list of proficiency-infused courses in the undergraduate (or graduate) catalog.

Since the inception of this process, the university has required that students take at least ten courses that are infused with one or more of the five proficiencies. As a result, each semester, faculty ask to take part in the workshops or, in anticipation that their courses will achieve proficiency-infused designation, just submit reworked syllabi to the group leaders, who are ultimately responsible for assessing and ensuring that each syllabus follows prescribed proficiency guidelines.

Monetary incentives for participation in the proficiency workshops have ceased; however, all parties benefit from the new Core Curriculum in other ways. Since the Core involves all campus faculty, once their syllabi have been certified proficiency-infused, they are assured that students will sign up for their courses. Students benefit in that they satisfy part of the ten-course proficiency requirement. The librarian group leaders perhaps benefit in a most extraordinary way. They have ultimate say in whether syllabi satisfy IF infusion requirements. Such influence reflects a power that few librarians enjoy.

Because of their role in establishing, participating, and leading core proficiency groups, librarians at Seton Hall have established a unique status among librarians in the United States. Their participation in the creation of the new SHU Core has established their position on campus as experts in IF training. As a result of their unique experience, they have also achieved the following:

1. Deeper communication with faculty, with the CCC, and in the workshops
2. Recognition of IF training as essential to general education at SHU
3. A permanent place for librarians in developing segments of the new Core
4. Evidence for faculty beyond their personal experience that students lack essential IF skills
5. A deeper understanding of IF that will benefit the students and university

The SHU librarians have profited due to their understanding that cultural change takes time. The Core Curriculum went through several iterations before the final one articulated in this article, several of which disregarded the need for IF instruction. The librarians on the CCC spent many months convincing other faculty of the importance of such training. They persisted in allowing faculty time to realize that computer literacy and information literacy are not synonymous. They also enlisted supporting forces and allegiances around campus. The library faculty have had a history of working with members of the English Department. In 1999, they participated in a grant provided by the TLTC, in which they used technology to work together to develop tutorials and other instructional objects for underclassmen and women. They collaborated on a plan to ensure that all seventy-five or so freshman English classes would have a library component. Clearly, the English faculty and librarians had already developed a mutual respect even before the Core proficiency workshops were planned. Most importantly, in core meetings, English faculty championed librarians, which helped establish the respect of other teaching faculty members.[15]

FUTURE PROSPECTS

Since the inception of the proficiencies, librarians at SHU have had more contact with students in classrooms. There has been much more collaboration between library and teaching faculty in those sections designated with the IF core proficiency. The question remains, however, whether knowledge about the successful relationship between these courses will influence faculty in other classes to include librarians in their curricula. Teaching and library faculty will no doubt partner in greater numbers, yet many faculty still see no place for the librarian in their classrooms. Consequently, gaps in the connection between librarian and students will persist.

In response to this, MSCHE, in its focus on outcomes, has specified that, to avoid marginalization of important proficiencies, various campus constituents should experiment with and practice new models of instructional collaboration.[16] Thomas P. Mackey and Trudi E. Jacobson describe an example of such successful collaboration at the University at Albany.[17] In this instance, a campus-wide Information Literacy Subcommittee has developed a "multitiered approach" to information literacy instruction. In other words, librarians and teaching faculty share the responsibility to instill information literacy skills. They have developed a system of progressive information literacy instruction, taught in increasing depth at various stages of the college experience. Trudi E. Jacobson and Carol Anne Germain focus on the Albany campus Information Literacy Subcommittee, consisting of members of the Center for Excellence in Teaching and Learning, the School of Information Science and Policy, and the University Libraries. Similarly to SHU, they have conducted a series of IF workshops. One of those workshops features faculty who have successfully instilled IF into their courses and who discuss their "best practices."[18]

A considerable portion of the library literature centers on the inclusion of IF in university curricula.[19] Various articles focus on collaboration, for instance, librarian–faculty partnership in developing IF courses,[20] including IF in coursework (curriculum),[21] or adding IF components to an existing course.[22] In addition, Weber State University has included its IF team leader as a member of a new general education reform committee.[23] Robert Miller, Ed O'Donnell, and Neal Pomea[24] have instituted online training workshops for distance education faculty with goals similar to those articulated at Seton Hall.[25] Like the librarians at SHU, they also review and provide feedback on their colleagues' assignments.

Since the official rollout of the new Core Curriculum in 2008, such courses as Freshman English 1202 were redesigned to include IF as an essential infused proficiency. Business writing and other prerequisite courses experienced the same transformation. Clearly, this has resulted from the successful partnership between librarians and other CCC members. The librarians hope that their successful part in the new Core Curriculum will lead to more collaboration with faculty at both the undergraduate and graduate levels. The architecture of the new Core stipulates that faculty should be proactive in large course redesign. Faculty members who have participated in the Core proficiency workshops will be training their colleagues in the application of these proficiencies. This will further necessitate librarians' expertise as partners in IF training. The librarians have established a unique place for themselves on the SHU campus. There, they hope that the best is yet to come.

NOTES

1. Lea Curie, Frances A. Devlin, Judith Emde, and Kathryn Graves, "Undergraduate Search Strategies and Evaluation Criteria: Searching for Credible Sources," *New Library World* 111, no. 3/4 (March/April 2010): 114. http://kuscholarworks.ku.edu/dspace/handle/1808/6700 (accessed April 20, 2013).

2. Melissa Gross and Don Latham, "Undergraduate Perceptions of Information Literacy: Defining, Attaining, and Self-Assessing Skills," *College & Research Libraries* 70, no. 4 (July 2009): 344.

3. Barbara J. Cockrell and Elaine Anderson Jayne, "How Do I Find an Article? Insights from a Web Usability Study," *Journal of Academic Librarianship* 28, no. 3 (May/June 2002): 129.

4. Gross and Latham, "Undergraduate Perceptions of Information Literacy," 344.

5. Alison J. Head and Michael B Eisenberg, "Finding Context: What Today's College Students Say about Conducting Research in the Digital Age," *Project Information Literacy Progress Report*, Project Information Literacy, 2009, 11. Available online at http://projectinfolit.org/pdfs/PIL_ProgressReport_2_2009.pdf (accessed April 2, 2013).

6. Evan I. Farber, "Working with Faculty: Some Reflections," *College & Undergraduate Libraries* 11, no. 2 (December 2004): 131.

7. The literacies do not appear in this table. This part of the Core was later removed by the Faculty Senate and placed within individual departments.

8. Eventually, the CCC formed subcommittees that composed guidelines for the proficiency courses.

9. MiddleStates Commission on Higher Education, *Developing Research & Communication Skills: Guidelines for Information Literacy in the Curriculum, Executive Summary* (Philadelphia, PA: MiddleStates Commission on Higher Education, 2002).

10. Jennifer J. Little and Jane H. Tuten, "Strategic Planning: First Steps in Sharing Information Literacy Goals with Faculty across Disciplines," *College & Undergraduate Libraries* 13, no. 3 (October 2006): 115. The authors describe a similar situation at the University of South Carolina, Aiken.

11. Nancy F. Campbell and Theresa L. Wesley, "Collaborative Dialogue: Repositioning the Academic Library," *portal: Libraries and the Academy* 6, no. 1 (January 2006): 96.

12. Carol Kuhlthau, *Seeking Meaning: A Process Approach to Library and Information Services*, 2nd ed. (Westport, CT: Libraries Unlimited, 2004), 82.

13. Jane Scales, Greg Matthews, and Corey M. Johnson, "Compliance, Cooperation, Collaboration, and Information Literacy," *Journal of Academic Librarianship* 31, no. 3 (May/June 2005): 233.

14. From a syllabus developed by SHU history professor Dr. Dermott Quinn.

15. Robin Lockerby, Divina Lynch, James Sherman, and Elizabeth Nelson, "Collaboration and Information Literacy: Challenges of Meeting Standards when Working with Remote Faculty," *Journal of Library Administration* 41, no. 1/2 (January 2004): 250.

16. Oswald M. T. Ratteray, "Information Literacy in Self-Study and Accreditation," *Journal of Academic Librarianship* 28, no. 6 (November/December, 2002): 369.

17. Thomas P. Mackey and Trudi E. Jacobson, "Integrating Information Literacy in Lower- and Upper-Level Courses: Developing Scalable Models for Higher Education," *JGE: The Journal of General Education* 53, no. 3/4, (July 2004): 202.

18. Trudi E. Jacobson and Carol Anne Germain, "A Campus-Wide Role for an Information Literacy Committee," *Resource Sharing & Information Networks* 17, no. 1/2 (January 2004): 119.

19. Bill Johnston and Sheila Webber, "As We May Think: Information Literacy as a Discipline for the Information Age," *Research Strategies* 20, no. 3 (January 2005): 108–21; Rui Wang, "The Lasting Impact of a Library Credit Course," *portal: Libraries and the Academy* 6, no. 1 (January 2006): 79–92.

20. Scales, Matthews, and Johnson. "Compliance, Cooperation, Collaboration, and Information Literacy," 229–35; Lockerby, Lynch, Sherman, and Nelson, "Collaboration and Information Literacy," 250.

21. Mackey and Jacobson, "Integrating Information Literacy in Lower- and Upper-Level Courses," 202.

22. Susan Kaplan Jacobs, Peri Rosenfeld, and Judith Haber, "Information Literacy as the Foundation for Evidence-Based Practice in Graduate Nursing Education: A Curriculum-Integrated Approach," *Journal of Professional Nursing* 19, no. 5 (September

2003): 320; Jeanne Galvin, "Alternative Strategies for Promoting Information Literacy," *Journal of Academic Librarianship* 31, no. 4 (July/August 2005): 353.

23. Shaun Jackson, Carol Hansen, and Lauren Fowler, "Using Selected Assessment Data to Inform Information Literacy Program Planning with Campus Partners," *Research Strategies* 20, no. 1/2 (January 2004): 54.

24. Robert Miller, Ed O'Donnell, and Neal Pomea, *Library-Led Faculty Workshops: Helping Distance Educators Meet Information Literacy Goals in the Online Classroom*, presentation before the University of Maryland University College, OCLS, Adelphi, MD, April 30, 2010. Available online at http://contentdm.umuc.edu/cdm/singleitem/collection/p15434coll5/id/1025/rec/11 (accessed December 19, 2012).

25. For example, they 1) define information literacy; 2) name information literacy objectives for students; 3) help students find, evaluate, and use information; and 4) design an assignment teaching information literacy skills in conjunction with course content.

Index

About the Editors and Contributors

Maria T. Accardi is assistant librarian and coordinator of instruction at the Indiana University Southeast Library in New Albany, Indiana, a regional campus of Indiana University Bloomington. She holds a B.A. in English from Northern Kentucky University, an M.A. in English from the University of Louisville, and an M.L.I.S. from the University of Pittsburgh. She served as a coeditor of and contributor to *Critical Library Instruction: Theories and Methods* (2010) and is author of the forthcoming *Feminist Pedagogy for Library Instruction* (2013). Prior to entering librarianship, Accardi taught first-year college composition and tutored in a university writing center, and these experiences inform her current practice as a librarian instructor.

Beth Bloom, associate professor/librarian II, received her B.A. in history from the University of Wisconsin–Madison, and both her M.A. in musicology and M.L.S. from Rutgers University. She has been a member of the Seton Hall University library faculty since 1992. Her main interests are information literacy, the research process, and the ways in which students learn how to learn. Bloom has published and presented both nationally and internationally on these topics. She has served as coordinator of information literacy; reference librarian; and liaison to the departments of art, music, nursing, allied health, women's studies, and communications. She has also served as faculty senator and member of the committee to develop a new core curriculum for the university. Bloom's outside interests include music, dance, and theatrical performance.

Stephanie Sterling Brasley took a position as dean of Academic Affairs at Los Angeles Southwest College two years ago, after sixteen years at the University of California, Los Angeles (UCLA) and four years at California State University's (CSU) Chancellor's Office. Much of her tenure at UCLA and CSU focused on coordinating and leading information and information and communication technology (ICT) literacy efforts. Brasley has presented and published topics related to assessment, information literacy and public policy issues, ICT literacy, and instructional design. She holds a B.A. in Spanish literature and an M.L.S. from UCLA. Her research and scholarship activities have targeted information/ICT literacy and diversity/social justice issues.

Barbara J. D'Angelo is assistant clinical professor of technical communication at Arizona State University. She earned her Ph.D. in technical communication and rhetoric from Texas Tech University and her M.L.I.S. from the University of Illinois at Urbana–Champaign. She teaches courses in technical communication, business communication, health communication, and intellectual property at Arizona State. D'Angelo has presented and published on topics related to information literacy, technical communication, writing assessment, and curriculum development.

Nancy DeJoy is associate professor in writing, rhetoric, and American cultures. Her publications focus on approaches to teaching and learning writing that favor participation and contribution over adaptation and consumption. She also writes and publishes poetry. For the past five years, DeJoy has been doing special projects to enhance undergraduate education at the college and university levels.

Marta Mestrovic Deyrup earned her Ph.D. from the Department of Slavic and East European Languages and Literatures at Columbia University and an M.L.S. from the Rutgers University School of Communication and Information. She is professor/librarian I at Seton Hall University and for six years served as the university's codirector of women and gender studies. In addition to writing *Successful Strategies for Teaching Undergraduate Student Research,* Deyrup is the editor of *Digital Scholarship* and *East-Central European Collections of the New York Public Library Research Libraries.* She is also author of *The Vita Constantini as Literary and Linguistic Construct for the Early Slavs* (2009).

James Elmborg is associate professor and former director in the School of Library and Information Science at the University of Iowa. He has an M.A. and Ph.D. in English from the University of Kansas and an M.L.S. from Emporia State University. Prior to coming to Iowa, Elmborg was the Andrew Mellon Librarian for Information Technology at Furman University and Wofford College in South Carolina. He was also head of library user education at Washington State University, Pullman. Before becoming a librarian, he taught English for twenty years at both the high school and university levels. Elmborg is author of several award-winning publications from the Reference and User Services Association and the instruction section of the Association of College and Research Libraries. In addition to his work with information literacy, Elmborg is active in digital humanities projects, specializing in collecting and digitizing literary readings.

Mary W. George is senior reference librarian for humanities and social sciences at Princeton University's Firestone Library. She attended the University of Michigan as an undergraduate for her library degree and an M.A. in English and worked there as a library instruction and reference librarian before moving to New Jersey. She subsequently completed coursework and qualifying exams toward a Ph.D. in library and information science at Rutgers University. George considers herself a generalist and is responsible for reference collection development, as well as library science selection. She is author of *The Elements of Library Research: What*

Every Student Needs to Know (2008) and teaches a special topics course, E-Humanities and Social Science Reference, in the Rutgers University School of Information and Communication.

Williamjames Hull Hoffer is a graduate of Harvard Law School and has a Ph.D. in history from Johns Hopkins University. He is associate professor of history at Seton Hall University, where he teaches various courses at both the undergraduate and graduate levels. Hoffer has authored or coauthored numerous books on U.S. legal history.

Heidi L. M. Jacobs is an information literacy librarian at the University of Windsor's Leddy Library. Prior to becoming a librarian, she earned a Ph.D. in American literature and taught English literature and women's studies. Her current research relates to information literacy, critical pedagogy, and digital humanities.

James M. Lipuma is senior university lecturer in the Humanities Department at the New Jersey Institute of Technology (NJIT) and has been the teacher education programs coordinator for NJIT since 2004. He holds a B.S. in chemical engineering from Stanford University, an M.S. in environmental policy studies from NJIT, and a Ph.D. in environmental science from NJIT. Lipuma also earned a postdoctoral Ed.M. in curriculum and teaching focused in science education from the Teachers College at Columbia University. He leads the Curriculum, Learning, and Assessment Studies (CLAS) Project and supports all NJIT teacher education initiatives, including the National Science Foundation Robert Noyce Teacher Scholarship Program and C2Prism project, and has overseen several curriculum redesign projects for secondary- and university-level programs. Lipuma is coordinator of the upper-division technical communicator course and has completed several curriculum redesigned projects at NJIT.

Sara D. Miller is head of information literacy at the Michigan State University (MSU) Libraries, where she partners closely with the MSU first-year writing program for classroom instruction, scholarly collaboration, and developing shared student learning outcomes. Miller has presented both nationally and internationally on the intersections of information literacy, writing, and inquiry-based learning. She received her M.L.I.S. from Wayne State University in 2005 and is a 2010 alumna of the MSU Lilly Teaching Fellows program for early career faculty.

Benjamin M. Oberdick is an information literacy librarian at Michigan State University, where he provides information literacy instruction for students taking a class in the first-year writing program and assists patrons through multiple reference services. Oberdick has presented both nationally and internationally on topics related to information literacy, creativity, and inquiry-based learning. He received his M.L.I.S. from the University of North Carolina at Greensboro in 2007 and completed two Association of College and Research Libraries Immersion Programs (Teacher Track in 2010 and Intentional Teacher Track in 2012).

Stephanie N. Otis is assistant professor and library instruction coordinator at the University of North Carolina at Charlotte. She earned her M.L.I.S. from the University of North Carolina at Greensboro, and an M.A. in English from the University of North Carolina at Chapel Hill. Otis teaches research instruction for students in first-year writing and freshman seminar courses, as well as for the departments of religious studies, philosophy, and international studies. Her past presentations have focused on and her current research focuses on curriculum integration of research skills and critical thinking in the research process/8.

Davida Scharf earned a B.A. in art and architectural history from Barnard College and an M.L.I.S. from Columbia University. She is completing her doctoral work at the Rutgers University School of Communication and Information in the area of educational assessment and information literacy. Scharf is director of reference and instruction at the New Jersey Institute for Technology. Her research interests include critical thinking, information literacy instruction and assessment, program evaluation, online communications, knowledge management, and digital libraries.

Roberta Tipton is business librarian, information literacy coordinator, and School of Public Affairs and Administration (SPAA) Librarian at the John Cotton Dana Library, Rutgers–Newark campus. She has worked in government, medical, corporate, and academic libraries. Her research interests include information literacy, organizational management, and the research/writing process.